D1452775

NICHOLAS CRABBE

By the Same Author

*

STORIES TOTO TOLD ME

IN HIS OWN IMAGE

CHRONICLES OF THE HOUSE OF BORGIA

HADRIAN THE SEVENTH

DON TARQUINIO

THE WEIRD OF THE WANDERER

THE DESIRE AND PURSUIT OF THE WHOLE

HUBERT'S ARTHUR

Nicholas Crabbe

OR

THE ONE AND THE MANY

A ROMANCE BY

Fr. Rolfe
(Baron Corvo)

WITH AN INTRODUCTION BY
CECIL WOOLF

GREENWOOD PRESS, PUBLISHERS
WESTPORT, CONNECTICUT

Library of Congress Cataloging in Publication Data

Rolfe, Frederick William, 1860-1913.
  Nicholas Crabbe : or, The one and the many.

    Reprint of the 1958 ed. published by New Directions,
Norfolk, Conn.
    I. Title.
[PZ3.R644Ni 1977]   [PR5236.R27]   823'.8   77-11680
ISBN 0-8371-9816-X

Originally published in 1958 by New Directions, Norfolk,
Connecticut

Printed with the permission of New Directions Publishing
Corporation

Reprinted in 1977 by Greenwood Press, Inc.

Library of Congress Catalog Card Number   77-11680

ISBN 0-8371-9816-X

Printed in the United States of America

CONTENTS

CONTENTS

Quam tu nuper eras, cum candidus ante fuisses, corve loquax, subito nigrantes versus in alas.

(Ovid, *Metamorphoses*, II, 534-5)

. . . . plerumque recoctus scriba ex quinqueviro corvum deludet hiantem.

(Horace, *Satires*, Book II, v, 55-6)

Sed tacitus pasci si posset corvus, haberet plus dapis, ex rixae multo minus invidiae-que. (Horace, *Epistles*, I, xvii, 50-1)

Effossos oculos voret atro gutture corvus.

(Catullus, *Carmina*, CVIII)

Oscinem corvum prece suscitabo, solis ab ortu. (Horace, *Odes*, III, xxvii)

Delius in corvo.

(Ovid, *Metamorphoses*, V, 329)

Introduction

"THE histories of his two careers (the ecclesiastical and the artistic) are already written"—that is how Frederick Rolfe, self-styled Baron Corvo, refers to *Hadrian the Seventh*—"so also is the history of his first literary period; and the curious may read who have the wit to find."

Nicholas Crabbe is that history. Now printed for the first time, it completes the semi-autobiographical tetralogy which begins with *In His Own Image*, continues with *Hadrian the Seventh* and ends with *The Desire and Pursuit of the Whole*. With that in mind, it is interesting to see how the two ends of his career, in a sense, join each other.

The story of Rolfe's life has already been told in *The Quest for Corvo* by A. J. A. Symons. Yet there are still gaps in plenty, and many dark places remain unlit. *Nicholas Crabbe* provides the indispensable documentation of this period of Rolfe's life, all the more important because during this period information is particularly scarce. Rolfe's Prologue to this book is in itself sufficient explanation of its genesis in his life, yet to some casual reader at least the background of *Nicholas Crabbe* may be unfamiliar, and some aspects of it surprising, and to such a reader a word of explanation may not be amiss.

Frederick Rolfe was born in 1860 in Cheapside, London, and died in 1913, in Venice. At the age of fifteen he left home and succeeded in earning a living as a schoolmaster for ten years. In 1886 he became a convert to the Roman Catholic faith, and, a year later, offered himself as a candidate for the priesthood. He spent a year at Oscott College, and then was sent to the Scots College in Rome. From here he was expelled, suddenly, without explanation of any kind.

The incident demands more than a passing reference since it carried with it the seed of great suffering later on. But more important than his ultimate exclusion from ordination was the

1

immediate reaction of the incident upon his mind and character. He suffered spiritual torments from his rejection from the priesthood, and he believed that it had been unjust. During the long years of restless wandering—Mr Graham Greene has called them the "purgatorial years"—he suffered, suffered terrible material misery in his attempts to earn a livelihood, by doing what he calls all sorts of "fatuous frantic excellent things".

Having, he says, "a shuddering repugnance from associating my name, the name by which I certainly some day should be known in the priesthood with these secular pursuits", he split up his personality and adopted pseudonyms. Under one he wrote and painted, under another he photographed, under another he designed furniture and so on. As he puts it in *Hadrian the Seventh* (to which one continually returns), "As Catholic malfeasance drove me from one trade, I invented another, and another". And he wandered everywhere. He left frescoes in the little Roman Catholic church of The Immaculate Conception and St Joseph's in Christchurch, Hampshire, and painted banners for the Shrine of St Winefride, Holywell, in North Wales; Aberdeen, where he worked as a photographer and a painter, turned him out to dress in the streets; in Wales he ended up in the workhouse. "For six years," writes A. J. A. Symons, "Corvo was driven by fate from pillar to post, and his life of bizarre misadventure has probably no equal among those of modern authors". Finally, literature being "the only outlet you Catholics have left me," he began to write in earnest.

Faced, as it seemed to him, by a hostile world, he learnt to pretend, even to himself; and, as soon as he began to write, he sought to project himself into his work as a form of dream-compensation for his unhappy life. Almost everything he wrote is disguised autobiography. Vincent O'Sullivan, himself a priest, wrote to Symons: "He was born for the Church: that was his main interest". Had he only had the opportunity to be accepted for what he longed to be—a priest—perhaps the pose would have become, if not actually genuine, at least so much a part of him as to serve as genuine. Certainly he would have ceased to torture himself and become a useful person. But the sudden interruption of his career wrecked his chance of imposing on himself the *persona* for which he yearned.

A contributor to *The Quest for Corvo* who knew Rolfe as a seminarian says that of his desire for the priesthood there was "nothing elevated or fine". In *Hadrian the Seventh* the man who had been found unfit to be a humble priest dreams that his superiors have come at last to his squalid lodging to offer amends and be forgiven by him. The poor pariah, George Arthur Rose, is ordained immediately, taken to the conclave then sitting in Rome, and there by the Princes of the Church, who know the story of his sufferings and persistence, raised to the throne of St Peter. Throughout this wishful autobiography Rolfe expresses a deeply sincere devotion to the Church that had rejected him. There is more here than a dream of "doing picturesque things in a picturesque way". That very different genius D. H. Lawrence wrote of *Hadrian the Seventh*: "The book remains a clear and definite book of our epoch, not to be swept aside. If it is the book of a demon, as Corvo's contemporaries said, it is the book of a man demon, not a mere *poseur*. And if some of it is caviare, at least it came out of the belly of a live fish". Mr Graham Greene has written of it: *"Hadrian the Seventh, a novel of genius, stands in relation to the other novels of its day, much as The Hound of Heaven* stands in relation to the verse".

In the Nineties we find him writing folk-lore, as he called it. These Toto stories, which first appeared in *The Yellow Book*, were "retellings of the legends of Catholic saints in the manner of Greek mythology", with "quaint attributions of human characteristics and motives to the saints in their heavenly functions". In 1898 these tales were reprinted by John Lane under the title *Stories Toto Told Me*.

Rolfe's Toto stories caused some sensation at the time, with the result that John Lane, the publisher, invited him to submit a second series of tales; and it was with the fate of this further collection that Rolfe first concerned himself when, in February

1899, he left the workhouse in Wales and tramped to Oxford and thence he travelled to London.

Nicholas Crabbe (Nicholas is a Rolfe family name and the crab plays a large part in the author's personal mythology) is Rolfe's own detailed account of the four dreadful years beginning with his arrival in London and ending in the early part of 1903. This "modern novel about friendship and literary life", as Rolfe called it, is surely one of the most singular books that strange man ever wrote. It is well described by its subtitle— *The One and the Many.* It is also one of the few books by Rolfe with an English background.

During this time he lived the life of an ascetic anchorite in the little den at 69 Broadhurst Gardens, Hampstead, which he describes in such minute detail in the 'Prooimion' of *Hadrian the Seventh.* His main benefactors during these four years were, first E. J. Slaughter (the languid Neddy Carnage of the present book), and later, when Slaughter went to the South African War, Harry Bainbridge—the Bainbrigge of the following pages. Bainbridge has told in his autobiography *Twice Seven* how Rolfe was introduced to him one evening, and stayed for four years. Incidentally, the sub-plot of the oil-prospecting in the Greek Islands is an allusion to Bainbridge's work as a chemist on the white lead process for Dr Ludwig Mond. Bainbridge recalls in his autobiography that it was Rolfe who prepared the material for his final report on the effects of white lead fumes.

All the *dramatis personae* of *Nicholas Crabbe* were suggested by real men and women, and readers may like to have a note as to who the originals were. The disguises are flimsy enough. The people themselves matter only for the part they play in the story. They are all dead, but out of consideration for relatives it may be as well to say that although most of the incidents described are transcripts from life, Rolfe's interpretations are often fantastic.

Among them are Henry Harland, the literary editor of *The Yellow Book,* who appears here as Sidney Thorah, the infamous editor of *The Blue Volume.* Harland was by birth an American who, before he came to England, had, under the pseudonym of

INTRODUCTION

Sidney Luska, obtained a considerable vogue in America, as a realistic novelist. He wrote a series of sensational novels dealing with Jewish life in the poorer districts of New York, including one entitled *The Yoke of the Thorahs*. In later life Harland did all he could to suppress both his early book and the name of "Sidney Luska". The "sub-editor of *The Blue Volume*", whom Crabbe describes as "an intellectual mouse-mannered piece of sex", is a fleeting reference to Ella D'Arcy, the assistant-editor of *The Yellow Book* and author of *Monochromes*. J. L. May, in his book *John Lane and the Nineties* (London, The Bodley Head, 1936), quotes a description by Ella D'Arcy of Henry Harland:

> Harland was the most brilliant, witty and amusing of talkers, the sweetest-tempered of companions. Never were there such evenings as those long-ago evenings in Cromwell Road! I see him standing on the hearth-rug, or sitting on the floor, waving his eye-glasses on the end of their cord, or refixing them in his short-sighted eyes, while assuring some 'dear beautiful lady!' or other how much he admired her writing, or her painting, her frock, or the colour of her hair. He would re-christen a golden red-headed woman 'Helen of Troy'; he would tell another that her eyes reminded him of 'the moon rising over the jungle', and thus put each on delightfully cordial terms with herself . . . and with him.
>
> The large drawing room, lighted by lamps and candles only—in those days electricity had not yet become general —would begin to fill up about nine o'clock.
>
> Two or three would have dined there. Others dropped in to coffee and cigarettes. One might hear Kenneth Grahame, Max Beerbohm, Hubert Crackanthorpe, Evelyn Sharpe, Netta Syrett, Ethel Colburn Mayne, the Marriott-Watsons, Victoria Cross, Charlotte Mew, George Moore, Richard Le Gallienne, Arthur Symons, occasionally Edmund Gosse, and Henry James.

The two scheming villains—Slim Schelm and Doron Oldcastle —whose plots Crabbe-Rolfe saw as the cause of all his misfortunes, are his publishers, John Lane and Grant Richards. But whatever Rolfe may have thought of them, it is on record that although they may at times have driven a hard bargain with an author, they were certainly good men and enterprising publishers. And in passing it may be remarked that Rolfe, who in these pages describes Doron Oldcastle as "a strenuous stripling in a spotty plush waistcoat", "a scorbutic hobbledehoy", and "an ostentatious tyrannical turpilucricupidous half-licked pragmatic provincial bumpkin", offered this novel to Grant Richards in 1905. Whether he offered it to Lane, whom he calls "a beery insect", "a snivelling little swindler", and "a carroty dwarf, with a magenta face and pendulous lips and a vermilion necktie" is not known![1]

The unedifying Abrahams who later becomes Church Welbeck is meant for an unflattering portrait of Temple Scott, who had changed his name from Isaacs. The original character appears for a moment on pages 74–77 of Grant Richards's *Author Hunting*. Robert Kemp, the telegraph-boy, derives from Sholto Douglas, who was in fact a graduate of Christ Church and a private tutor. Rolfe adopted the guise of a telegraph-boy for him because Douglas had a friend named George Browning who was a telegraph-boy in Oxford. The series of twenty-seven essays, referred to as "Notes on Posthumous Literature", written by Crabbe and Kemp was in fact the "Reviews of Unwritten Books", several of which were published anonymously in *The Monthly Review*. The manuscript of part of their "Thirty Naughty Emperors", which remains to this day unpublished, is preserved in the Bodleian Library. A full account of the growth and decay of Rolfe's friendship with Sholto Douglas, and their literary collaboration, appears on pages 145–153 of *The Quest*. The original of the fateful Captain Theophanes Clayfoot was a man named

[1] Rolfe was not their only satirist. It may be remembered that Wilde liked his publisher so little that in *The Importance of Being Earnest* he called Algernon Moncrieff's manservant by the name of Lane; and Richards was the prototype for the ever-worrying Barfleur in Dreiser's *A Traveller at Forty*.

INTRODUCTION

Arthur Smith Graham, who lived at Great Ambrook, Ipplepen, in Devon. The well-meaning and interfering Painter, who is also The Divine Friend, was, in real life, a painter named Trevor Haddon. The search for the true, permanent companion was perhaps the personal tragedy of Rolfe's life. The literary agent, Vere Perkins, is an unkind portrait of Stanhope Sprigge. Kenneth O'Lympos is of course Kenneth Grahame, the creator of the Olympians in *The Golden Age*; and Mrs Arkush Annaly is Mrs Hubert Bland, better known as E. Nesbit, the writer of children's books. Those whose memories go back to the Nineties may be able to identify Odoys the publisher, the "witty Irishwoman"[1], the "lovely Florentine", Gervais Quair, the Tooveys and the rest. Is the "insistently celebrated critical caricaturist in a frayed waistcoat" an allusion to the creator of that Rolfean character Enoch Soames?

Rolfe's life is not idealised here, as it is in *Hadrian the Seventh* and *The Desire and Pursuit of the Whole*, and is therefore more real and convincing. Even though his portraits are either ruthlessly cruel or superbly silly caricatures, the meaning they convey is horrible in its realism. And if Rolfe's outlook is distorted by hate and bitterness, there are perhaps moments of unclouded vision when he sees himself as he really is. Towards the end, he writes: "Let it be quite clear that I make no excuse for Nicholas Crabbe. I simply am telling you patently of the things which he did which he ought not to have done, and of the things which he left undone which he ought to have done; and, that there should be no health in him, is not singular". Nowhere else in his work—into which he put so much of himself and his aspirations—does he appear so authentic. Here his faults and virtues are shown in a fiercer light. Even his physical appearance, his manner of speech, his likings, his pleasures, and his habits are all vividly recorded. When Rolfe describes Crabbe's appearance—Thorah

[1] The sobriquet is almost certainly derived from page 193 of Henry Harland's *The Cardinal's Snuff-Box*, where she makes a brief appearance as "a young, pretty, witty, and voluble Irishwoman, Mrs O'Donovan Florence, from an hotel at Spiaggia".

"looked all over the tea-leaf coloured garb, the corduroy trousers and jacket, the jute-soled canvas shoes frayed and stained and amorphous with a thousand miles of walking, the withered cloak, the dreadful cap; but he noted that the socks and finger-nails were clean, and that the whole arrangement was concise. He revolted at the thin unkempt beard and hair, wondering what the face would look like after shaving. The voice attracted him, low and minor, with its delicate swift vibrant enunciation." —that is nothing but a bare record of fact. Naturally, there are qualifications. But, whatever discounts have to be allowed, one can always be certain that Rolfe is presenting a faithful account of his own feelings at the time. The world of Rolfe is not very far from that of Rousseau's *Confessions* and Hogg's *Memoirs* and even the early volumes of *À la Recherche du Temps Perdu*. And although it is possible for the reader to regard Rolfe as from the outside, one is readily drawn into his nightmare world—as he intends—in which every man's hand is against him; and it is sometimes with pity, sometimes with amusement, often with dismay and occasionally with admiration that one follows the poor, worn Crabbe, taking "his imperscrutable face and his grim air and his sensitive longing soul, here, there, and everywhere, expecting sooner or later to have an opening offered to him," until the memorable final line, when the One, who has been failed by the Many is, in Newman's phrase, all alone with The Alone.

No exact date can be assigned to the composition of this work, but it probably belongs to the year 1905, being written after the historical novel of the Borgia epoch, *Don Tarquinio*. Possibly it was this that Rolfe was referring to when in a letter to his brother Herbert, dated March 15th, 1905, he says he has started four new books, including *Rose's Records* and *Ivory, Apes and Peacocks* ("successors to *Hadrian*"). Later on, in correspondence he sometimes referred to *Nicholas Crabbe* and *The One and the Many* as two separate books. From internal evidence, I am rather inclined to think that the Prologue was written some years later, in Venice, towards the end of his life. *Nicholas Crabbe* could not have been published sooner in this country for reasons connected with the law of libel. It was high time that this novel saw the light.

The text given in this edition is based on Rolfe's own typescript which is now in the Walpole Collection of the Bodleian Library. No manuscript is known to exist. The Walpole typescript, which lies on the desk before me, consists of a typescript on three hundred and seventy-four folio foolscap leaves with corrections in Rolfe's handwriting, preceded by four folios of Prologue written in Rolfe's own beautiful Petrarchan hand, the whole bound by the author in cream buckram with his decorations of crabs and moons, in red and black, on the front cover. The title-page bears Rolfe's own name. There is another coetaneous typescript, with the first three leaves and revisions throughout in Rolfe's hand, in the Library of Harvard University; and a typescript of the Prologue only, with a few variants, in the Martyr Worthy Collection, in Hampshire.

And now, at this distance of half a century, one notices some things in this book which might have been suppressed, or added, or altered. But bearing in mind my duty to the reader as well as to the author, the original typescript has been strictly adhered to, excepting in a few instances where obvious clerical slips have been silently altered and superfluous hyphens and dashes eliminated. On the whole Rolfe has had his own way in the matter of spelling, punctuation and the use of capitals and italics. Novel-readers have a natural antipathy to footnotes. I had at first intended to put none, but was gradually forced to the conclusion that a complete absence of explanation was even more irritating to the reader than the occasional distraction from his reading. Of two evils, I hope I have chosen the lesser. Words within square brackets have been supplied to complete the sense.

The reader fresh to Rolfe's writings must not be affronted by Rolfe's eccentric vocabulary. To his novel *Don Renato* he appended a fifteen-page glossary of new words he had coined, prefaced by this note: "Kipling appends a glossary to his *De-*

partmental Ditties. I suppose that that great writer also knows how gladly The Public takes a little trouble over its higher pleasures." Such monsters as "rhypokondylose", "tolutiloquence" and "dicaculous" need to be treated with indulgence.

I must end this Introduction by recording my gratitude to the Curators of the Bodleian Library, who afforded me every facility for transcribing the Walpole typescript.

CECIL WOOLF

London, February 1958

Prologue

OUR late Lord the Paparch Hadrian (Seventh of the name) when He was plain George Arthur Rose, had a friend called Nicholas Crabbe. I use the word "friend" here in a modern sense. Nicholas Crabbe was a man whom George Arthur Rose might address in the streets, without receiving the slash of a cane across his face for insolence: a man whom George Arthur Rose might slander, subvert, swindle, without anyone finding such proceedings singular. Friendship (in the old-fashioned sense of the word) by no means would describe their connection. They were aware of each other's existence. The gods of their stars had endowed them with similar temperaments, placed them in almost identical circumstances, afflicted them with equally frightful experiences. They liked (or loathed) the same things and persons: they were in short on speaking terms. But they lived their lives apart: they secretly admired each other. But, not till the very end, did they really come together. George Arthur Rose could not be useful to Nicholas Crabbe; and Nicholas Crabbe knew it, and expected someone who could. Nicholas Crabbe could not be useful to George Arthur Rose; and George Arthur Rose clothed himself in icy mail. Together, they might have moved mountains. But they remained apart: for each one went in ignorance and terror and distrust of himself, and in knowledge and faith and love of the other.

That was the comic tragedy with which the present history is not concerned. The gests of George Arthur Rose are related in another place.[1] It is his friend's experiences which (with permission) I am to set forth here.

I believe that I knew these two amazing creatures rather better than anybody else. Otherwise, I suppose, I should not

[1] *Hadrian the Seventh*, the story of George Arthur Rose, a spoiled priest who becomes Pope.

11

have chosen to write my short account of George Arthur Rose's paparchate, by explicit command of and in accordance with data supplied by our late Most Holy Lord, personally conveyed to me by Sir John Devine, under seal in a pigskin portfolio, nine weeks after the martyrdom at the Castle of Santangelo.

It seems to be my lot to be chosen, by my most intimate friends, as their biographer. For, when the other man (Nicholas Crabbe) became utterly tired and sick to death of all people who on earth do dwell, and determined to go in peace and live in peace and touch up his lovely *Toward Aristocracy*[1] in peace on board a cargo-liner, he (in turn) gave me an oaken copper-cornered chest of papers, enjoining me to make a literary use of their contents when nineteen months should have elapsed without news from himself. He found no difficulty in getting a Swansea captain to take him as sole passenger, giving him a cabin to himself, deck-space for a cane chair, dry hash and boiled tea at regular intervals, the freedom of the ship, perfect privacy, and no society whatever; and he made no bones about "signing on" as a stoker: for his tastes were simple, and his wants most modest, and his income permitted him to pay his way and to make life tolerable by means of the contents of a dozen little packing-cases.

His first voyage was a complete success, I know: because he told me so. Beside, I saw his face after it; and I suppose we all know what sort of a book it enabled him to write.

On his second, he posted me a letter from each of the ports where he was able to hear his Mass: viz., Barcelona, Marseilles, Palermo, Ancona, Trieste, Corfu, Zante, and Larnaka (Cyprus.) But from the last place, he did not return to the ship. So much I glean from the captain.

I have scoured the island: but I have not found him, nor any trace of him beyond his visit to the Post Office. I have laid my facts before his bankers: who naturally—(and I thank Heaven

[1] Rolfe was working on this counterblast to Edward Carpenter's *Towards Democracy* when he died in Venice in 1913.

12

that there is still some chance of privacy open to mortal man)—
refuse to give me a single shred of information.

And so, as the nineteen lunar months elapsed last February,
and as Nicholas Crabbe's history is frightfully interesting and
highly discreditable, I will begin to set it forth.[1]

It falls, I think, into four divisions:—

(α) The period of his previous incarnations:

(β) the period when he was driven out into the wilderness:

(γ) the period when the vernacular multitude came about
him (like bees) and were rapacious:

(δ) the period when Love brought him wings wherewith to
flee away and be at rest.[2]

The First Period contains so many surprising histories, that
I am going to collaborate with other writers. The Second,
Third and Fourth Periods, I rather fancy I had better tackle
myself. But I am certain that it is the Third Period which ought
to be perused first.

So here you have as much as I have done of it.

[1] In the Walpole typescript Rolfe has written "far from discreditable", and scored it out and written "highly disceditable". In a
typescript in the Martyr Worthy Collection, Rolfe has written "by
no means disceditable".

[2] Rolfe writes of these four periods in *The Weird of the Wanderer,
Hadrian the Seventh, Nicholas Crabbe,* and *The Desire and Pursuit of the
Whole,* respectively.

Chapter One

WHEN Nicholas Crabbe had cashed the lawyer's cheque for the legacy of £250, he dug himself out of the nethermost hell; and came back to town. He started with one predominant idea. He had a horror of those next to him: "closed he was, captious, intolerant. He would sweep a space round him; and sulk in the midst of it." He would acquire some sure and secret cranny of his very own, some hidden crevice beneath a shelving rock, whence nothing could dislodge him, and wherefrom he might watch the world and seize the flotsam and jetsam floating by.

He found a top-floor of four rooms in Lincoln's Inn Fields. There was a large room in front, and a kitchen and a bedroom across the landing at the back: the set was enclosed by a door at the top of the stairs. The rest of the house was let in suites of offices; and there was no resident housekeeper. That functionary occupied the corresponding attics in the adjacent house, only coming to No. 96[1] for daily duties and at call. Crabbe had no use for a housekeeper.

He went to the agent at the corner to make a bargain. The rent was £40 on a three years' tenancy. The clerk was inclined to be brusque: but the crepitation of bank-notes caused him to summon his principal.

"I'll give you £140 cash down for four years' rent in advance," Crabbe said; "and I'll begin my tenancy on Monday."

It was noon on Saturday when he said that; and, by a quarter to one, he left The Fields with the agreement signed and duplicate Yale latch keys of the front-door and his own door in his pocket.

[2] In the original typescript Rolfe first wrote 69, then struck it out and wrote 96 above. During the period covered by this book, Rolfe lodged at 69 Broadhurst Gardens, Hampstead, but when he wrote it he lived at 15 Cheniston Gardens, Kensington, and, being engaged in litigation, probably paid frequent visits to his solicitors in Lincoln's Inn Fields.

So was the first step taken. Now he would have a roof over his head for four years, privacy, a place where he could agonize in secret anyhow. His ideas only came one at a time: for he still was trembling and stunned with the horror behind him. He went and bought a bed, a table, an easy-chair, a mug, a plate, a bundle of blankets and towels; and ordered them to be delivered on Monday. He made a penny aluminium door-plate "N. Crabbe" at Saint James's Park Station; and he would nail that up when he retired into his cave.

Meanwhile there were thirty or more hours to be passed, plans to be made, thoughts to be thought. London struck him as being crammed: the din and the rush and the swirling eddy of people, respectable, cold mutton-faced, dazed him. He was frightfully tired: but he did not care to sleep on a chair in Kensington Gardens, because of the money which he carried on his person, and because it was ten chances to one that some one who knew him would see him. He did not wish to be seen. He was shabby; and his old brown-check mackintosh was a most unsuitable garment for June. However, he was not going to part with that: it covered deficiencies; and it admirably concealed a canvas haversack which contained his worldly goods—soap in a box, nail-brush, tooth-brush, sponge, a large Selvyt duster, three classics, and a MS. book. No: he would not alter his outer garb. By and by, when he had crept into his cave, he would permit himself the luxury of some new grey sweaters and socks, perhaps; but now he must have sleep. He looked at himself again. Would an hotel take him in? A station-hotel might. He went on to Victoria; and commandeered a bedroom, paying for it at the office. People stared benignly; and made him angrily nervous. He told the chambermaid to call him at 10 o'clock at night: locked the door and stripped; and instantly slept.

On waking, he was fresh, alert, and very self-possessed. He strolled up into Piccadilly; and had a good big supper of chops, sea-kale, vegetable-salad, at Hatchett's. An *omelette-au-chasseur* gave him much joy. He lingered till closing-time: filled his tobacco-pouch; and walked the streets all night, thinking hard, and wondering incidentally whether London ever went to sleep. In Charing Cross Road, he was much exercised in mind by the number of different gangs of lads and youths, who seemed to be taking the air. They were plebeian: but comfortably dressed, and with great pretensions to style. And they seemed to have nothing to do: except to expatiate in sixes and eights, chatting and smoking, noxious to none. He wondered whether they would give truth to an inquiry accompanied by half a crown; and deliberated not to compete for rebuffs. The thing was (and is) a mystery.

Soon after three it was light. He had no object, except to pass the time; and he thought that the air in the park would be delicious. Alexandra Gate was open at half-past four. He entered; and went toward the Serpentine, slowly, absent-mindedly. Down at the water's edge, an obscene tramp was dipping nameless rags. A short-legged fat German waiter puffed up on a bicycle: undressed by the railings; and plunged in knee-deep to splutter. Crabbe retreated. There was going to be some fun then. He found a chair on a bare patch in the grass under a big headless elm, thick-trunked, low-foliated; and made an inspection. The spot was near the east-end of the bathing-place, midway between the railing and the water. Thus, he avoided the crowds which, later, hung their clothes on the one in order to use the other. The tree also protected his back; and, directly in front of him, another large polled elm cut his view in two. To his right was a great tree on the grass, with a seat between it and the bold sweep of the gravel path. Beyond, the railing curved, completing the enclosure. In front, the wide stretch of still water glittered like a silver shield in the rays of the sun. Over by the island, a number of boats were moored. To his left, occasional trees, large and small, dotted the greensward. A huge elm in the distance had a wooden seat right round its base; and there was another seat by a nearer tree. Through the foliage, exquisitely lush and vivid, he could see the arches of the bridge which crosses the Serpentine. Before him was the green grass, the gravel-path, the silver water, and the microscopically clear expanse of the other side, verdant, brilliantly bright. The air was clean and warm.

Three boats came from the opposite boat-house; and took up stations at regular intervals near this side. The boatman nearest to the bridge rowed almost inshore; and a turning movement transformed a diving-board on three posts into a spring-board on one post. Miscellaneous males, of all ages from seven to seventy, came hurrying by many ways: shed dun-colours; and slipped pink into the water. There were yells and splashes; and the heads of swimmers appeared like black pin-points on the silver shield. Toward the spring-board, the throng grew thicker and thicker. Newcomers dotted themselves along the gravel and the grass. The seats were soon and constantly occupied: but Crabbe was left alone. Certainly, people came near; but not too near. He was very pleased; and intently watched the animated scene.

It seemed to him that someone was looking at him—that someone had passed round him two or three times, taking stock of him. He concentrated his attention.

A very slim boy, in dark-blue Norfolk jacket and knicker-bockers, encountered his gaze—quite a little fellow, of fourteen or thereabouts, very pale, with dark wide brows and bright-green eyes and perfectly white hair. Crabbe instantly decided that this was the most vivid and most dainty personality which he ever had seen. There was something so keen and crisp and sparkling about the air of it.

"Will you be so kind as to look after this for me, sir, while I am in the water?" the boy said, laying down a towel-wrapped bundle by Crabbe's chair. He did not wait for a reply: but raised his cap, and ran off toward the bridge.

"Well—I—am—damned!" Crabbe grimly ejaculated, turning to follow the runner with his eyes.

He watched the lithe little figure darting away; and lost it among the crowd by the spring-board. His eyes came back; and considered the bundle entrusted to his care. Horrible thoughts,

18

of babies deposited upon receptive strangers, were dismissed by the happy thought that the depositors never are boys. The stunned feeling (which was habitual) now returned; and grabbed and gripped his mind. He felt that he was fettered to his seat for at least an hour; and he set himself intently to watch the distant spring-board. It was such a long way off: an almost continuous stream of pink humanity, girt with scarlet or partly clothed with blue, hurled itself therefrom. A tiny form like a flash of pearl-coloured flame dashed up it: issued from it: descended: and disappeared in the water; and a shining head moved toward the opposite shore. Crabbe fixed his gaze on that. It was so very very small, and as insistently pallid as a moonstone on silver. It went shifting in the direction of the eight silly little Noah's Ark plane trees on the distant bank, swiftly for a swimmer, slowly for the watcher. Crabbe conceived an image of the complicated effort and energy which produced the movement, straining his eyes so as not to lose sight of the little white dot even for a moment. The lake was sprinkled everywhere with moving dots, red and yellow, grey and black and brown; and pink arms threshed the water also everywhere: but the white head went on, near to none, avoiding all. At a few yards from the other side, it turned eastward. The boy evidently was a splendid swimmer; and Crabbe noted that he used a breast-stroke all the way, swimming by the far shore, past the four small plane trees and the large one. At length he turned southward again, bearing straight toward the place where he had left his bundle. Every moment, the heat of the sun was augmenting. He dived, and swam a few strokes beneath the surface, from time to time. Once Crabbe lost him in the middle of the lake for quite two or three minutes. He did not come up at the expected place, but several yards off; and then he had turned again, and was swimming away toward the further shore. He did not touch it: but bore to the right, past the Humane Society's lodge, past the easternmost of the four boat-houses where he made a final turn, by the end of the island and between the fleet of moored boats; and now he was swimming straight to the near bank.

19

NICHOLAS CRABBE

As he came up out of the water, Crabbe noted the extremely pure diaphanous whiteness of him, the whiteness of his skin, the whiteness of his hair—the one warm as living ivory, gleaming, fire-concealing, the other cold as snow, glittering, water-waving. He was walking delicately across the curved sweep of the gravel, and deliberately across the grass toward his bundle. Crabbe sat perfectly still and silent, rolling and lighting a cigarette with the air of one who is all alone. The boy picked up his bundle; and threw it down by the tree just out of Crabbe's range of vision. He began to dry himself with the towel, strolling from the shadow into the sunlight. Crabbe noted his manliness, and the airy poise of his winged gait, light-limbed, mercurial: making no sign, but taking in all with the corner of his eye, the wonderful pallor, the supple yet rounded tenuity of form. He settled with himself that the boy must be seventeen for certain; and surmised what (in the Name of Goodness) so finished a piece of work might have in the shape of a history, past and future. When the boy was dry, he looked at Crabbe: but, finding no responsive glance in the set impassive shaded face, he stood still in the burning intolerable sunlight, straightening his limbs and watching the crowd. After a few minutes, he went out of sight to his bundle behind the tree. Crabbe could have included him in his gaze with a head-turn: but he would not move. Nothing ever should make him seek or speak unnecessarily to a fellow-creature any more—not even curiosity. His curiosity was intense: but his firm resolve, to do nothing until someone else did something, kept him as grimly as imperscrutably immovable as the sphinx. His eyes remained withdrawn and directed straight before him.

The boy finished dressing out of sight a couple of yards away; and presented himself to Crabbe. He dangled his wet towel; and he wore the uniform of a telegraph-boy. Crabbe shot out both eyes; and stared at him up and down.

"I suppose that you know how to keep another man's secret when it is confided to you, sir?" the boy said, rather haughtily. Crabbe noted a slight trembling of the lips and the knees, which might be due to cold, and which might not. The boy bore inspection bravely.

"Oh yes," Crabbe at length responded: "I know how to keep a secret, when I know what the secret is."

"Then that's all right. You have seen mine. Please keep it." And, turning round, the youngster ran off across the grass, vaulting the railing and going toward Rotten Row and Knightsbridge.

"Come back, you young devil," Crabbe growled, his voice sinking to *diminuendo*: for he saw that no words were suited: and only uttered them as it were automatically, obeying an impulse. But the young devil was out of hearing; and, in another minute, was out of sight.

"Well—I—am—damned!" Crabbe iterated. He resumed his impassive attitude; and considered the thing from many points of view for an hour. He could not make anything of it—beyond this, that a boy in blue had arrived, that a boy in nothing-at-all had swum about a mile, and that a telegraph-boy had gone away: and yet not three boys, but one boy. Then what had become of the blue Norfolk jacket and knickerbockers? Crabbe rose; and slowly went towards the spring-board, auguring that they must have been deposited in that neighbourhood. The boatmen were clearing the bathers out of the water; and the spring-board was being returned to its three posts: it moved on a pivot, and was secured by a padlock. Crabbe crawled along, avoiding the groups who were dressing; and anon he saw a little heap of clothes lying by the railings right at the western end. No one was near them: no one seemed to note them. There was a policeman on the gravel thirty yards away: his back was turned. Crabbe thought of grabbing the bundle, of concealing it under his cloak, of examining the clothes elsewhere at leisure for a name or initial or any kind of clue to identity. But then—no. The secret was the boy's. Suppose that he were to leave the clothes,—the policeman, or the boatman, would discover them when all the bathers were gone away; and would imagine that their owner had been drowned. Anyone easily might be drowned, or might drown himself, in all that mob. Then they would drag the lake; and make no end of a fuss, looking for the body. Crabbe laughed abruptly and unpleasantly. He well knew—oh he jolly well knew, what an infinity of pains men will spend to redeem, and how strenuously men will exert themselves not to prevent.

"Let the fools drag their beastly lake!" he said; and sidled away to the right to hear the eight-thirty Mass at the Brompton Oratory.

When he returned at a quarter-past nine, he was just in time to see a dreadful young hag come from the arch of the bridge and snatch up the clothes and scuttle away with them. The place seemed quite deserted now. He crossed the road into Kensington Gardens: made for the enclosure where tables and cane armchairs are shaded by Japanese umbrellas; and ordered breakfast. All the morning, he sat there smoking and thinking furiously.

"Well—I—am—damned!" he at length reiterated.

Then he began to turn attention all to his own schemes.

Chapter Two

O n Monday morning, he presented himself to his publisher. Slim Schelm (a tubby little pot-bellied bantam, scrupulously attired and looking as though he had been suckled on bad beer,) was both interested and afraid. The two never had met before. The publisher had a curiosity to see the writer whose first book he had published;[1] and, knowing the past, he also had his qualms. The writer, on the other hand, took no more interest in the publisher than one takes in the chopper which one seizes at random for hewing out steps to fortune: and he had no fear at the back of his mind: and he had something quite definite to say. Slim Schelm expressed in words his pleasure at the meeting; and put on a mask which was intended to represent sympathetic commiseration. Crabbe brushed all veils aside.

"I am come to see you about my new book," he began.[2] "Don't think though that I wish unduly to occupy your time," he continued with an arctic highness which strangely contrasted with his frightfully shabby garb. He thought that he saw a spark of patronage in Schelm's watery china eyes; and made haste to quench it.

"Last March," he began again, "you commissioned me to write a second book. I delivered the MS. to you in October; and since then I have not heard from you. You know what has happened to me in those nine months; and I think that you have had sufficient time for deliberation. So will you kindly tell me whether you are going to publish me or not?"

"Of course, Mr Crabbe, what I mean to say is I shall be most happy to publish your book. I was thinking of writing to you about it. It has been very favourably reported on, you know."

"I don't know. You have not told me. However, I am glad

[1] *Stories Toto Told Me*, published by John Lane in 1898.
[2] *In His Own Image*, published by John Lane in 1901.

that you are going to publish; and I shall be much obliged if you will settle terms with me out of hand."

"I'm afraid I'm rather pressed to-day. If you could—. Would not any of your friends—?"

"Oh, lots of my friends would be happy to. But I don't propose to approach them."

"What I meant to say was would not any of your friends put you up for a week or so while I am considering—."

"No. Please look at the thing in this light. Take it that I have no friends, that I have nothing in this world except that book. If you, after nine months, are not able to make up your mind to buy it, please give me the MS.; and I will take it to some other publisher."

"By the by, let's see. Have you ever met Sidney Thorah?"

"No. But I am going to see him to-day. He wrote, a year ago, when he was publishing those stories of mine in the *Blue Volume*, and said that (if I ever wanted a man to talk to) he would like to be the man."

"And I'm sure you'll find him a very useful party to know, Mr Crabbe. Now let me advise you to wire him at once that you're coming; and then go and have a good long talk with him."

Crabbe meditated a minute; and consented. A clerk was summoned; and a telegraph-form filled and dispatched. Slim Schelm continued, "I suppose you intend to settle down to write in earnest, Mr Crabbe?"

"Yes."

"Well then, you cannot have a better introducer to literature than Sidney Thorah. He can get you no end of work, because he's on the staff of the *Daily Anagraph* and in touch with all the literary lights. Besides, you know, he thinks very highly of your folk-lore stories—."

"Or he would not have printed six—." [1]

"I know. And what I mean to say is they were very well received."

[1] Henry Harland had published six of Rolfe's Tato stories in *The Yellow Book.*

CHAPTER TWO

Crabbe inwardly glowed. He had been buried in a desert; and never a word of praise or of encouragement had come to him so far. But he kept his satisfaction in his shell, merely poking out his inquisitive eyes.

"In fact," Schelm continued, "I see nothing to prevent you making a huge success. Any introductions I can give of course I shall be most pleased to. For example, I advise you to take a copy of your first book—."

"How is that book selling?"

"Well what I mean to say is we never expect a little book to be a pecuniary success. You see a shilling book is not worth advertising. But it's an excellent advertisement of your future work; and I advise you to take a copy to let's say Odoys and tell him you're the author of it, and ask him to give you employment as a reader to his firm. And while you're in the neighbourhood you might as well go and see Doron Oldcastle Limited. Tell him I sent you. Show him your book. He's a very pushing young publisher; and I'm sure he'll be only too glad to give you some MSS. to read. Unfortunately my own reading staff's quite full; otherwise I should have been most happy. And by the by, you might go to *Appleton's Weekly*[1] offices—you know where they are—and ask for Mr Giddy. He was one of my clerks once. Tell him I sent you; and ask him to get you something to do on the paper. And meanwhile depend on me to do everything in my power—."

A clerk stuck in his head announcing a visitor. Schelm turned to the grim figure in the mackintosh.

"I'm afraid I must ask you to excuse me, Mr Crabbe—a most important appointment. You go and have a good long talk with Sidney Thorah. You know his address? And come in to-morrow morning about eleven and then we'll settle about the book. Meanwhile, don't set me down among the friends you seem to scorn so: but please put this in your pocket. This way, Mr Crabbe, please."

Crabbe emerged from a side door with a sovereign in his

[1] *Pearson's Weekly*, to which Rolfe contributed.

hand. His impulse was to dash it in the gutter. His second thought led him to pouch it: for Schelm actually owed him £3. A year before, the editor of the *Blue Volume* had told him he was to have ten pounds for his last contribution; and the publisher had sent seven. Besides, he was come to London to make money —fairly, if possible: but to make money. It was no good to be more difficult than was necessary. So he pounced on the coin as a bit of flotsam; and sidled away to the left, calculating whether Thorah would have had time to receive his telegraph if he were to go straight off to South Kensington bus-wise.

Chapter Three

CRABBE waited a couple of minutes in a large and very dainty drawing-room. There were a couch and a piano and lots of weird and comfy chairs, and a feminine atmosphere. Sidney Thorah suddenly fell in, with a clatter and a rush; and began to talk-on-a-trot. He was a lank round-shouldered bony unhealthy personage, much given to crossing his legs when seated and to twisting nervously in his chair. He had insincere eyes, and long arms which dangled while he was silent and jerked and waved when he spoke. He spoke a great deal, in eager tones inlaid with a composite jargon which was basically Judisch but varied with the gibberish of newly-arrived American students of the Latin Quarter. He wore a fawn-coloured dressing-suit and a silk handkerchief; and Crabbe, noting the big jacinth on the little finger and the wide upturned nose, suspected an apostate Jew.

Thorah was delighted. He never looked his guest in the face; but made play with his eye-glasses, fiddled with his slippers and the fringes on carpets and chairs, provided cigarettes, and finally settled down with one leg tucked under him and the other dangling in a manner which indicated mitral regurgitation. He evidently was a hard man on trousers. All the time, he was darting side glances; and his shrill clamour lashed Crabbe like sleet. He talked of books and people. His conversation was amazingly witty, pleasant, ephemeral, and insincere. But he seemed to be a man of power; and Crabbe deliberated to give him a chance of being useful.

Crabbe's main characteristic was a most retentive memory. Living, as he did, entirely in himself and in the past, gave him an old-fashioned habit of mind. Consequently his progression was always lateral and somewhat slow. At the same time he was sure: for nothing could exceed his tenacity. He yearned for sympathy; and he would have purred to proper appreciation. He was

27

timid in most things, reserved, fearful and impatient of ridicule
and disapproval; and, hence, he was conventional in his dread of
publicity. If he had had his will, he would have elected to live
alone (with a few slaves). Forced into public life, he was in
difficulty. He encased himself more or less in a carapax of
secrecy and mystery, watching the world and waiting for an
opportunity. He had found his natural predilection for a gre-
garious existence to be a complete failure; and he was resolved
to ally himself to no person and to no company any more. With
the development of his individuality had come a remarkable
development of his imagination. With the growth of his personality had come a fastidiousness which was composed of
boredom, aloofness, contempt, and fine feeling. He was a
bundle of inconsistencies. Keenness of sensation, carefully
cultivated, made his tender core easily accessible to wounds; but
his proud hard (not to say) crusty demeanour concealed them.
To his enemies he was enormously exasperating; he never let
them see that they had drawn blood. Psychically, he was quick
of perception: he could sum up a person or a problem in a
minute, and generally accurately. Physically, he gave the impression of being phenomenally obtuse, indurated, ferocious.
In the matter of money, he was extravagant, chimerical, quixotic, noncurant, to a degree: but he collected and hoarded odds
and ends, books, papers, gems, facts, under all circumstances,
even impossible. He was very conservative. Radicalism and dissent filled him with scorn and contempt beyond utterance: the
fierce and mordant pungency of his comments on the methods of
methodists were quite unequalled. Yet he himself unscrupulously
would part with his own most cherished illusions or opinions
when new light came to him. I have said that he was tenacious: I
must say also that he was a most persistent persequent ruthless
foe. He never attacked for the mere sake of attacking: but people
who poked at him, or trod on him, had reason for bewailing the
cruel violent unexpected inevitability of his crunching grip. He
never let go; and he never ceased to persecute and harass. He
never forgot anything at all. Although he was not averse from

fame and public recognition of a quiet kind, his ambitions were extremely modest. His wants were those of Martial:—

> A wine merchant, a butcher, a bath, a barber, a chess-board and chess-men, a few books (but give me to choose them), one comrade not too unpolished, a tall servant who long preserves his youth, a damsel beloved of my servant —secure me these, o Rufus, even though it be at Butontum, and you may have the baths of Nero.

He was, then, reserved and sensitive, sympathetic and tenacious, persistent and impatient, impressionable and emotional. He was beginning to understand the necessity of selfishness for the protection of his individuality; and, on these lines, he was becoming self-possessed, self-reliant, strong, and potent. He fully realised that a success would be obtained by tenacity; and that failure would attend hyper-sensitiveness. With this frame of mind, the knowledge that the moon was in her first quarter and that the day was Monday, and a fervent invocation of Saint Gabriel Archangel, he confronted Sidney Thorah, ready to hear, frank to speak, quick to note, and relentless against yielding an inch.

"I don't want to be intrusive," his host said, "but do tell me, if you will, why you went there, and how you came away."

"It doesn't much matter," Crabbe responded, "but, to prevent charitable people from reaching their conclusions, I'll say what I will say; and then you'll know what to think when you 'hear people of importance bleat,' as the important Newbolt says. I went into the workhouse for just this reason. A man, for whom I had slaved, defrauded me of my promised wages. He was strong: I was weak. When I demurred, he swore that he would ruin me, prevent me from earning a living ever, and have me hounded out of the town. I retorted that he might be able to do the first and the second; and that he was free to do both: but that the third was beyond his power. 'I will stay here,' I said, 'and rot here, and let you kill me here: but I never will go away from here unless I am carried away dead, or until I have seen

Your Reverence slink away in disgrace.' That's what I flung at him. I went to my lodgings: finished the book which Schelm had ordered last March twelvemonth: sent in the MS. and began another. Four months passed. Then I saw my persecutor convicted of fraud and conveyed to a lunatic asylum. Then also, I was at the end of my own resources. I asked everybody I knew to give me work. None would. No word came of my book; and I surmised that to mention the matter to Schelm would mar my chances of publication. I don't know the ethics of publishers, beyond that 'Bar-Abbas was a Robber': but I opined that a man of business would be likely to take advantage of necessity. I had no friends upon whom to lean. All my goods were pawned. I had no money, and no prospects beyond that book—.''

"I've read it," Thorah interpolated. "It's going to bring you £700 in six months."

"How delightful of you to say so!" Crabbe adjoined. "That would be proper! However, there I was, stranded, naked, exhausted. I posted all my pawn-tickets to myself at St Martin's-le-Grand.[1] I didn't want to die before the appearance of my book: because, then, someone else would reap the profit of my exertions, and I should stand a chance of being *Dylymyled* as a pathetic and romantic failure.[2] It wasn't the dying which I minded. No. 'If we are happy asleep in bed, it must be exquisite to be dead' says that silly O'Sullivan. But I wasn't going to have all my previous sufferings wasted. I made up my mind that someone would have to pay for those. So I went into the workhouse, just to live and pass the time. Then, I managed to see the next step: so I came out, and walked here."[3]

"How ghastly—how hideous—how frightful!" Thorah gabbled.

"Oh yes, as ghastly and all the rest as possible this side of

[1] The headquarters of the London Post Office.
[2] This alludes to *The Daily Mail*.
[3] Readers of *The Quest for Corvo* will need no telling that Rolfe is following the lines of his own life very closely in the description he gives of Crabbe's career.

hell. But we are not going to talk about it any more, at present," Crabbe concluded.

Thorah, twitching with excitement, mentally summed up his guest as a very clever and thoroughly impracticable man who had been beaten down into the mire by the terrible force of circumstances opposing an unconventional personality. He looked all over the tea-leaf coloured garb, the corduroy trousers and jacket, the jute-soled canvas shoes frayed and stained and amorphous with a thousand miles of walking, the withered cloak, the dreadful cap; but he noted that the socks and the finger-nails were clean, and that the whole arrangement was concise. He revolted at the thin unkempt beard and hair, wondering what the face would look like after shaving. The voice attracted him, low and minor, with its delicate swift vibrant enunciation. He was interested in the misadventures of an identity: for his visitor was a most distinct identity. Crabbe answered all questions clearly: seemed to be ashamed of nothing, and to have nothing to conceal. Undoubtedly he had been treated horribly and neglected abominably. Undoubtedly he had it in him to do something notable; and might have to be reckoned with some day.

Bent on hospitality, Thorah apologised for his own practice of taking nothing but a glass of milk for lunch; and commanded eggs and bacon for his guest. Crabbe thought it funny: but a large old housekeeper produced eggs and bacon on a tray; and he ate and talked, making no signs of wonder. It appeared that, as regards taste, especially literary taste, he and his host were in sympathy. Thorah indicated his impatience of most things. Crabbe manifested his possession of much curious and valuable knowledge. It was all quite pleasant.

Presently, Thorah wished to make his visitor known to the sub-editor of the *Blue Volume*. She was an intellectual mouse-mannered piece of sex, inhabiting a neighbouring flat; and a verbal message brought her. The men carried on the conversation while she played the chorus. Thorah at last introduced the question of ways and means. Crabbe described his interview with Schelm.

"Did you tell him what you were going to do?" Thorah inquired.

"I said that I was going to write for my living."

"And what did he propose?"

"Oh he advised me to apply to Odoys and Doron Oldcastle for a reader's berth. And I'm to ask one of Schelm's late clerks, who's on *Appleton's Weekly,* for something to do in connection with that paper. And Schelm's going to do everything in his power. And I'm to see him about my book to-morrow morning."

"M—ym! Don't have anything to do with Odoys if you want money. He never pays. Ask Gervais Quair whether he does. And I hardly should think *Appleton's Weekly* the kind of paper you'd care to appear in."

"My dear sir, I don't care where I appear, I've got a living to earn."

"But you couldn't write that kind of stuff."

"But I can write forty-two different kinds of stuff; and, if *Appleton's Weekly* doesn't like any of those, I'll invent a forty-third. What about Doron Oldcastle, though?"

"Well, he might put something in your way, perhaps. I used to know him when he was a pimply bumpkin in gorgeous vests. He was office-boy to the *Earthly Arbiter,*[1] then. Four years ago, he took to publishing on his own account; and seems to be successful. You might do worse than go to him. The joke is he's Schelm's rival and mortal enemy."

Crabbe abruptly laughed. "Thanks. It's well to know that," he said.

The sub-editor nodded silent sympathy; and would have squeaked a tale upon request. Thorah said that there was lots of work going begging: the thing was to get to know the proper people. He offered to arrange a hundred introductions; and, when Crabbe rose to go, asked him to accept a sovereign. This was too comical. Crabbe gaily rejected it, saying he had no need of it, in view of what Schelm had done and was going to do: but Thorah insisted—it was due for the last story printed and

[1] *The Review of Reviews.*

never paid for properly—no man ever was the worse for an extra sovereign—the next few weeks might be a little troublesome, and it was always well to be provided—and so on and so forth. Crabbe said that, if he put it like that, of course—in time he would collect his £3; and he came away from South Kensington godlike, golden, breathing ambrosial odours.

He cabbed it to Lincoln's Inn Fields; and arranged his furniture. He bought a little mirror, and a case of oranges, and a sack of coarse oatmeal; and ordered a quart of milk a day from the dairy. In the evening, he had his hair cropped within half-an-inch of his skin, and his beard trimmed in the Vandyke mode. The barber was in raptures of the natural upward wave of the chestnut-hued moustachio; and Crabbe purchased a small pair of scissors for future private use.

All the evening, he sat in his easy chair by the open window of his big bare room, gloating over the new green of the trees and the fusky splendour of the sunset sky. At last he had a place of his own, a garden enclosed. The house beneath him was empty for the night. He was alone with his soul within shut doors. When darkness devoured the twilight, he went and had a good wash at the kitchen sink—a lovely wash under a running tap; and, soon, he slept.

About five o'clock in the morning, he awakened; and ate an orange: afterwards returning to bed and lying at rest in that delicious warm freshness when the limbs quiesce and the mind is at easy activity. He revised his memory of yesterday; and erected his schemes for to-day. Thorah seemed well disposed: but—there was something Judisch about him, and he was worth watching. In fact, he needed watching—all the time. What was the relation between him and the mouse-mannered sub-editor? Obviously they were not man and wife. But that drawing-room had a feminine air. True, Thorah himself was an effeminate sort of male. Still—. But the lady looked clever. Oh, she certainly was not one of that kind. Yet Thorah had not mentioned anybody's wife. Was there a wife? Oh, what did it matter? Think of something else. Think of Slim Schelm. Now there was a beery insect for you, a snivelling little swindler if you gave him a chance. Crabbe always did think a carroty dwarf, with a magenta face and puce pendulous lips and a vermilion necktie, hideous. Still, that insect was going to buy his book. Well; if Schelm treated him decently, he would treat Schelm decently. Crabbe knew that he had the ability to do something uncommon in the way of literature; and, if Schelm had the sense to make a success of this book, as any publisher with ordinary wit can do with any extraordinary book, he was quite ready to let him have all his future work. He knew very little about these things: but he supposed that, when one found a publisher, one stuck to him. That would be so admirably satisfactory all round.

Crabbe permitted himself to enjoy a day-dream of rosy hue.

Chapter Four

AT eleven o'clock, Slim Schelm presented a silver cigarette-case containing a single cigarette. Crabbe took the latter; and lighted it. They were sitting in a little dirty-green room full of framed drawings in black and white. A clerk brought in the precious MS. of *Daynian Folk-lore*;[1] and reverently laid it by the publisher. Schelm tapped it.

"I have been thinking what I can do for your best interests, Mr Crabbe," he said. "I should like very much to publish your book, you know; and what I mean to say is I'm willing to give you twenty pounds for it—ten now, and ten on publication. If you consent to accept those terms, I'll send it to the printers at once."

Crabbe's features wore a stony mask. He was hiding his bitter disappointment. He had written and rewritten that book ten times, in order to make it a perfect work of art; and now somebody was talking about twenty pounds.[2] Thorah had said that it was going to bring him seven hundred in six months. Supposing that he refused Schelm's offer, and took the MS. to another publisher. Then there would be another long delay. No. Better seize what was floating before him. No doubt but that, if Schelm sent the book to the printers at once, it could be published in a month; and then, in six months' time—.

"Will you accept my offer, Mr Crabbe?"

"It's not a matter of 'will I'. You know I must."

"Then you do?"

"Oh yes, I do. But I sincerely hope—."

"Well, if you're agreeable to sign a contract to that effect,

[1] *Daynian Folk-lore* is *In His Own Image.*

[2] Here again Rolfe is, of course, drawing from life. Lane offered him £20 for *In His Own Image* and, because Rolfe needed the money, he accepted, but he never forgave Lane. Later, the publisher was persuaded to buy a few more stories concerning Toto for £10.

I'll let you have a cheque now." Schelm turned over the first page of the MS.; and produced agreement and cheque both ready for signature.

Crabbe wrote his name, not attempting to understand the document he was signing: for his mind was full of other things. Schelm performed an autograph on the cheque; and handed it to him, saying, "Now Mr Crabbe, I hope that'll give you a good start. We'll soon have the book out; and that will help you to dispose of as many magazine articles as you can write. I think you'd better take a little room somewhere, and apply yourself to writing seriously. You'll find lots of cheap lodgings in the by-streets off the Euston Road; and that ten pounds ought to keep you comfortably until you're making a regular income."

"And I'm sure that you will remember—."

"Oh certainly, certainly. But I'm afraid I couldn't go into that now. Fact is I must ask you to excuse me, Mr Crabbe, a most important appointment—."

Crabbe drew in his eyes; and crawled reservedly away. Anyhow, he was £10 to the good; and his book really was coming out. Then there would be £10 more. He did a sum on his fingers. He had now a matter of £109 in his pocket. He opened a current account with a hundred at the nearest bank; and went the round of the people whom Schelm had recommended.

At *Appleton's Weekly*, a very bland young man smiled on him; and placed personal questions. Crabbe frankly responded; and became excessively interesting. The very bland young man begged permission to retire; and returned with another smiling and interrogative youth. Inquisition proceeded. Other derisive and deridable popinjays strolled in: inspected Crabbe's horrible attire: stroked their satin ties; and fingered their orient-pearl pins, listening violently. Crabbe began to hear his own voice: began to be conscious that he was making no sort of impression by what he said: became sure that he was simply a curiosity on exhibition. The light went out of his eyes; his animation languished: he was silent, stolid, armed, once more. The first bland young man said that he was happy to have made his acquaintance. He came away, speechless with rage. This was a most damnable thing of Schelm to do—to make a show of him. It was plain that nothing was to be hoped for from *Appleton's Weekly* and Slim Schelm must have known it.

He went to Odoys in the next street. A hoary old person presented a mask indicating alarm. Crabbe exhibited his first little book: announced that Schelm was issuing a second and a larger one immediately: briefly described his qualifications; and asked for a chance of showing his skill as a judge of commonplace literature. Odoys fearfully gibbered that, at that moment, there were three MSS. on which he would be glad to have Mr Crabbe's opinion: they should be sent to him at Slim Schelm's; and the fee was four guineas a MS. Then the old thing tottered so very dreadfully that Crabbe benignly beamed, and terminated the interview.

When he was admitted to the presence of Doron Oldcastle Limited, there was a little crash of falling and breaking glass. A scorbutic hobbledehoy rose from a roll-top desk: dropped and smashed a stringless monocle; and shook Crabbe's hand, gravely saying to the clerk who introduced him, "Syren, please will you have the courtesy to at once go and purchase me an eyeglass and charge it to Petty Cash."

Crabbe suppressed a snort of joy: squirmed at the diction; and began to narrate his business.

"Ha yes!" Oldcastle meditatively said. He was a strenuous stripling in a spotty plush waistcoat; and he seemed to find his own smile most alluring. "And so you want some literary work, Mr Crabbe. Well now, have you any proposals to courteously specify to me?" He split all his infinitives with conscientious insistence.

Crabbe said that his present need was such regular literary employment as would enable him to produce several books which he had planned.

"I know your first book very well, Mr Crabbe; and I think most highly of it," said Oldcastle. "But if you'll allow me to just pass the remark, I don't think you have been ever properly published yet. Let's see. How many of these *Daynian Folk-lore* stories have you now written?"

"Six, in the first book; and seventeen, in the second which Mr Schelm has bought today."

"Exactly. Well now: have you any more?"

"I collected forty-nine stories altogether."

"Twenty-three of which you have already disposed of. Well now: would you not like to obligingly write the remaining twenty-six for Me?"

"Very much indeed."

"I personally would be very glad indeed to immediately purchase those which you have previously sold to Mr Schelm, and publish the lot in one volume. I happen to (between ourselves) know that your work has been very well received in the best quarters; and I believe that I could so to speak do a great deal better for you in the way of honoraria than Mr Schelm."

A broad-nosed dough-faced dwarf, with thin woolly hair scattered over his big head, entered; and was presented as "Mr Abrahams, My Manager." Oldcastle continued, "I've just been telling Mr Crabbe, that I should much like to publish his *Daynian Folk-lore* series. It seems that Schelm has made a book of those six stories which originally appeared in the *Blue Volume*; and he's just bought a further instalment of seventeen stories for a second book. But Mr Crabbe has been courteous enough to just specify to me that he still has twenty-six stories of the same series left; and I've been saying that I should like to Myself purchase the lot."

Crabbe inserted a sentence. "It will be necessary for you to approach Mr Schelm concerning the twenty-three stories. But the twenty-six are mine to sell."

Abrahams enquired, "Can you let uth have a look at them? Are they written?"

"Yes; in a way: but they are not in a fit state for you to see. You can have them though in the time required for making a fair copy of them."

Syren, the clerk, came in with a new monocle. Doron Old-

castle wedged it into and blinded one eye. "Well now: that
comes within the range of what I may call practical politics. You
let Me see (say) a specimen story and the concluding story of the
series; and I shall be happy to definitely make you a handsome
offer."

"But I'm afraid that you don't quite understand my position,
Mr Oldcastle. There's nothing which I should like better than to
write books for you—the *Daynian Folk-lore*, for example,—if
you can square Mr Schelm: but at present I am seeking the
means to live. I want regular employment, of any kind, on the
proceeds of which I can live while I write my own books. It is
suggested that you should employ me to read the MSS. which
are submitted to you."

"Unfortunately there is not a vacancy on My staff of readers
just now. But look here: perhaps I could as it were put something
else in your way. Why not dash off a few *Globe Turnovers*? I
could get them accepted for you. Or a few magazine articles?"

"I am not facile at dashing off casual rubbish. I can do it: but
it's harder work, and takes a longer time than respectable
literature."

"No, don't say that, Mr Crabbe. Anyone can do it like wink-
ing. Why, when I was fifteen—I'm twenty-five now—I used to
every week review all the books for the *Earthly Arbiter*."

"That's precisely what I would like to do. I can't write
original rubbish, without taking enormous pains; and I must
keep my pains for something worthy of them: but I can criticize;
and I only want enough criticism to live on."

"Ha yes. Well now: courteously think over what I have
specified; and come and see Me again. It would give Me much
pleasure to as far as in Me lies be of service to you, Mr Crabbe:
for I think that we might work together to our mutual advantage."

Oldcastle rose, extending a damp hand. Crabbe internally
vowed that he rather would kiss a cold poached egg than touch
it again. Abrahams conducted him toward the outer office. As
they passed, there was the tinkling crash of a smashed monocle;

and a sweaty voice murmured, "Syren, please will you have the courtesy to at once go and purchase me an eye-glass and charge it to Petty Cash."

"Your work ith quite well known to me, Mithter Crabbe. I think it'th shplendid," Abrahams said.

"Thank you very much," Crabbe coldly responded.

Abrahams tried again. "Pleathe don't think me intruthive, Mithter Crabbe, I really thould be glad to therve you. The *Globe* givth a guinea for a Turnover, you know; and I could get anything of yourth into a magathine. I know thutth work'th not worthy of you: but jutht for the prethent, you know."

The little man's manner was not disrespectful: it was anything but that. His black bead-like eyes were almost genial. His opinions certainly were most right and apt. Crabbe looked down on him, with as much urbanity as he could collect, though he was rather sick at heart.

"Thank you very much," he iterated, "I'll think of what you are good enough to say."

On the way back to Lincoln's Inn Fields, he bought a lamp and an oil-can, a ream of standard linen bank-paper, a ream of green blotting-paper, a large bottle of Draper's Dichroic Ink, a Japanese letter-copybook, and a ream of letter-paper and envelopes. He tried to get a fountain-pen holding a quarter of a pint, like the one used by the barbarian Elgar: but failed; and had to be content with the largest Waterman Ideal in the shop and world.

As he ate a meal of oranges and dry oatmeal, he pondered his morning's work. It appeared certain that, in order to evade a charge of dereliction of duty, he would have to produce the magazine work desiderated by Doron Oldcastle. If he did not, the publisher might aver that he had refused work. So, with infinite trouble, he contrived (during the next few days) to excrete certain rot of the kind which is dear to the magazine-editor, to wit:— *The Romance of a Raphael, The Confessions of a Carnation, Alligator-hunting in the Andaman Islands, Burke's Stranded Gentry,* 800–1000 words each, and a new Daynian

Folk-lore story about Judas Iscariot of 2,500 words. The last was an afterthought, done to cleanse his clogged and slimy pen. He delivered the sheaf to Oldcastle; and expected guineas. None came. Instead, a note from Sidney Thorah gurgled:— "Do come to T and meet my wife who returns from New York to-morrow. What have you been a-doing of these last days?"

Chapter Five

THE wife was a dark pale tired timid little thing, with a secret and the voice of a nightingale. Crabbe was very shy: for there was a party. The mouse-mannered sub-editor also was there, squeaking unobtrusively;—and that settled that. There was a very handsome large young woman, bright-haired, azure-eyed. There was a curate, obese, olive-skinned, curatical, with a dazzling soft red-haired wife, who answered to the name of Helen of Troy.[1] There was a rather pretty worn Irish woman, excruciatingly and incessantly witty. There was a thin wide-mouthed suffragist of thirty, coy and silent, whose huge black eyes yearned for the secretary of a bank. A solemn young Slav, and a male lath conscious of a likeness to Professor Lecky, and an insistently celebrated critical caricaturist in a frayed waistcoat, completed the company. Sidney Thorah skipped and hovered and sat on his hind leg everywhere, like a cricket, a bluebottle, a toad, clicketty-clacking, buzzing, and rarely dumb.

Crabbe was silent and grimly shy. At first, he really found little to say. He folded his claws as tidily as possible, and drank his tea, and ate his farthing bun, gravely reticent, alertly vigilant. The cackle around him was wonderfully inconsequent and amusing. Everyone (except the tired little hostess and himself) seemed to be dancing on the apex of light-heartedness and irresponsibility.

Thorah blared at him questions as to where he was living and what he had been doing. Everybody pinned their gaze on him and listened with phrenzy.

"I have taken a modest lodging in town. You can write to me at Schelm's. I shall go there for my correspondence every other day," he said; and rapped out a concisely categorical response to the second question. This was punctuated by inappropriate shrieks of laughter. Luckily he had cultivated his keen sense

[1] Possibly Percy and Mabel Dearmer.

42

of the ridiculous; and had a dryly witty way of describing his sensations. In a forest of trees without heart-wood, the castor-oil plant is king, says the Burmese adage. Crabbe felt himself able to swim in the present company. The titles of the articles, which he had written for Doron Oldcastle, elicited roars: but, when he named the Daynian Folk-lore story, Thorah demanded why he had not brought it.

But he had brought it—at least, a copy of it; and he produced the MS. from his haversack. Thorah grabbed: commanded silence; and began to read aloud. He read most beautifully and sympathetically, without a trace of the Judisch sibilation.

Crabbe presently found himself thinking that he had done something which was as good as possible. The description of the thunderstorm was quite impressive: it had marmoreal majesty and the divine ether of the empyrean. Silence followed the reading—silence which was more convenient than applause.

People eyed Crabbe as they took their leave. He, in turn, rose to go: but Mrs Thorah put out a small hand of detention. They talked very quietly until her husband came back from assisting his guests' departure. Nothing of import was said: but Crabbe was aware that the lady was trying to come from the depths, in which her own soul was concealed, in order to comfort and encourage him. He believed that this was a case of simple sympathy. He would have liked to have corresponded with the vibrations which he distinctly could feel. But he was afraid. His desperate fear of women restrained him. His unreasoning instinct, against anything like near relations with his fellow-creatures, barred reciprocation. The idea, that there was anything in him, psychically or physically, which could attract the esteem of another, never entered his mind. He had accustomed himself to count all kindness, all praise, as the offspring of pity or of envy or of contempt; and, as such, he rejected it utterly. So, he remained unresponsive, gravely attentive and urbane; and maintained the progress of the acquaintance merely upon the surface of things.

Thorah returned, screeching, "My dear soul, do you know

you've done something really great? Fancy, Eileen, our friend Schelm's only going to give him twenty pounds for a book full of stories like this!"

"Oh they're not all as good as that!" Crabbe interrupted. "But that one's not the best of the rest by a long chalk. I've only been feeling my feet so far. Wait till I shew you some of the new ones which I'm going to begin to-morrow; and then you'll tell me some news."

"I hope you won't let Mr Schelm have these new ones," the lady affirmed.

"Why not?" her husband peremptorily inquired." It seems to me that he can't do better than offer them to Schelm on the nail. I'll tell ye for why, as Mrs Toovey would say. Isn't she adorably funny? Well, I'll tell ye for why. Schelm and Oldcastle hate one another like poison. Don't ask me the reason. Oldcastle's jealous of Schelm; and Schelm says that Oldcastle steals his authors. He's really trying to steal you, Crabbe, now; and you may take this for certain—if Schelm thinks that Oldcastle wants your *Daynian Folk-lore*, nothing on earth short of barratry, the King's enemies, or an Act of God, will persuade him to part with it. So you can put Oldcastle out of your mind altogether, as far as *Daynian Folk-lore*'s concerned. What I advise you to do is to try and make better terms with Schelm. How many stories can you get ready in a month? Six? *Bien!* How big's the book now? Eighty thousand words? *Très bien!* Then look here. Tell Schelm that you'll write him six more stories for it, and make it a hundred thousand words. The public likes a big book—something fat for its six shillings. Your aim is to get published as precipitately as possible and as perfectly as possible. So I say put all you know, all your very best work into this book for the sake of your future. Never mind what Schelm gives you now. You give him a good book; and you'll find it worth your while."

"Consider two things," Crabbe said. "If I add six stories to *Daynian Folk-lore*, I shall have to rewrite the whole thing for the eleventh time, in order to fit them in. That's one. I'm afraid that

I've sold the book outright to Schelm; and that I shall have no claim on him for further remuneration if it's a success. That's the other."

"Never mind. Schelm's a smart man of business; and he's taken a shameful advantage of your poverty—don't fly down my throat. I'm only speaking as a friend. Schelm's a smart man of business, I say: but he's not a blackguardly bandit like some publishers I could mention—."

"Oh Sidney, how can you say that, when you know what a wretch he was to you before you made your own name. Mr Crabbe, don't believe him, Mr Schelm's a—."

"Eileen, you know he's not. Do be careful: or we shall have a writ for libel. One must be very cautious in this country, Eileen, don't you know. Listen, Crabbe. When a book succeeds, the publisher makes the author a present in proportion to the book's success. That's what Schelm will do. So you let him have all your work now for anything he likes to give you; and by and by you'll reap the benefit. And, if you must rewrite the book, rewrite it. That's what I say," Thorah concluded, rising, and lighting a Three Castles cigarette.

Crabbe looked hard and glum. The prospect was not alluring.

"You know more of these matters than I do," he stated, "and I'm content to take your word. If I knew what I was going to live on, while I'm doing all this work, I'd make no bones about it. But don't you see that I must have something certain?"

"I'm sure, Sidney, if you were to speak to Mrs Toovey," the lady said, "she could make her husband give Mr Crabbe plenty of regular work."

"The very thing!" Thorah screamed, with a bound in the air. "Crabbe, if you've made a friend of Eileen, you can look upon yourself as safe. She never makes a mistake; and she's the cleverest woman in the world."

"What can Mr Toovey do?" Crabbe inquired.

"Do? Why he's the London editor of the *American Orb*; and he can do anything—give you a fifteen-pound article a week to write. I'll put him on to you by this very night's post as ever is."

"Because you're clever, and you're good, and you're charming; and we're going to help you to get on as you deserve," Mrs Thorah exclaimed, with sudden and Kirkean animation.

Crabbe walked on air down the Brompton Road and Knightsbridge and Piccadilly. The way seemed clear. He was going to have the happiness of writing the stories which he loved. No more dancing attendance on publishers. Yoicks! He could live on the article a week for the *American Orb*—could live well, and dress properly, and have chops at will, and save money too. Even if that didn't come off quite, still he had a hundred pounds in the bank. But no one was to know of that hoard. It was for an emergency, for a last resort. And there were the four articles which Oldcastle and Abrahams had promised to sell. Oh yes: things were shaping beautifully. And he was going to write the stories which he loved.

While he was waiting to cross Piccadilly Circus, he became conscious that someone was eyeing him from the top of an omnibus. He shot up an eye of his own; and beheld a very pallid telegraph-boy intently gazing.

He instantly mounted. The top was empty, save for himself and that one. No one else was there: but only himself and the youngster.

Chapter Six

THE boy occupied the back seat on the near side. During his ascent, Crabbe's impulse had been to sit beside him, and to put questions. Second thoughts caused him to use a distant disengaged unrecognising air; and to take the seat which was just in front of the boy. The omnibus moved on; and turned down Regent Street toward Pall Mall. The course was fairly easy. Crabbe sat very still, in a state of wondering expectation. He could not conceive what was going to happen: he only could determine to see the thing out to the end, that is until the boy alighted. Manners would forbid him to alight as well: but there was no rule against riding on a public omnibus. Of course the two were perfect strangers; and so, perhaps, they would remain. In no case would Crabbe seek. He simply would not avoid a sending. Nay: he even would go so far as to make his address more unfindable than was necessary.

Just as much as that. The omnibus was bowling gaily down Whitehall. A quiet thin and clear voice behind him said, "I believe, sir, that I owe you an explanation."

Crabbe waited a few seconds. Then he turned round, and gravely said, "How do you do? I am very pleased to make your acquaintance. My name is Nicholas Crabbe."

"Mine is Robert Fulgentius Kemp."

"Have you anything particular to do for the next hour or so, Mr Kemp? The top of an omnibus is not the best place in the world for explanations."

"No. I am off for the night, after I have delivered an express letter in Victoria Street."

"Then perhaps you will do me the pleasure of dining with me. There is a restaurant by Victoria Station where one can eat a chop."

"I will be pleased to accept your invitation," the boy quaintly and frankly concluded.

47

Under the lights of the restaurant, Crabbe secretly noted that an undesirable change had come over his guest, during the couple of weeks which had elapsed since their first meeting. Under and at the corners of his long green eyes, sundry fine lines were beginning to trace themselves. The wonderful white skin was whiter: but it was not so radiant or so warm. It seemed to have become sore and frozen. The cheeks had lost their delicate roundness. The cloven chin was imbared. At the back of the bright eyes lay a nameless haunting wistful terror: they were hot and sad and tired: they sparkled mysteriously. The hands were like the hands of an old priest, very attenuated, sacred, pure.

"I conceive, sir," said Kemp, with rather weird directness, "that you are in error concerning my age."

"Perhaps."

"I am much older than I look."

"You look about fourteen or fifteen now: but I know that you are older than that."

"Well I told the Post Office people that I was fourteen and a half. As a matter of fact, I will be twenty-three in September."

Crabbe shot a swift side glance over him: admitted to himself the possibility: produced an air of sympathetic respectful attention: but uttered no word. The boy seemed to consider such reception of his news correct. Further communication, however, had its difficulties. The two ate their meal in silence. Crabbe knew that the interview was none of his seeking: although nothing could have jumped more accurately with his desire. He did no more than to shew himself in the character of blotting-paper, unasking and essentially receptive. Kemp's hesitation was caused merely by a scruple at stripping one's soul to a stranger. He found it hard to select, from his experiences, enough to give a just account of himself; and also it was very hard to put the same in words. Still, the stranger did not disgust him by banal verbosity, had not shown any kind of disposition to intrude; and Kemp seemed to feel at length that he was side by side with one of those lonely men to whom one can unbosom oneself with satisfaction and with security.

CHAPTER SIX

"No doubt, sir, you consider all this very strange," he began.

Crabbe decided to shift the conversation on to a suitable and convenient plane. "Will you believe," he said, "that you are only an incident in my life? When you are present, I admit that you interest me: when you are absent, I do not permit myself to consider you at all. I have no right to consider you. My own life belongs to myself, and to no one else. I concede an equal respect to you. I can see that your stars, or mine, or both, have thrown you in my way. I'm bound to say that your proceedings the other morning excited my curiosity—and my admiration. But you spoke of a secret; and so you sealed the door of inquiry or of interest on my part. Now, you are urged, somehow, to offer an explanation. Let me say that an explanation is unnecessary: unless you desire to explain. If I can serve you by hearing you, it will give me pleasure to listen. But I have nothing, not even an explanation, to offer you in return."

"I think I shall tell you, all the same."

"I am honoured by your confidence. Will you let me make you one of my cigarettes: or will you prefer those which they sell here?"

Kemp accepted the former; and produced a ring-clip which he attached to his finger. He licked the paper, deftly closing the cylinder; and shared a match with Crabbe. He blew a few clouds in silence, seemingly hesitating still.

"Did you ever write a short story?" Crabbe inquired.

Kemp darted a brilliant glance at him. "Perhaps. Why, though?"

"Treat it as the scheme of a short story, told in the first person," Crabbe responded.

"That's a capital idea." He quickly arranged his materials, and began. "A description of myself and my early life is not cognate matter. You shall be pleased to take for granted that I was born and went to school and did things in the ordinary way. At the end of last year I was sent down from Oxford. I was at the House. I wish you to know that there is no necessity for placing an unwarrantable construction upon the reason given for my being sent down."

The eyes were wonderful.

"I was allowed to come up and take my degree a couple of months ago. But, meanwhile, my last relation had seen fit to die. Everything pointed to a severance from all my past life and from all my plans for the future. I had to leave something behind me —it was very little—in order to affect some such severance: but there was nothing else—at least I knew of nothing else to do beyond what I did do. You happened to see the transmigration of my personality. That's all I want to say."

"But, Gracious Powers—," Crabbe began. Ideas rushed confusedly about his mind; and oozed out in the remonstrating ejaculation. He pulled himself together.

"Pardon me," he said, "I see so many possibilities of sadness in that story."

The two sat smoking in silence, each rapt in his own thoughts.

"Pardon me again," Crabbe said at length, "but was there really nothing else for you to do but this?" He lightly touched a button on the other's uniform.

"No doubt there were lots of things. But my head was in a whirl; and I followed the first idea which seized me. I wanted to get away from everyone and everything."

"But your friends?"

"Most of my former friends deserted me. Most of those who remained were not friends of my choice. The rest—they were two—should have damaged themselves by associating with me; and I gave them the slip. I have no friends."

"But yourself?"

Crabbe found himself confronted by 'the tense glittering eyes never swerving a moment'. There was another longer pause of meditation.

"I did the only thing which occurred to me," Kemp put in.

"And what next?"

"There is no next."

Crabbe made another effort. He changed his manner to one

of conventionality. "How do you like the life?" he inquired.

"It's not bad, so far. One gets about a good deal; and one sees a lot of people; and it's rather fun to look on from the standpoint of an outsider. Now and then, I want to stop and puzzle and ponder a bit: but of course that's out of the question. On the whole, though, the life's not bad."

"How do you get on with the others?"

"I don't get on with them. I had to pull a few ears at first, I'm afraid. So now they leave me alone."

"Is the work long? Or tiresome?"

"Oh no, it's not tiresome—at least, yet. There's nothing to do but to run about: nothing intellectual, I mean. And my shift only lasts nine hours—."

"Only?"

"Well you see that leaves fifteen to be filled."

"And those?"

"Say that I sleep seven."

"That leaves eight."

"Yes. Eight hells."

"What do you do?"

"Walk about—anywhere but in Hyde Park."

Crabbe laughed with understanding. "Do you live anywhere?" he pursued.

"I've got a bed of sorts, not far from here."

"Not a room?"

"Yes: a room."

"Pleasant? Convenient?"

"Certainly not."

"What do you live on?"

"My pay."

"That's not much."

"No."

"What did you do at the Varsity?"

"First in Mods: second in Greats."

"Couldn't you have got a tutorship?"

"Perhaps. But I didn't. Well: I'm exceedingly pleased to

have met you; and thank you very much for a most delightful evening."

"Oh rot! Don't be in a hurry. Let me make you another cigarette."

"I'll make one myself, if you'll let me."

"Please, I beg of you." Crabbe proffered tobacco-pouch and a book of papers.

"I'm so glad you like these huge ungummed papers," Kemp remarked: "but I confess I've never seen this particular brand before. Hedderley used to get some for me in a black cover marked 'Job'."

"Hedderley in the High? Now if you wanted to be really kind, talk to me about Oxford. I haven't been there for nine years."

Kemp nodded. He seemed to know instinctively that intense undying adoration of the sacred exuberant exquisite place which inspires all those who have lived there. He talked gently and beautifully. His reminiscences were scholarly, virile, delicately fresh and stainless as a primrose.

Crabbe heard: but did not listen. He was tossing the circumstances over and over in his mind. His companion had won him strangely. He was attracted to the dainty little person who sat beside him, to the mercurial ingenious critical intellect which was expressed by the keen quiet sensitive voice, full of minor vibrations like a muted lute. His impulse was to offer help and friendship: but second thoughts denied the latter. He remembered what friendship actually is, as at present understood; and would have none of so foul a thing. He had his own way to make. Besides he could not and would not give confidence for confidence. Had not personal experience taught him that personal intimacy, of any satisfactory kind, is impossible without pecuniary independence? He remembered a former sentence of his, to the effect that a truly happy marriage only could occur, when the husband and the wife each bought the other out of slavery. Such might be the case with friends too. And he could pay no price. No. He must avoid intimacy. It would distract his attention, just at the time when he wanted all his powers for other purposes. And then, of course, there would be the throat of the usual reptile to be clutched and torn into bleeding tatters. Oh no. He had all his work cut out without that. Still——. He sighed, because of the hardness and the straitness of his own shell.

About eleven o'clock, Kemp's discourse came to a natural conclusion. There was a moment's silence. Crabbe called for the bill. As he put the remainder of his change into his trousers' pocket, his fingers came into contact with some idea-inspiring things. He drew out his latch-keys, the duplicate keys of his doors. He laid them on the table; and turned to Kemp, with an air which was at once kind and repelling.

"I have been thinking," he said, "whether there is anything which I can do to help you without offending you. It is difficult: but I will venture to make a suggestion. If you will accept what I offer, you will do me a very great kindness: because you will make me feel that I owe you nothing for the extreme pleasure which your conversation has given me this evening. Now listen. At the top of No. 96 Lincoln's Inn Fields, there is a kitchen and a bedroom and a landing and a large front room, all enclosed by a private door. The place is mine for four years. You see that I have two keys of the house-door and two keys of my own door. I occupy the front room; and use the kitchen for washing and cooking. The bedroom is unoccupied. You must know that I am, and intend to continue to be, a perfectly solitary creature. I have a lot of work—writing—to do; and I cannot be bothered with other people's affairs: nor will I permit any interference with my own. I think that I understand you to be in a verisimilar condition of mind. So this is what I have to say."

He sorted the four keys into couples: not pairs.

"There is the vacant bedroom. If you will do me the favour of accepting these keys," he pushed one couple toward Kemp; and pocketed the other, "you can go and look at the place to-morrow evening after seven. You will find a bed, a chair, a table, and a lamp. If you care to make shift with that, and the use of the kitchen, it is yours. No one will interfere with you, as long as you do not interfere with anyone. I certainly will not. Come, boy, I'm old enough to be your father—."

Kemp looked up. "I'm thirteen years older than you are; and—Precocious."

"Never mind that. I'm going to be brutally frank with you. You're starving; and you're carrying your troubles bravely. Don't add to mine by making me know that you won't let me help you. You're thin and weak since I last saw you. You couldn't swim across the Serpentine to-morrow morning anyhow. Do take what I offer; and spend your money on food. Try the experiment. Let me leave you to-night with a clean heart and an even mind. I have such a frightful lot to do to-morrow; and I don't want to be worried with wondering what has become of you. Take those keys; and let's be strangers who happen by chance to dig in the same house. You are not to know me; and I shan't know you. It's merely a matter of convenience for both of us."

Kemp was looking down at the table-cloth. His wan face was like alabaster, gleaming, immoveable. He suddenly and deliberately lifted the lashes from his eyes; and flashed a bravely steadfast glance of comprehension at Crabbe, taking up the two keys in silence.

They rose to go. Out in the street, they touched hands for the first time.

"I beg you to believe that I am infinitely obliged to you for your kindness and for your perspicacity. I am proud to know you," Kemp said.

"Ah, but you do not know me," Crabbe responded; and, turning round, he disappeared, swiftly striding into the dark night.

Chapter Seven

SAYS Carlyle:—

Persons are mentioned, and circumstances, not always of an ornamental sort. It would appear that there is far less reticence than was looked-for . . . unornamental facts of him, and of those he had to do with, being set forth in plain English: hence "personality", "indiscretion", or worse, "sanctities of private life" etc. How delicate, decent, is English Biography—bless its mealy mouth!

Chapter Eight

T H E witty Irishwoman was evidently moved to move her husband. Toovey sent for Crabbe at intervals; and gave him "specials" to write for the *American Orb*, dissertations on The Death and Coronation of a Pope, Parr's Bank Robbery, Poisoners Past and Present, The Dreyfus Case, The Mosaics of Saint Paul's Cathedral, and (what the editor was pleased to call in writing) "a not too spicy article on the Decadence of the French *Jeunesse Dorée*." There, inspiration apparently gave out: for he cried to Crabbe for suggestions.

"If you could suggest any subject with a personal note, something novel, striking, calculated to attract attention, I should be very glad to have it. The most attractive stories are those woven round some prominent individual, which should include the Earl of Glastonbury (formerly Lord Richborough, who married Tottie Cholmondeley), Lord Frank Faulconbridge (who married Maudie Marjoribanks) and any others that you can think of."

Crabbe's thoughts did not rove in these directions. He was willing to write American-orbically on decent subjects, even though he received less than half of the regularly allotted remuneration. Nor did he trouble to inquire what became of the balance. Regular work was what he cared for; and he assiduously laid himself out to obey legitimate orders: for, as he was not permitted to gain credit by signing his contributions, he did not deem it worth while to waste originality. Toovey then made an effort; and sent him to report the lantern service held at Saint Deipara-on-the-Mount. Crabbe's predilection being against the vulgar and ostentatious, he went to scoff; and came away to write in admiration of earnest dignified simplicity. He tried to tell the truth. His article was very promptly rejected. The editor called for a burlesque "of the entertainment which the Rev. Mr Cumberland is pleased to call a religious service with a description of the female orchestra in mortar-boards, and a picture of them, and all the other odd features of Cumberland's ceremonies.'' Crabbe respectfully begged to be excused from making a gibe of decorous (if unconventional) sincerity in religion: his attitude was denounced as "unwarrantable impertinence"; and his employment by the *American Orb* abruptly terminated.[1]

An anonymous parcel had been left for him at Slim Schelm's. It contained cast-off clothes: a dinner-suit and sundry jackets and trousers and innumerable waistcoats, some coloured shirts, some odd boots and shoes, and a bunch of neckties. These garments bore the unknown name of 'Arkush Annaly'. Sidney Thorah summoned Crabbe to tea; and admitted that he himself had asked Henry Jacobs for the things, naming no names. Crabbe cursed his cheek: made convenient acknowledgements, with a mental note of inaccuracy; and provided what was necessary. Thereafter, insued a series of invitations to dinner at Thorah's flat. He met the same people, and some others. The red-haired Helen of Troy glowed in apple-green. An excessively beautiful girl, with a face like a Fifteenth-Century Florentine child, strong, delicate, hardy, voluptuous, dark and mysterious as night, wore black with old amethysts; and was attended by a plump yellow-haired mother in bugled satin. Conversation at these dinners was exclusively personal, gay, and frivolous to phrenzy, exhilarating and narcotic as benedictine and cigarettes (and as utterly innutritious). They talked ignobly of noble things; and summed you up in simple subtraction. And there were secrets (not always nice ones) in the depths of all eyes. An excellent port (called 'The Porchester') was drunk after

[1] Prebendary Wilson Carlile, founder of the Church Army and rector of St Mary-at-Hill, on the east side of the City of London. Here he held lantern services on Sunday evenings and a brass band paraded the streets. Carlile's unusual but effective methods made a considerable stir at the time. H. C. Bainbridge in his autobiography *Twice Seven* recalls that Rolfe was offered twenty guineas by an editor if he would write a series of articles ridiculing Carlile. Rolfe went to two of his services, and instead of mocking Carlile he extolled him—and his article was rejected.

dinner; and, at the fourth glass, the host would begin to shout reminiscences which caused right men to move toward the drawing-room. Crabbe could not understand these good people; chiefly because none of them ever seemed to be serious. None of them ever had done anything great, or even pecuniarily successful; and none of them gave signs of having any work of that kind in hand. Thorah indited occasional quips for the *Daily Anagraph*: as quondam editor of the *Blue Volume* he was selected to criticize the first number of the *English Quarterly Miscellany*; [1] and he damned it for its imitation of the *Blue Volume*. Under a pseudonym, he had published several Judisch novels written in a masterly caricature of a Judisch dialect. That was before his avatar on the south (or only) side of the Park. Of later years, under his own name, he had become an expert writer of short stories— expert, because his work bristled with solecisms and he never contrived to persuade himself that 'chirography' and 'calligraphy' are not synonymous terms. He had published three books full of these: which remained in their first editions. And Crabbe noted that (apart from his core-known Jews) he had only one set of characters and only one plot in his whole literary equipment. Thorah bragged of dancing on the crater of an active volcano: boasted of duns; and vaunted himself of writs received. And there were neighbouring shops into whose windows he durst not stop and stare. Crabbe could not understand this kind of thing. He himself was so grimly in earnest. The affair of living was so desperately solemn to him. His talent, of which he was by no means unconscious, impelled him to use it. He wanted to do a thing which would justify his reincarnation as a crustacean; and he could not see, for the life of him, that this particular set of literary people were at all likely to show him what to do or how. He got Thorah and his wife alone several times; and named his difficulty. He disclosed his schemes. Were these the right ones? If not, what were? They said that he was coy, savage. Why couldn't he be nice and charming; and believe that people were doing their best to help him? Both lauded him and his work and

[1] *The Savoy*, edited by Arthur Symons.

his schemes for future work, until he felt as though he were glossed with lard. The annoying thing was that the praise seemed perfectly sincere; and it indubitably was perfectly merited. But it cut no ice; it was not helpful or incentive.

He spent the summer days in green glades in Kensington Gardens, writing the extra set of *Daynian Folk-lore* stories. He loved the warmth of the sun, and the flicker of leaves in the shade of the trees. Schelm very willingly agreed to the addition to (and complete revision of) the book; and would pay £10 more for the same—£10 for 20,000 new words and a fair copy of 100,000 words. Crabbe said to Thorah that this was making things easy for the publisher with a vengeance; and again was assured that he himself would reap the benefit of concession when the book was published in the autumn. But, meanwhile, what was one to live on; and where was that regular work? Schelm did nothing; and regretted inability; and was afraid he must ask to be excused just now—a most important appointment. Oldcastle did nothing with the magazine articles which he had promised to place: returning them after three months and recommending Crabbe "to tentatively send them to the *Outline*[1] or *West End Budget*[2] or similar paper." But little Abrahams did serialize a *Daynian Folk-lore* story in the *Flutterby*.[3] Thorah (invited by Crabbe to advise as to the price to be asked for it) said "I imagine that they have no superfluity of tin, so I shouldn't ask for much more than 'the usual two gs'. I should try them with three gs. The great thing at present is to appear." This was sound sense; and Crabbe deliberated to appear at all costs. However, the *Flutterby*, of its own accord, sent him £3.10s.; and promptly demised in the odour of sanctity.

The real work, which Crabbe wished to do, seemed impos-

[1] *The Outlook*, for which Rolfe wrote book reviews. His remuneration was 8/6d. a review.

[2] Probably *The Westminster Review*, which published at least one of Rolfe's articles.

[3] *The Butterfly*, in which Rolfe's story *About What is Due to Repentance* appeared.

sible of accomplishment. He hesitated about beginning without certainty of being able to finish. As a matter of fact, he had not yet found his singular and proper handicraft, which actually was rather solid and very brilliant and picturesque historical fiction based on unusually extensive researches in historical fact. This thing was adumbrating in his brain: he was not clearly conscious of it: but the shadows fast were fleeing away. He had two or three excellent schemes in skeleton already. On these, he passed the time. But he could obtain no regular work anywhere; and of course old Odoys belied his voluntary promise of reading.

Thorah clamorously asseverated that Crabbe ought to (and must) have a patron, a new Maecenas to give him an easy mind and a fair field for the cultivation of his genius. Crabbe found the notion not unpleasant, provided that it was understood that a *quid pro quo* would be given when success was reached. Thorah was in love with his idea; and would try to give it form. The husband of the tall fair handsome friend whom Crabbe had met, for example, and he was a financier in the city and a patron of Whistler and Otomaro. Why should he not be a patron of Crabbe?

Dinners insued; and an all-one-summer-night party in a garden in Kensington, when the flower-beds were outlined with fairy-lamps and everything was lovely and amusing.

A feuilletoniste (who, according to Thorah, kept a staff of 'ghosts' and earned £200 a week) told Crabbe in gasps that shewishedshewasaman — becausemenweresobrave — butshewhenshesatinhergarden — writing — jumpedoutofherchair — everytime — arabbitranacrosstheturfinthewood. She had a pink face and eyes like a doll's and a tame husband; and Crabbe thought her rather a fool with champagne. The host, an emaciated Sims Reeves minus the moustachio and plus a little iron-grey lip-tuft, spadged with the mysterious Florentine in amethysts. He was charming to Crabbe, respectful, lavish of hospitality. The frolicsome Thorah screamed pseudepigrams everywhere. He rushed up to Crabbe; and dragged him off to present him to a lovely Frenchwoman, whispering that she was the wife of the editor of the *Daily Anagraph* and useful. Crabbe did not know quite what he was expected to do with an editor's wife: but he found her frock a miracle of taste, her person inchanting, her wit amazing, and her voice and accent and broken English bewilderingly pretty; and he did not tell her so. Thorah tore at him again; and boosted him across the grass to make him known to Mrs Slim Schelm who was seated near the bandstand. She said (above the trumpets) "Ow Mr Crabbe, I wish to have you know that I've read your book; and I guess it's vurry— *vurry—vurry* clever!" Slim Schelm himself crept near, flicking (with his little finger) tiny pustules fringing red-rimmed nostrils.

"What! You here?" he kindly exclaimed to Crabbe.

"You mustn't mind his manners," Thorah expostulated, snatching the latter away.

"I didn't note any to mind," Crabbe replied.

He drifted over to the group surrounding the hostess. She was very radiant in turquoise silk chiffon and diamonds. There had been some talk in the papers about a peerage for her husband; and her friends were disputing as to the title most apt for her. Thorah incontinently soared to strawberry-leaves.

"Look at her!" he chattered. "Isn't she lovely and stately and splendid and fine and large and altogether inevitably and incomparably magnificent? Of course she ought to be a duchess!"[1]

"No," Crabbe gravely denied.

"Not a duchess? Then what?"

"A marchioness."

"And do you mean to stand there and tell me that she isn't fit to be a duchess?"

[1] E. Nesbit, the prolific author of children's books, and her husband Hubert Bland, entertained lavishly at Well Hall, Eltham. In his *Experiment in Autobiography*, H. G. Wells says, "Those who loved her and those who wished to please her called her royally 'Madame' or 'Duchess', and she had a touch of aloof authority which justified that." He mentions that Rolfe was among the many people present at the Blands' parties.

"Nothing of the kind. But, you see, if she becomes a duchess, you will have to *call* her Your Grace."

"Ha-ha! He means that you are our Grace already, Mrs Annaly, without the duchy."

Crabbe often dined at this house, wondering whether the servants recognised his dinner jacket. Thorah insisted on his coming here, saying that he was being inspected for a purpose. Time passed; and nothing more than hospitality was offered. He did not know what to think or do.

The Florentine's mother asked him to dinner at the Metropole. Afterwards, they took him to their Chelsea flat. The girl was a very clever artist; and exhibited innumerable productions, singular works of singular genius. He had a delightful evening; and came away utterly failing to understand what it was all about, or what return was expected from him. He took it for a great deal more than granted—nay, he had the man's word for it—that Thorah had explained him and his need to all these people; and he obediently took his imperscrutable face and his grim air and his sensitive longing soul here, there, and everywhere, expecting sooner or later to have an opening offered to him.

Finding none, he himself moved toward the editor of the *Daily Anagraph* and the financier. Annaly had been tapping his store of knowledge of precious stones, especially of that very rare and precious gem called alexandrite, alexandrolith—the stone which is Man's Defender. Crabbe wrote to him a little dissertation on this subject; and told him where specimens of the lovely thing could be seen. Annaly acknowledged his obligation, expressing a hope that he might serve Crabbe in return. Crabbe promptly displayed a literary scheme in detail, indicating the advantage of the co-operation of (what Thorah called) Maecenas. The reply was staggering:—

"Your question opens up the realm of high finance—that exceeding great height from which the kingdoms of the earth and the glory of them are looked down upon with a view to their being given unto or taken over by the discreet worshipper. And the names of those who are found there are chiefly of the tribes of

Israel. It is to such as these, I am afraid, that you must make resort and not to a mere crawler upon the common level as I am."

But Thorah showed to Crabbe another letter from Annaly, wherein it was written:—

"Is your friend Crabbe trying to get at my cheque-book?"

Then the fierce claws came together with a clinching crush. "Damn him," Crabbe growled: "of course I'm not—at least, not in that way. I thought that you put me in the man's world in order that he might become my literary patron. I detest the notion: but, as I'm in your hands, I've been polite to him; and have given him a taste of my quality; and now I've offered him a chance of immortality. I did it delicately; and he has tralated it as vulgarly as possible. Never name the man to me again!"

A letter, to the editor of the *Daily Anagraph*, recited Crabbe's qualifications; and suggested that they might find expression in the literary columns. The editor sent curt refusal. The same day, the *Anagraph* printed an article full of historical errors. Crabbe noted it; and again wrote to the editor, indicating the blunders, and saying that (if historical accuracy came within the scope of a Radical periodical) it would give him much pleasure to provide, from original sources, an accurate statement of the affair. To this, he received no response; but Thorah wrote: "Oh, my dear, my dear, whatever have you been and gone and done! You are so violent and so obstreperous and so ferociously impossible, that you make enemies wherever you go. First, you fall out with Toovey; then, with Annaly; and now here's Gripeys cussin you for all he's worth, wanting your guts for a neck-tie, swearing that he'll put you on the newspaper black-list and damn all the books you ever write. What's the good of making enemies like this?"

There was nothing to be said. Crabbe grimly drew in his eyes and folded his claws and retired into his cave. No one should know how deep were the wounds in the soft kernel of his carapax. He gave no sign of life or energy. Only the palpi, antennae, feelers, continually and silently vibrated, seeking legitimate prey which he might devour, and live.

NICHOLAS CRABBE

He saw the summer die in autumn's arms, while he sat at his window looking out over Lincoln's Inn Fields. He finished the work for Schelm; and expected proofs. Not to be idle, he worked upon one of his minor skeletons. He studied a great deal at the British Museum. Writing was perdifficult to him; and he detested it: but his stars forced him to write; and the overcoming of difficulties was not unpleasant. From time to time he heard of Thorah; and occasionally saw as little of him as possible.

On the other side of the landing, Kemp scrupulously kept the bargain. A consistent sensationalism must be speechless. He and Crabbe rarely met: when they did, they favoured their tongues. Crabbe liked him awfully. He seemed happy and healthy: his dignity was so very dainty. Besides, it was nice to know that there was [someone] within call. This is the ideal solitude. Crabbe had picked up enough books, at second-hand bookstalls and out of twopenny boxes, to line the wainscot of his big room and to fill the tops of the cupboards by the fireplace. He selected an armful; and piled them on the landing which led from his door and the staircase-door to Kemp's room and the kitchen. On the top of the pile, he placed an envelope inscribed "Something to read." The pile and the envelope promptly disappeared.

Another day, inquiry of the housekeeper taught him that he also owned a coal-cellar in the basement. He procured two keys of it, and went out and bought five tons of coal (while coals were cheap), a couple of buckets and shovels, a load of firewood, a broom and some house-flannels, and a case of Lifebuoy soap. He labelled one key "Coal-cellar No. 6"; and put it, with half his other purchases, where Kemp could find them with another envelope inscribed "For use". These also were absorbed; and still no word was said.

Crabbe thought it fine; and bent, steadily warily working.

Chapter Nine

As autumn became gloomy, a period of psychical depression afflicted him. That ideal diet of oranges and oatmeal and milk no doubt would have been all very well in a land where there was a sun: but in the grey and grisly filth and fog of London it was inadequate. Man is a little soul bearing about a corpse, says Epiktetos. Crabbe's ill-fed body dragged down his soul. Yet he did not change his habits: for he worried apostolically little as to what he should eat or what he should drink or wherewithal he should be clothed; and he knew that he was living on his capital.

Abrahams cultivated his acquaintance. It had begun to grow when he was dancing at Oldcastle's door. That publisher bought a set of illustrations of certain early hymns by Browning, the copyright of which was about to become eligible for piracy. Abraham's influence got Crabbe the job of correcting the proofs of the pirated edition from the original in the British Museum; and gained him thirty shillings. The little Jew used to chat with him in his room at the office, worming himself into Crabbe's confidence by expressing sympathy and praising ability. From time to time, Crabbe put in a Sunday afternoon and evening at the Bloomsbury flat, where talk ran on literary lines. It was clear that Abrahams was convinced of Crabbe's utility as a publisher's asset; and it was equally clear that the manager was trying to find a means and a way of exploiting and using the writer. Abrahams' professions of friendship became perfervid. Crabbe reciprocated the sentiment to this extent: he only would accept friendship on terms of equality: if Abrahams were certain that, by helping him to do his work, he would benefit himself, then Crabbe was quite willing to be helped and would co-operate to the utmost of his power; and, out of such a soil, the flower of friendship might bloom. But the two things must be kept apart: the one thing, i.e. the mutual obligation, might produce the other, but not inevitably, and not if the two were confused. Beyond the charm of Crabbe's personality (which was undeniable when he chose to display it), and the force of his works (which editors, publishers, reviewers, and the public, emphatically acknowledged, though they did not know exactly how to describe it felicitously), there was nothing which could make him interesting to Abrahams. Beyond the fact that Oldcastle's manager spoke kindly and appreciatively and shewed a desire to find an opening for him, there was little which could attract him to Abrahams. Physical beauty was the only 'Open Sesame' to Crabbe's heart; and there was nothing even passable here. The two men diametrically were opposed in philosophy, in process and mode of life. Abrahams harped on friendship. Crabbe was not ready for that; and Abrahams completely failed to realize the situation. He would force what will not be forced. Crabbe tried to explain: did his level best to correspond: implicitly followed directions; and worked as Abrahams designed. He was quite unable to do more. After all, his was a rational and philosophic and very sagacious and sensible attitude.

In mid-November, Doron Oldcastle suddenly invited him to obligingly drop in on Monday at eleven.

"I understand," the publisher interrogatively said, "that you are not very busy just now, Mr Crabbe?"

Crabbe grimly froze the man (who had made him a pack of broken promises and neglected him for six months) with a look of silent and fiercely angry contempt. Oldcastle awkwardly flushed (for he was still young): coughed mortification at such a check to his carefully prepared gambit; and tried again.

"I have been wondering whether you would like to courteously undertake a historical work for me?"

Crabbe mitigated ferocity; and continued to look silently.

"Do you know anything about the Medeechy Family, Mr Crabbe?"

"The Medici? Oh yes: something."

"Well now how much do you know, Mr Crabbe?"

"Perhaps a little more than most people."

CHAPTER NINE

"Do you consider that they are an interesting family, Mr Crabbe?"

"Oh, immensely."

"Will you courteously specify why you think that they are interesting?"

Crabbe shot up his memory; and ran over the names of Cosimo and Lorenzo and Giovanni and Giulio and Piero and Alessandro and Catarina, and of the divine geniuses with whom they had to do, appending little salient incidents and characteristics. He sat as still and alert as his eponym in a crevice: the words flowed from his lips: the matter which he uttered was pregnant and pointed. The publisher extracted his monocle; and watched him with attention.

"But of course," Crabbe concluded after about ten minutes, "if you want me to write a book about the Medici, I should have to study the subject for two or three months."

"I think that you would write admirably, Mr Crabbe, without much study. Well now: yes, I do want you to kindly write such a book for me."

"What sort of a book? Serious history? Or a book of stories? How big a book?"

"Suppose we say 100,000–120,000 words. And I wish to in fact have you write something as vivid and picturesque as what you've been specifying, to as it were suit the Library Public."

"Very well. I must think about it."

"Well now: as to terms. What sum would you expect to precisely receive? And when could I expect to actually have the book?"

Crabbe was in a quandary. He cogitated during some moments.

"I could write a book on the Medici in six months," he said. "As for the honorarium, I don't know what to say. You must make me an offer. Perhaps I had better tell you frankly that I want enough to live on. As this is the first book which I am doing for you, and as I hope that it will not be the last, I do not want to place undue obstacles in your way. But I must have no pecuniary worries while I am doing the book; and I should like to have an interest in making a success of it."

Oldcastle instantly dropped and smashed his monocle on the fender; and touched a bell. To the clerk who appeared, he said, "Syren, please will you have the courtesy to at once go and purchase me an eyeglass and charge it to Petty Cash. And, Syren—send Miss Meaking with her typewriter."

Crabbe resumed his impassivity, while the publisher pragmatically dictated to the girl:—

"November twenty comma eighteen ninety-nine full-stop—Dear Mr Crabbe C-r-a-b-b-e comma—(Ha yes)—We have to-day discussed—a work that I have proposed to you—on the Medeechy family M-e-d-i-c-h-i comma—"

"There's no h in the word," Crabbe interrupted.

"Mr Crabbe tells me that there is no h in the word, Miss Meaking. I suppose that he has reasons for so specifying as he is going to now write me a book about them. Kindly put your pen through the said h; and continue—(ha yes)—and you told me of your willingness—to carefully undertake it full stop—On the understanding—that it should not be less—than a hundred thousand (letters not figures)—words in length—and not more than a hundred and twenty thousand (as before)—words comma—I undertake—to regularly pay you—from to-day—one pound (letters not figures)—a week—until the book is finished comma—but that the whole period—must not be greater—(you said six months, didn't you, Mr Crabbe? Well now: let's say seven, to so to speak make it easy for you)—than seven months full stop—On the day of publication—I pay you—a farther sum of ten pounds (letters as before)—comma—and—on the book going into a second edition—in England—I pay you a farther sum of—twenty-five pounds (letters not figures) full stop—For these payments—all rights (underlined)—in the work are mine—and mine only comma—and you have no farther interest in it full stop (next line)—Kindly send me an acceptance of these terms full stop—(Next line middle) Believe me—(next line again) Very sincerely yours—comma—."

CHAPTER NINE

He took the sheet; and dribbled an autograph on it, before sending it in to be press-copied in the letter-book.

"There you are, Mr Crabbe. Well now: just let me have your acceptance of that letter to-morrow. You can draw your week's salary in advance, if you like. I wish to really get up a friendly understanding with you from this auspicious day; and I hope that our connection may do us both good. Come in pretty often will you, Crabbe; and specify how you're getting along. (Thank you, Syren. Did you charge it to Petty Cash? Right. Then will you courteously tell the cashier to once a week pay Mr Crabbe a sovereign, and take his receipt; and let him have the first now.) Good-bye, Crabbe; let me hear from you to-morrow; and come in and see me in about ten days' time."[1]

Crabbe pouched his pound; and asked for Mr Abrahams. The manager was away, at Cardiff. The traveller was sick; and Abrahams was persecuting country booksellers in his place. Crabbe obtained his address; and gave him news; for he guessed what influence had been at work.

The little man wrote:—"I am glad to find that you have settled the book on the Medici. I think you now have the opportunity of your life. Put all the best work you can into it. I am sure if you do that it will be as good as anything that has been done of its kind. And once finished you need fear nothing for the future. At any rate for the next seven months you are secured against starvation. Above all utilize the peace of mind this will give you to do the rest of the *Daynian Folk-lore* stories and let Mr Oldcastle have them. He will deal kindly with you, I am sure. You have it in you to make lasting and abiding friendships, which will serve you in good stead, and make us all proud of the faith we had in the genius that we felt to be yours. I do hope you will look after your health. This is essential to your success.

[1] The *Medici Book* was in fact Rolfe's *Chronicles of the House of Borgia,* commissioned and published by Grant Richards. Rolfe wrote the book in seven months and his remuneration was a pound a week and ten pounds on publication.

Make up your mind to keep well not for your own sake alone: but for mine. All benedictions be upon you."

The course was plain. Crabbe rearranged his life.

All day long, he lived in the British Museum, studying, discovering unknown Medici MSS. and some unpublished holographs, following clues, and generally collecting the atmosphere and the background on which to place his figures "vividly and picturesquely to suit the Library Public" (whatever that chimaera might be). When the Museum closed, he went back to his cave, and grappled with his day's notes. He denied himself all society: except for an hour or so on Sundays when he went to see Thorah or Abrahams. The remainder of the day of rest was spent in sweeping and scrubbing and washing and darning. The change of life affected him. The abominable electric light of the Reading Room damaged his eyes. The enormous consumption of cerebral tissues (which his work involved) demanded augmentation of nourishment. His carnal appetite astonished him; and his pound a week went almost all in food. In the course of his work, it became necessary for him to go about the country after Medici documents; and his means did not suffice. He went and bullied Oldcastle into giving him authors' MSS. to read in the evenings. He read, judged, and advised on, fourteen frightful tissues of rubbish; and was remunerated with twenty-eight shillings. He decided to do no more. Thorah was no help to him: being himself in grave straits, and about to write a real book in a frantic attempt to keep his own head above water. Thorah's desperation and incessant tolutiloquence made him impossible as the quiet gentle healer needed to allay Crabbe's fever. During these months, he put so much upon himself that he needed someone on whom to lean at times. *No woman ever had the sense to shew him that she needed him.* After all, a man can not work eighteen hours a day during seven days a week, on insufficient food and with total absence of recreation, without feeling the strain. The only relaxation which he permitted himself was the emotion of putting new books on the landing for the other lonely hermit: watching them disappear; and wondering—wondering, sometimes.

Chapter Ten

WHEN he had been for three months at this kind of game, he found that he had collected enough material, had licked it into shape, and had got a first copy of his work down on paper. Oldcastle developed the vile and suspicycious habit of sending frequently for him, to make him read aloud his synopsis and many chapters in detail. These were applauded without reserve. Crabbe consoled himself with the reflection that his publisher perfectly knew what he was writing, and (consequently) never could pretend dissatisfaction later. Though he often believed himself to be on the verge of physical collapse—his eyes went one to the bad; and his hair became streaked with grey—still he managed to keep afoot and to continue his undertaking. But he was frightfully wearied and worried.

Schelm said and did nothing about the book of *Daynian Folklore*. One publishing season had been missed; and Crabbe had not a minute in which to look after his interests. Though Thorah's schemes for a patron had fallen through, it was arranged that *Daynian Folk-lore* would be dedicated jointly "To Sidney and Eileen Thorah, and to Arkush and Alys Annaly" in acknowledgement of hospitality. Whether any good would come of that foolery remained to be proved. Anyhow, Crabbe himself had not seen even the first proof-sheets of his book.

The relations between Oldcastle and Abrahams became tense. There were rumours that the publisher's papermaker wanted something on account. Certainly, Oldcastle suddenly went to Monte Carlo (according to the *Dylymyle*) for a fortnight; and the cashier couldn't pay Crabbe's weekly sovereign at the regular time; because his principal had left him short of cash. The manager muttered objurgations on the megalomaniacal fatuity of the red-rashed publisher; and Crabbe perceived, not without joy, a prospect of eruptions and conflagrations in the near future. When a certain class of people fall out, another class come by their own.

Thoughts and ideas are things; and undoubtedly they get about. Oldcastle had played Schelm several very scurvy tricks in the way of business, enticing his authors, and so on. Now, the facts, (that Oldcastle had recognised the genius of Crabbe, had given him a commission, was trying to obtain a monopoly of his works), inspired Schelm to determine to stick to the *Daynian Folk-lore*; and to initiate retaliatory measures. "Let the booby bear the cost of making a successful author of Crabbe; and then the book (which I got for a pittance) will become valuable property. The arrogant young fool is giving me a chance to reap what he sows." So Schelm argued. And then he proceeded to steal Oldcastle's right-hand man. He invited Abrahams to become his New York representative. And—the inducement which he offered was wages quadrupled.

Chapter Eleven

A FIGURE arose out of Crabbe's past life; and sought a renewal of relations. It answered to the name of Neddy; and seemed to have something up its sleeve. Its air of benign self-satisfaction appeared to say to all and sundry, *Strip-me-naked-if-you-please: but-you'll find-the-names-of-none-but-Bond-Street-tradesmen-on-me-garments.* Also, it carried itself with the assumption of one who has caught hold of Fortune's skirts.

Things, quoth Neddy, had been goin on much the same as usual,—until lately. He loathed the Law more than ever: but he thought that he soon would be in a position to chuck it. And what he meant to say was his dyeuced liver let him know more often than he liked, begad. Then a queer effectual look invaded his vacuous and strenuously fascinating eyes; and he announced that he was about to become a multimillionaire.

Crabbe took it with grim impassivity. Neddy watched him with increasing attention.

"Begad, I believe you're just the rotter we want," he burst out: "you know Greek, don't you?"

Crabbe did not deny his guilt of that felonious misdemeanour.

"Here, let's turn in somewhere where I can ask you questions," Neddy hurriedly burbled.

Crabbe conducted him to the cave in Lincoln's Inn Fields: put him in the easy chair; and sat down on the bed. He knew that, when an effete homuncle requests permission to pick your brains, it's hard if he doesn't give you more than he takes. Neddy gazed about for a little while; and then began.

"D'ye know what pitch is? Where does it come from? D'y'ever hear of it comin out of a well? What else is there in the well? D'y'know anything about the Greek Islands?"

"Vaguely. Know not. M-yes. Don't know: but could guess. Some things about some," Crabbe categorically responded.

"Thenks. What price Zante?"

"Zante? M-m-m-m, Homer's ὑλήεις Ζακυνθος, Vergil's nemorosa Zacynthus, called The Golden Isle, twenty miles by ten, mountains and woods, currants and olives in valleys, city of Zante on east coast, clean, aqueduct constructed by Englishmen, subject to earthquakes, twenty thousand people a mixture of Greek and Italian, and—by George, yes—and pitch-wells at south end!"

"Thenks: that's what I mean to say. Now wasn't there one of your historical rotters who wrote about those bally pitch-wells? Beerbohm Tree, you know—the rotter who scragged the babies, begad. Ah yes, name of Herod!"

Crabbe picked a brown calf duodecimo: found a page: passed it to Neddy.

"Thenks. What's this stuff. Oh, I say what I mean to say is I can't read this rot."

"It's Herodotus's *History*, book IV, Ἡροδοτου Ἰστοριων Τεταρτη, paragraph 195, I'll read it to you. Εἴη δ' ἂν πᾶν, ὅκου καὶ ἐν Ζακύνθῳ ἐκ λίμνης καὶ ὕδατος πίσσαν ἀναφερομένην αὐτὸς ἐγὼ ὤρεον—;"

"What sort of blithershights is 'hydatos pissan anapheromeneen,' begad? Read it so that I can understand, there's a good chap."

" 'I myself have seen pitch extracted from the water of a pool in Zakynthos. At the place of which I speak there are several pools: but one is larger than the others, being seventy feet each way and (m—m—m—διόργνιος—) twelve feet deep. Here, they let down into the water a pole having a bunch of myrtle tied to one end;' —I say, how essentially artistic these dear Greeks were! '—and, when they draw it up, there is pitch sticking to the myrtle, resembling bitumen in smell, but otherwise it excels the pitch of Pieria. They pour it into a ditch dug by the pool-side; and when they have collected a quantity, they take it out and put it in casks. Whatever falls in that pool passes underground; and comes to light in the sea; which is not less than (m—m—m) half-a-mile away——' "

"Oh my godmother's ghost! And what's the 'pitch of Pieria'?"

"A very superior brand."

"Thenks. Is that all? D'ye know any more?"

"Oh yes. I know a lot more. But what is it that you are getting at, my boy?"

"Never mind now. I'll tell you by and by. What I mean to say is when was all that written?"

"About four hundred *ante Christum.* About twenty-three centuries before you were born."

"No, begad, was it really? And is that bally pool there yet?"

"It's shrunk into a well about five feet in diameter—a well filled with oily scum, which flows more freely when there's an earthquake. They still get pitch from it, which they use on boat-bottoms. And there's another oil-well in the sea, near the shore. The oil floats on the water in calm weather."

"God—frey—Dan—iel—Simp—son! What kind of oil is it?"

"Well I suppose that Herodotos was writing about some kind of mineral pitch, such as bitumen or asphalt—he mentions the odour of bitumen—. Both of these simply are forms of petroleum; and I imagine that the oil, in which his pitch occurred, was in fact petroleum."

Neddy became very cheerful. "Now we're getting warm," he said. "Have you got a map of the place?"

"No: but I can give you a rough idea." Crabbe went to the table; and did a diagram on a bit of paper, which he handed to his guest.

"And what's this little island in Kieri Bay?" Neddy inquired.

"I don't know its name: but it's only a barren rock, containing about four square miles of nothing. That doesn't signify——."

"My ant! Doesn't it though, begad? Well: I'll tell you what it's called. It's called Marathonisi."

"Devil! How much of all this did you know?"

"Nothin. Except by hearsay. And vaguely."

"Have some lunch?" Crabbe went to the cupboard; and produced brown bread, cheese, and a weird root on a plate, with a winchester-quart of distilled water.

"No, thenks. What filthy stuff you eat, Crabbe! And garlic, begad!"

"I can't afford snipe and chocolate creams and potted stenches, like you. And garlic's most wholesome."

Neddy elaborated the lighting of a cigarette, surveying his companion. At length, he said, "What a bally lot you know, Crabbe!"

"Do you remember what George Arthur Rose once said about my knowledge? 'He knows all that there is to be known about a handful of out-of-the-way useless things; and nothing at all about everything else.' That's quite true. And now I want to know what you know."

"Well then what I mean to say is there's a syndicate of Scots rotters who've got hold of that Greek writin-rotter's yarn about the pitch-wells: so they've sent a genealogical—no geological rotter, Borrodale Blackstone, and another rotter, name of Bainbrigge, out to prospect. Bainbrigge's nobody: not a gentleman you know; just a good little cad. He says the Scotters treated him shabbily: so did what he'd contracted to do, and no more; and he kept his eye skinned for himself, begad. What I mean to say is when he and Blackstone had found out all about the pitch-wells—and there's half-a-dozen of them—they came home: and made their reports; and there the matter ended. Bainbrigge had nothin to do next; and went to stay with a friend in Devonshire. There, he met my brother Bill——."

"What's Bill doing in Devonshire?"

"Brewin. Well: there he meets old Bill: and spins him such a yarn that Bill says 'Begad man, why don't you cut in and make your bally fortune?' 'Got no money,' says Bainbrigge. 'What'll you give to anyone who'll find you the money?' says Bill. 'Half,' says Bainbrigge. 'Well, you'd better run up to town and see my guvner,' says Bill—keen old dog! So Bill writes him a letter of introduction; and, a week ago, Bainbrigge presents himself at the office and spins his yarn to the guvner. We make a few inquiries; find all serene—and what you've told me corroborates it; and then the guvner resolves to put his shirt on it. So do we all, begad—Bill and me and the whole bally crowd of us.''

"But what was this infernal yarn?''

"I'm tellin you now. Those two rotters were sent out to report on pitch wells. That, they did. But Borrodale Blackstone discovered that the source of them was not on Zante, but on Marathonisi, four hundred yards away. He said nothin about that in his report: because he was sent to look for pitch, not petroleum. But he told Bainbrigge that the oil-spring in the sea, and the pitch-wells on Zante, were fed from an inexhaustible supply of petroleum which might be tapped on Marathonisi——.''

"How did he know?''

"Oh, these biological what I mean is geological rotters go by the lie of the land somehow. Suppose it's a layer of gravel on a layer of rock. Well, they'll tell you where it ends, or breaks off, by the way it lies. Fault, they call it. Oh, they're deuced smart, I can tell you.''

"Is that abominable blighter's opinion worth anything?''

"It's worth everything. It's infallible. You can get vouchers for it on the Stock Exchange.''

"Well?''

"The guvner's bought a short lease of Marathonisi from the rotter who owns it—a Greek rotter called Count Anaxandron Stephanophoros; and what I mean to say is we're going to bore for oil, begad.''

"What good will that be?''

"Oh-my-ant-hear-him! Why, you blinkin old rotter you, come out of your shell for a minute and think!! Where does all the petroleum come from, now?''

"Please sir, Standard Oil-wells in America for the West: Baku in Asia for the East.''

"And Marathonisi lies between the two. What I mean to say is, for one thing, the Admiralty daren't use oil-fuel in the Navy: because, if we want to go to war with Russia, she'll shut her bally oil-wells, and the Yankees will put the price of oil up. But, if we have an inexhaustible supply of oil in the Mediterranean, near our base at Malta, and in English hands—why then there you are you see you know, begad."

"I see. Well: here's luck to you," Crabbe said, quaffing a mug of distilled water.

"Thenks old man. And what sort of luck are you havin yourself?"

"Middling. I'm doing some hack-work for a publisher—writing a history of the Medici."

"History? Will there be any conversations in it?"

"No," Crabbe snorted.

"Ah then I'm afraid it isn't much in my line. Why do you do this stuffy kind of thing?"

"For bread and cheese and garlic."

"I hope the publisher rotter's goin to pay you well."

"He's going to pay a pound a week for seven months."

"God—frey—Dan—iel—Simp—son! Couldn't you have made a better bargain with him than that?"

"I didn't have a chance of making a bargain. The job was offered to me at that price; and I suppose that I had either to take it or leave it."

"I bet I'd have got better terms for you. It wants a business man to tackle these things. You're the cleverest man I know, Crabbe: but you're a baby in business matters."

"If you think that you can do better for me than I do for myself, I'll gladly let you manage all my business for me; and give you half the profits."

"Done!" Neddy cried.

"No: will you though?"

"My dear chap, I'll do it with pleasure. Just let me know exactly how you stand, and what's to be done; and I'll do it with pleasure. I'm goin to make a bit worth talkin of out of this oil-shop: but I'm always open to turn an honest penny."

"I shall be frightfully obliged to you."

"Don't name it. Well: I'm afraid I must be movin on just now to go and get a bit of lunch somewhere: but I'll tell you what. You come and have some tea with me at the Club some day next week; and we'll put the thing in writin. Will Toosday soot you?"

Tuesday would; and the meeting took place. Neddy's air of importance was five times magnified by the lapse of five days. He clearly knew that his mere existence was a national asset. He said that he had been looking at a pearl pin in Streeter's, price £250.

"Are you going to buy it?" Crabbe inquired.

"Yes: I think I will, now that I've struck ile. D'ye know," Neddy earnestly continued, "I've been tottin up the profit we ought to net on Marathonisi; and find we shall scoop" (with grandiloquent sonority) "fifteen thousand seven hundred and thirty-three and five-eighths per cent!"

All the men in the tea-room of the Club instantly dropped their crumpets with a crash; and began to glare in one direction.

"How?"

"Begad, we bore for oil: find it all quite quietly: buy the place outright; and sell it to a company."

"Why not work it?"

"Oh we're modest. The guvner wants to retire and play in his garden. I hate the Law; and I'm sick of bein a junior partner at £250 a year. What I mean to say is I want a little shootin and fishin of my own. Well: we can all have what we want out of four millions and a quarter."

"But what's your share?"

"One eleventh. I've blued a legacy the firm held in trust for me. We've all done it. It's quite a family affair. Look here, Crabbe, if you've got a hundred, I'll put it in for you in my own name. You know I'm straight."

"Oh yes: you're straight enough as far as you know. But I haven't got a hundred."

"Beastly sorry, old man. I should like to do you a good turn."

"Well: as my business-manager and partner, you'll have plenty of opportunities. But we'll talk of that afterwards. What's the next step, though, in this oil-affair?"

"Bainbrigge and I are goin to Athens to bribe some of the government rotters. We've got to get a concession before we can begin borin; and there's goin to be a game of baksheesh played on Athenian backstairs, begad."

"Who's going to play it?"

"Why I am."

"In what language?"

"Begad, I never thought of that! Damn all niggers, I say. Anyhow, Bainbrigge can do the talkin."

"Does he know Greek—Modern Greek—French? Can you trust him?"

"Oh I suppose he knows their cursed lingoes. And we shall have to trust him. I say, Crabbe, you shunt your bally books and come along with me. You might pick up a bit for yourself you know. It'll do you good to have a change; and you could make yourself no end useful. It won't cost you much, you know, begad."

"And what's to become of my *Medici Book*?"

"Oh damn your *Medici Book*!"

"What's the good? Won't the pikrantic and pyopoiose geron-tomaniacs of the *Anagraph* and the *Minervium*[1] anonymously damn it quite soon enough? However, the idea of seeing the Akropolis smells like violets. I'll think about it. Meanwhile, I'll tell you what you are going to do for me."

Crabbe proceeded to give a concise account of the present state of his affairs. Schelm had bought *Daynian Folk-lore* for £30. Two-thirds of that sum had been paid. Schelm had promised publication six months ago: but had not sent even the first proofs yet. Oldcastle was paying a pound a week for seven months for the *Medici Book*. There were four months of that to run, and another £10 due on publication. Those were the only definite things in hand. Crabbe also told Neddy of the literary people, into whose set his stars had thrown him, who had expressed a wish to help him. He described them, and especially Thorah, in detail: stating his instinctive conviction that they all

[1] *The Athenaeum.*

were impotent for good. The act of putting these ideas in words caused him himself to see them in a new light, and not a pleasant light. Thorah had published three books of short tales through Schelm; and had edited the *Blue Volume* for the same publisher. Thorah did no serious or regular work: he merely buzzed about as the *koryphaios* of a chorus of literary bounders, all fantastically chattering. Yet Schelm took and deferred to his opinion and advice on literary matters. Crabbe suddenly asked himself (and Neddy) what the precise relation between Schelm and Thorah really was. Was the latter the publisher's official adviser? Or what? Was he Crabbe's friend? Or Schelm's? If he were Crabbe's friend, why did he not use that influence, which he undoubtedly exercised over the publisher, in order to procure better pay and regular work for the writer? Why did he not agitate for the instant publication of *Daynian Folk-lore*, which was dedicate to himself and his friends? On the other hand, if his interests were Schelm's, what kind of game was he playing with Crabbe? Here, forsooth, were mysteries. Only, it became quite plain that Thorah would have to define his position at the earliest opportunity.

Neddy intuitively perceived, and proclaimed, that Schelm could afford to delay publication until he had evidence that Crabbe was likely to become a successful writer; and, if he could obtain that evidence gratis, (as he was likely to do from Oldcastle's experiment), he certainly, as a business man, would wait for it. Crabbe conceded the consequence, with a wet finger; and began to talk about Abrahams.

This gave Neddy a chance of pronouncing another judgement. Schelm and Oldcastle, he said, resembled Michael and Satan contending for the body of some Moses-rotter or other: in that they both were after Crabbe's work. The dodge would be to play one off against the other; and this was where Abrahams came in. He possessed knowledge of Oldcastle's plans and affairs; and he was going to acquire knowledge of Schelm's. Obviously, Abrahams would be a very useful man; and, as he already had shown himself well-disposed toward Crabbe, it would be as well to cultivate him. Let Abrahams, then, have whatever literary work he wanted; and, when it came to the question of pay, let him, or Schelm, or Oldcastle, or any other bally publisher with money to spend, be turned over to Neddy. That sage would undertake to get good terms; and to arrange all Crabbe's affairs on a sound financial basis.

"And Crabbe, old man, don't you write any letters. You've got the gift of rubbin people the wrong way, you know, begad. Let me write your business letters: or at least let me draw up the drafts of all you write."

Crabbe very thankfully agreed. He knew how prone he was to pinch people with his frightful nippers when they poked at him; and he had the sense to see that he had not been the gainer from this proclivity. If only he could work at peace, he asked nothing better; and Neddy might do his business and welcome, and share his profits.

So they wrote letters to each other in these terms, offering and accepting, all in a legal agreement.

Chapter Twelve

ABRAHAMS' accession, as the New York representative of Slim Schelm, was accompanied by alarums and excursions. The little man intended to be a Power. Fate, he said, had put a clean slate into his hands; and none but himself was going to write on it. He stayed a few weeks in town, thoroughly acquainting himself with the condition of Schelm's business. He told Crabbe that it was on the verge of bankruptcy. But he was going to save it; and to raise it to a pitch of prosperity, envy-inspiring, pocket-filling, hitherto undreamed-of by any publisher. He astonished the London House (principal and all) by his masterful (not to say imperial) manner. He had all the tricks of the trade at his fingers' ends. He made changes in the staff. He initiated enterprises daring and enormous. He formally changed his name to Church Welbeck Esquire; and arrayed himself in shepherd's plaid trousers and a pilot jacket veiled by a covert coat and embellished by a silk hat, a lemon satin necktie, yellow ochre gloves, and brown umber boots with pearl-buttoned spats. Crabbe drew in both eyes at this garb: but gravely listened to all which its content had to say.

A mellifluous summons to an interview with Slim Schelm was issued. Crabbe was received with subservient grins. Church Welbeck Esquire was present: he had the air of the Jesuit General's *socius* (on the watch for the utterance of heresy) combined with that of The Power Behind The Throne. Schelm was gracious, diffident, obsequious, and perhaps slightly uneasy. Crabbe retained himself in his shell, his claws tidily folded, his eyes alert and imperscrutable, his feelers vibrant.

"Mr Church Welbeck and I have been discussing your new book, Mr Crabbe," the publisher said. "What I mean to say is things have been in such a muddle in my New York House that I haven't been able to send you proofs yet. But I'm going there myself next week to instal Mr Church Welbeck; and I'll see that it's sent to the printer's immediately. You know I print all my books in America; and send half here to be bound for the English market. It saves the terrible tariff which I should have to pay if I printed them here and exported them to America."

Crabbe nodded comprehension.

"I hear that you're doing a book for Oldcastle," Schelm continued.

Crabbe nodded assent.

"I've been telling Mr Thchelm that it'th going to be a Great Book," the new manager interpolated.

Crabbe nodded acknowledgment of the audible majuscules.

Schelm turned over a few papers: pulled forward three octavos: locked his fingers on the petty rotundity of his waistcoat; and took up his parable again, smiling beerily but benignly.

"I have been thinking that I should like to have another book of yours, Mr Crabbe, something besides what you've done for me already. I'm very pleased with *Daynian Folk-lore.* Everyone who's seen the MS. speaks most highly of it. Kenneth O'Lympos went into raptures over it, only the other day. But, you know, it's very difficult to make a success out of a single book."

"I hope that you will try," was Crabbe's first word.

"Of course I shall do my best; and so will Mr Church Welbeck, I'm sure: but what I mean to say is I don't want to leave anything to chance. You see, I am interested in you, Mr Crabbe. I'm very proud of the distinction of being your publisher." (Crabbe gasped.) "And the fact is I'm anxious to make you a great commercial success as you already are a great artistic success."

"I'm sure that I shall not prevent you, Mr Schelm. I didn't know that I was an artistic success: but I do know that I want to be a commercial one. If you are going to make me that, you may count on my collaboration."

"Then that's all right:" with a festive fundamental bound and bump on a roomy site. "You may look upon the thing as done, Crabbe. Well now, tell me, have you any time on your hands just now?"

CHAPTER TWELVE

"My work for Oldcastle practically is finished. The book's on paper; and I've still three months before me. In writing a book, I find it desirable to give quite half the time to revision. That's what I'm doing now—revising, making a fair copy, and revising again. By this method, I get unity and perspective. I would like to make a third fair copy: but there won't be time."

"How many hours a day do you give to Oldcastle's work?"

"For three months, I worked twelve to twenty hours a day—eighteen was the average—and I nearly killed myself. But lately I have turned over a new leaf and I only do eight to ten."

"Do you think you'd have time to do a book for me?"

"If you make it worth my while. I can work fourteen hours a day easily. What sort of book do you want?"

Welbeck pushed the three octavos nearer. Schelm handed them to Crabbe.

"Do you know anything about this book, Mr Crabbe?"

"Brunch's *Greek Anthology*. M-yes."

"Would you mind telling me something about it?"

"It's a collection of the love-poems and epigrams of a lot of Greek minor poets."

"Quite so. What I mean to say is it's been suggested to me that we might make a very nice little poetry book, by selecting all the works of one of those poets; and translating them, and printing the Greek text with them. I'm told it's never been done before."

"I don't know that it has. And you want me to do it?"

"Can you?"

"Oh yes. Which poet have you chosen?"

"The one who was mixed up with the place where the swine in the Bible came from, has been named to me."

"You mean Kalliphonos of Gadara?" Crabbe laughed. "Yes: I should say that there's enough of him to make a book. And I know that there's no complete edition of him. He's just here among a lot of others. But you know, Mr Schelm, that some of these poems are quite unprintable in English."

"Ah: but I want you to wrap the spice up in some sort of fantastic rhythmic prose which I'm sure you can invent."

Crabbe meditatively looked at the book. "Perhaps I might."

"Don't you think you would like Mithter Crabbe to translate thome of the poemth to uth, Mithter Thchelm, tho that we could form an idea?" the manager suggested.

The publisher corruscated in assent.

"Very few people can read Greek into English at sight," Crabbe protested, "but I'll try." He turned over the pages with, convincing random. "I'll tralate literally at first; and then try to give the thing an English shape afterwards. Now listen to this:—

'Terrible Love, terrible: but what the profit if I say it again, and again, wailing often, terrible Love? For indeed the boy laughs at these things; and frequently being reviled rejoices; and, if I say abusive things, he even is nourished: but a marvel to me how you, O Kypris, having appeared through grey swelling sea, have borne fire out of wet-stuff.'

"Don't dare to laugh, either of you! That's literally what the thing means. Well now, I should dress it up in some such guise as this:—

'Oh, Love is dire, is dire! But what do I profit by saying it over again and again, and railing him times without number? Oh, Love is dire. For indeed the imp laugheth at words; and hath pleasure in frequent revilings: he'll feed on abuse if I give it. O Kypris, this is the wonder to me, how that thou, from the grey swelling billows emerging, hath borne from the water a Fire!'"

"That'th not bad," Welbeck pronounced.

The musical minor voice went on. "Let's try this one:—

'Not a lock of Timo, not Heliodora's sandal, not the balsam-scented threshold of Timarion, not a dainty smile of cow-eyed Antikleia, not the buddy garlands of Dorothea: no longer thy quiver holds winged shafts, Love, for in me are all bolts.'"

Schelm guffawed. "This'll be a funny book, Welbeck! Make 'em laugh, eh? What can you do with 'the buddy garlands of Dorothy,' Mr Crabbe, gaw—gaw—gaw!"

CHAPTER TWELVE

"This," Crabbe sonorously declaimed:—

'Not Timo's tresses, nor Heliodora's sandal, nor the balsam-scented threshold of Timarion, nor a delicate smile of ox-eyed Antikleia, nor Dorothea's garland of rathe bloom—O Love, thy quiver holdeth no more winged shafts, for all thine arrows are in me.' "

"It sounds very pretty: but I don't quite see what he's driving at."

"Lovers and poets are expected to rave a little sometimes. However, here's another:—

'Was I not yelling these things to you, o soul, o misloving soul, by Kypris, you will be taken, constantly on-flitting the snare? Was I not yelling? Trap took you. Why vainly do you struggle in bonds? Love himself has bound your wings and set you afire, and sprinkled you breath-failing with balsams, and gave to you, thirsty, hot tears to drink. O heavy-woed soul, you are just indeed burned with fire: but just you resoul, having recovered breath. Why do you weep? Did you not know that you were nurturing the unmeltable Love on breasts, that he was being nurtured on you? Did you not know? Now learn a requital of beautiful nurture-wages, having received fire and at the same time cold snow. You yourself chose these things: bear the toil. You suffer things of those worthy of those which you did, being burned in roasted honey.' "

Schelm protested, "Oh I say Welbeck, now you can't possibly call that poetical! What I mean to say is it sounds like damned rot. 'Roasted honey' indeed!"

"You'll excuse me," Crabbe interpolated, "but that's really the most poetical song we've had so far. The pathos of its imagery is quite wonderful. But you've only seen it in the rough. With a little polish, you'll see what a gem it is. Look!

O soul of mine, o love-lost soul, did I not cry to thee as thou wast fluttering over and over the snare, that it would catch thee? Did I not cry to thee? Thou art caught in the trap: thou art bound: thy struggles are vain. 'Tis Love, Love, who hath fettered thy wings, casting thee on to the fire, with spices

besprinkling thee breathless. Thirsty, he gave thee hot tears to
drink. O soul, which art laden with woe, thou art burned of the
fire: thou revivest, regaining thy breath: ah, why dost thou
weep? On thy breast, thou wast cherishing Love, wist thou not,
the Implacable One? Wist thou not he was nurtured upon thee?
Wist thou not? Now learn a requital of goodly cheer. Fire hast
thou got, and chill snow withal. Thou hast chosen; and thine was
the choice: the burthen thou needs must bear; and suffer daily
for what thou hast done. Thou must burn in the honey-sweet
flame.' "

"*Braviththimo*, Crabbe! Why you're a good deal of a poet
yourthelf!" Welbeck cried.

"It certainly seems rather like that," the publisher admitted.

Crabbe was striding along now. "Try another," he said; and
continued with quietly intense animation, "Here's a lovely
thing, addressed to his girl Zenophila:—

'Let him be sold, even still sleeping in mother's arms. Let
him be sold. Why for me to rear this rascal? He is naturally
snub-nosed and winged. And he scratches with nails tiply: and,
weeping, he laughs much meanwhile. Besides still for the rest
an obstinate, always speaking, swift-looking, cruel, not even
gentle to dear mother herself. In all points a monster. Therefore he shall have been sold. If any sailing-away merchant
wishes to buy a boy, let him come hither. And yet he prays. Be
bold, having wept. I no longer sell you. Cheer up: remain here
as comrade to Zenophila.' "

"Really I haven't the faintest notion what that's about,"
Slim Schelm objected.

"Haven't you? Well, it's about Love—Cupid—Eros—and
it's delicious. Why it melts into sapphics as it stands. Listen:—

'Let him be vended, even while he lieth sleeping in mother's
arms: let him be vended! Why should I rear this rascal, who by
nature turneth his nose up; and who hath wings; and scratcheth
with his nail-tips; and, weeping, laugheth at the very moment;
and who is also obstinate, loquacious, quick-eyed, and cruel,
not even gentle to his own dear mother, and at all points a

88

monster. Oh, he shall be sold! If a merchant, sailing hence, desireth to buy a boy, oh let him come hither. Ah, look how he prayeth! Look how he weepeth! Lo, I'm no more for selling. Be of good cheer; and stay here as the comrade of Zenophila!' "

"Well I don't see anything particularly what-shall-I-call-it you-know-what-I-mean about any of those bits of poetry!"

Crabbe shot a bleak glance at Schelm. "There will not be anything particularly oh-yes-I-know-what-you-mean-and-you-can-call-it-whatever-you-damn-please about my tralation, Mr Schelm," he ferociously affirmed. "Here and there, where Kalliphonos is not in accord with modern mealymouthiness notions, I shall give you his Greek with the note '*Deest tralatio*', 'There is no tralation'. That will suffice. Now favour me with your attention again:—

'I saw on-the-road noon-tiding Alexis going, just as the summer was cutting the hair of fruits. And rays from two sources down-burned me: one set indeed of Love from a child's eyes, the other from sun. But one set night again lulled: but the other a phantasm of form rather uplighted in dreams. Sleep, painloosing for others, wrought pain on me, an inbreathing fire, having imaged beauty in soul.'

"The magical myth of this song calls for strenuous effort, especially in verse two, which I shall fail to reproduce at all. Did either of you ever hear anything more wonderful than the labialism of the last couplet? Well: here's the best which I can do now:—

'I saw Alexis going on the noontide road, just when the summer scorched the foliage of fruits. The splendour of two fires did burn me through and through: one flame, indeed, was from the sun; and one was Love's from a child's eyes. The one, night lulled again: the other, a phantasm of fair form, blazed yet more fiercely in my dreams. And care-relaxing sleep brought care to me—a breathing fire which limned a form of beauty in my soul.' "

"That'th very fine!" was Welbeck's pondered judgement.

"Do you wish me to go on?" Crabbe inquired.

"Perhaps you might give me a couple more," Schelm responded.

"Pass me your opinion on this one then:—

'O misweeping soul, why burns up again for you through inward parts the ripened wound of Love? No no, by Zeys, no, by Zeys, you, o loving ill-counsel, do not stir fire low-burning in ash. O forgetful of troubles, at once Love will please you again, if He take you fleeing, having found a she-runaway?' "

"Gaw-gaw! Did you hear him say 'found a she-runaway', Welbeck? Gaw-gaw!"

Crabbe produced silence by a sweep of a menacing claw; and continued, "Sapphics again, quite naturally:—

'Soul sorely weeping, why anew now burneth that wound of Love which in thine heart hath ripened? Nay, nay, by Heaven, o thou wilful scorner of all good counsel, by Heaven, nay, I do intreat thee, stir not fire which yet lurketh underneath those embers. Love will torment thee, who so soon forgettest all recent evils, if He shall catch thee as once again thou fliest, if He shall find thee fugitive, o wilful scorner of counsel, o soul so sorely weeping, Love will torment thee?'

"And for the last, I will give you:—

'One beautiful thing I know altogether. My greedy eye knows one thing only, to see Myïskos. And as to all other things I am blind. He visionizes all things to me. Do eyes inlook for the soul as a favour, the flatterers?'

"Or in other words:—

'One lovely thing I know: I know it well. One thing alone my greedy eye doth know, to see Myïskos: to all else I'm blind. He is the vision of all the world to me. Mine eyes, then, are they sycophants to see out of complaisance to the soul of me?' "

"Thith ith going to be a Great Book," Welbeck solemnly pronounced. "How long will it take to do?"

"To collect all the poems, copy the Greek text, and tralate as I have done; oh, about a couple of months in my spare time."

"If you'll bring it to me in three months, I'll give you five-

and-twenty pound," Schelm cried, making his pendulous lips vibrate with excessive rotundity.

"Very well."

"Please, Welbeck, will you draw up a memorandum to that effect in the form of a letter to him. Now, Mr Crabbe, as I said before, I intend to make you a commercial as well as an artistic success; and this is how I purpose beginning. This translation is going to have a tremendous sale. We're going to force the sale up by all the means we know: because we think that Kalliphonos can be made a first-class rival to that blasphemous old drunkard whom people call 'Umar Khaiyam. You know very well what a vogue 'Umar Khaiyam has. Everybody translates him at some part of their lives. Societies are formed to study him. And all this is due to the chance work of Edward Fitzgerald. So now we're going to set up Kalliphonos and work him up commercially as 'Umar Khaiyam has been worked up; and we want you to be his Edward Fitzgerald. You seem to appreciate him; and I want you to do your very best for him. Give me a translation as tasty as what you've given me to-day, only for Gord's sake make it as fantastic and striking and mysterious as you know how; and what I mean to say is I'll publish it at once . . . As soon as it's out, I'll publish *Daynian Folk-lore*. That will secure a certain success for both books."[1]

"If that's your candid opinion—."

"That is my candid opinion. I give you my word of honour as a gentleman that you shall have two successful books to your name before six months have passed over your head. And what I mean to say is that this five-and-twenty pound, which I'm

In fact, Lane commissioned Rolfe to make a prose translation of *The Rubáiyát*, from the French of J. B. Nicolas. Kalliphonos is, of course, Meleager of Gadara, whose songs in the Greek Anthology Rolfe later translated into English prose in collaboration with Sholto Douglas. Earlier, when Crabbe translates several random passages from Kalliphonos, Rolfe is giving us exact transcriptions of parts of his own translation of Meleager, which was published in 1937. Rolfe believed that Meleager's songs, in his version, would enjoy the popularity that had attended Omar's *Rubáiyát*, in Fitzgerald's.

agreeing to pay you, is a mere flea-bite to what I'll take care you net eventually. That's my solemn promise. (Thank you, Welbeck.) Now just write me a note acquiescing in this; and let's look upon your fortune as made. Well now, I'm very sorry that I can't go into any more just now: so I'm afraid I must ask you to excuse me, Mr Crabbe—a most important appointment."

Crabbe went out with Welbeck. "I suppose that I owe this to you," he said; "and so I'm taking for granted that it's all right."

"I'll thee to that. Take my word. I manage thith thhow," Welbeck responded.

"Well of all the rotten old rotters!" Neddy shouted, when the proceedings were narrated to him. "Signin agreements without submittin them to me!" He calmed down, however, when the exceeding definiteness of the new promises became clear to him.

"Now, sonny, take my tip. Just you cut round the corner; and buy a bally big diary; and write down a full account of this affair. And you'd better make a rule of keepin a diary of your business doins. In case of the case comin into courts, as you haven't got a written agreement—at least not one worth mentionin—a regularly written-up diary is the next best piece of evidence—notes of interviews made as nearly as possible on the bally spot, begad."

Crabbe drew away to the right, alone, confirmed in imprudence. What was the use of discretion, to the slave of a snob?

Chapter Thirteen

THORAH focussed his energies, during six weeks, upon a new arrangement of his one plot and single set of characters in the form of a long novel. It was not a very long one—perhaps fifty thousand words. He was a past master in the art of logodaedaly or verbal legerdemain; and his style was very romantic, very pretty, very suggestive—very. On technical details, he picked the brains of Crabbe. The book was to be issued by Schelm, as usual; and it was expected to reach a third edition within the year.

Publishing is a stupid business, conducted on a system which is simply archaic. The waste of force, and the absurd risks cheerfully incurred, are quite staggering to the scientific investigator of other people's affairs. Books may be divided into three classes: those by authors whose names alone induce the public to purchase or to besiege libraries: those whose publication confers distinction upon the authors and the publishers: and those, by unknown writers, which may or may not catch on. The first two classes need not be considered: they do not represent 10% of the annual output. They, however, may be placed under the head of Certainty. The third class, representing 90% of the annual output, goes under the head of Uncertainty. From which I deduce that 90% of the publishing trade is simply silly gambling. What prevents transformation of Uncertainty to Certainty? Four faults on the part of the pitiable publisher, viz., the Influence of Fragile or Unworthy Authority (*fragilis et indignae auctoritatis exemplum*), Custom (*consuetudinis diuternitas*), the Imperfection of Undisciplined Senses (*vulgi sensus imperitia*), and Concealment of Ignorance by Ostentation of Seeming Wisdom (*propriae ignorantiae apparentia*). It never seems yet to have occurred to a petty publisher to limit his output to (say) ten books a year: to select (from the myriads at his disposal) just ten books which (in his judgement) ought to succeed; and to concentrate his force on those ten. No publisher ever dreams of selling an equal number of all of his publications. The gods (with inextinguishable laughter) know why he does not so dream. The philosopher, watching the world, knows why he does not convert the undreamed dream into reality. He is a very silly pig-headed unsystematic unscientific unbusinesslike little person. His neglect of the uses of advertisement is purely shameful. His feckless efforts in that direction are spasmodically paroxysmal and aridly geometrical at best. He publishes from fifty to a hundred books a year, in the faint and feeble hope that he may clear cost of production of the aggregate; and, to this end, he only concentrates his energies on one or two. If he can sell twelve editions of one of those, he crows cockily: if he can sell thirty editions, he talks of nothing else all through dinner: if he can sell fifty editions, the man of sense goes up a turning rather than encounter him. Whatever were the relations between Slim Schelm and Sidney Thorah, it obviously was determined to make a brilliant success of the latter's new book. Crabbe's private opinion ascribed much to the new manager. Welbeck was a thorough and unscrupulous man of business; and, as far as his own nature permitted, he was scientific. He clearly had resolved to justify his transformation, by redeeming Schelm's tottering business. The steps which he took, during his last weeks in London, showed this. He grasped the notion of the value of concentration. Hence he selected, from the list of Schelm's authors, those whose work was notable; and, having collected a bunch of their MSS. and promises of MSS., he sailed with his principal to be installed in the New World.

There, the couple had a howling time. Girt in their most gorgeous paludaments, and followed by the alalagmos of little lions, they promenaded through archways of literary lunches and dinners; and the publisher's roseate countenance became more insinuatingly piggy as his rotund protuberance augmented. Welbeck found the MS. of *Daynian Folk-lore* safely stowed away in a drawer in the New York office. Schelm was for keeping it there; but his manager sent it to the printers'; and announced to Crabbe that he would receive proofs immediately and regularly.

They actually did begin to come. With them, during some months, also came astounding rhodomontades of ten and twelve pages of Welbeck's tiny writing, proclaiming heterodox philosophies pertinent to nothing, and a new religion, and news of gargantuan preparations for gigantic and coruscating happenings; and to these were super-added urgings that Crabbe incontinently should write on this and that and the other, sending all his MSS. to Welbeck, who promised prompt and plentiful remuneration.

Crabbe's head whirled round and round and round.

In late spring, he became conscious of the existence of his lodger. He was working very hard indeed, completing the *Medici Book* and the tralation of *Kalliphonos*. May and June did their duty with weather which blazed with gold. Crabbe could not afford to waste even an hour on journeying to Kensington Gardens to write in shady glades; and the day-time was too hot for work. So he slept daily from eleven to four; and worked round the rest of the clock. His carapax seemed to soften; and all his hypersensitiveness became intensified.

He noted that, when Kemp went in and out, he had the habit of sliding his hand along the wall of the landing. Once, it crossed Crabbe's very door. He distinctly felt the flesh slipping along the wood. That was late at night; and he supposed that Kemp had no matches. Also, he noted certain fumblings with the lock of the staircase door. These also, no doubt, were due to darkness. Crabbe felt no annoyance: on the contrary, he experienced the pleasure of a new emotion. He used to watch for the sound of Kemp's going out and coming in; and to chuckle over extreme irregularity. Sometimes, he wondered what was happening, and what was coming, and what would be the end of it all.

And then, one day, just before white dawn, without any previous notice, the Manager, the ’Αρχιτέκτων, sent him the leading part in a tragedy.

Chapter Fourteen

HE was writing swiftly and easily by the open window. The cool morning air was fresh and clean. He had kicked off his shoes; and wore just a silver-grey sweater and violet flannel trousers. Round his neck, his chalcedonyx amulet hung by a cord. The lamp had been extinguished about a quarter of an hour before: for the room was brightening with the glowing light. The world was all so sweet and quiet and daintily lavender in hue. A distant clock struck four.

Very gently, a hand came sliding along the wall: there was a slight sound of the difficult opening of the staircase door—then it carefully was closed. Some daimon of impropriety urged Crabbe to go and peep over the stair. He knew that it was desperately irregular, and an infernal liberty: but he did the thing. He wanted to have a look at Kemp. Why shouldn't he? He had not seen him since—when was it?—certainly since Christmas. He only wanted to have a look. That was all.

On the floor of the landing outside the door of his room, there lay an envelope. On the envelope was pencilled roughly, "Believe that I am grateful to you."

Crabbe snatched a box of matches; and pattered barefoot down the stair. The staircase and the hall were silent; and the light was dim twilight. He struck matches as he ran; and he saw no one. The street door closed from the outside as he approached it. He tore it open; and looked out.

A small slight figure in dark-blue mufti was walking away westward. Otherwise, the Fields were quite deserted. Crabbe stepped out on the cold stone; and hesitated about following, because his feet were bare.

"Kemp!" he said, in a strong low voice like the pang of a lute-string (F♯ minor).

The other spun round with the terrible silent scream of a martyr in mortal agony, showing the most hideously wrung face which a connoisseur in expressions ever could wish to see. It was a face of fright, suffering, outrage, despair, twitching and writhing into a mask of stone.

What happened next, happened in a moment. Kemp threw up his arms; and began to run like a hunted hare, turning off the pavement at a right-angle and dashing blindly across the road. On reaching the opposite double kerb, he tripped; and fell with a thud, lying at full length with his head toward the garden-railings. Crabbe darted at him; and pawed him for broken bones: but found none. The youngster's nose was bleeding; and he had swooned.

Crabbe picked him up; and carried him across to No. 96. He was an astonishing light weight even though he was such a little fellow. Crabbe estimated him at under seventy pounds, as he turned him face downward, interlaced his hands under the breast, and slung the limp loins and legs over his left shoulder so that the extended arms and drooping head remained in front of him. He mentally thanked the Etruscan athlete who had taught him the trick of using hypogastric and psoas in conjunction with meriaiose and podal muscles, when handling inert human weight. The ascent of the stairs was slow; and, when Crabbe put down his burthen on the floor of the front room, he panted a little, bathed in sweat. But he noted that the nose bleeding was stopped; and he laid out the body and loosened the collar and shirt, applying a cold wet towel to the cervical vertebrae. Then he seized a sheet of paste-board; and kneeled down to fan, mopping his own brow at the same time. He gave a soft laugh when he saw that his sweater was saturate with blood: his left breast and shoulder and arm might have been an executioner's. He skinned off the garment; and wiped his body as clean as might be, continuing the fanning, and cursing because there was no brandy.

Kemp was most exquisitely pale. The tiny blue veins on his temples and on his delicate eyelids had a most tender colour. The darker lashes lay on the cheeks; and there were dark shadows beneath them. The fine brows were not straight, as

Crabbe remembered them, but contracted slightly upward—very slightly—over the inner corners of the eyes. The fierce cold dignified determination of the expression was wiped away completely: the face was not the face of the dead, who know all, and are perfectly satisfied: it was only very young, very sad, very full of the remembrance of vivid pain. And this morsel was a man·

Crabbe noted it with intense interest: an interest which took a turn toward tenderness and sympathy—and a very little turn— as the moments passed. Gradually, he noted also that Kemp was frightfully thin, thinner even than he had been that night at the restaurant. The chin might have been chiselled. The wrists and hands were simply attenuate. Crabbe thrust his own hand under the bosom of the shirt: there was a faint heart-beat—but the breast, the asarkose breast and ribs—why the child was fleshless! He was starved again! What an exquisite skeleton he had, though: clean little bones, most beautifully done!

Crabbe lighted the oil-stove under his kettle; and hurriedly collected the remains of last night's milk, a bottle of Bovril, an egg, a loaf, and some oranges. He saw the serpentine veins on the temples beginning to throb; and he wetted the towel again. He got a basin of cold water and a sponge; and gently damped the skin, washing away the bloodstains. He thought that perhaps the nose was a little swollen: but that was natural. Still he beat the morning air into a breeze with the sheet of paste-board.

Kemp quivered all over: sighed; and opened vacant eyes.

"I'm afraid you've had a bit of a fall," Crabbe instantly began. "Luckily I happened to be on the spot; and I took the liberty of bringing you into my room. Now would you mind lying on the bed for a minute, while I get you something to drink. You see it's early yet; and there's nobody about. I think we can manage very well by ourselves, though."

While he was speaking, he assisted his patient to rise, whisking away the towel, and drawing the clothes together. He almost carried Kemp to the bed, using a masterful and irresistible manner: for the body hung limply, and lassitude encumbered the limbs. He went on talking all the time, as though the affair were quite ordinary: indeed, up to the present, he himself had not had time for realizing how extraordinary it actually was.

"You'll be good enough to overlook my unexpectedly horrible appearance. The fact is I've been up working all night for coolness' sake in a pair of bags and a sweater; and an accident has happened to the latter, so I've had to peel. Now do lie down and rest. I'll be about, in case you want anything."

Kemp sank on the bed with the graceful abandonment of a tired kitten. He closed his eyes again; and turned toward the wall with a little catch of breath, hiding his face in the crook of his right arm. The left drooped on the bed by his back, the palm turned upward and outward most pathetically. His shoulders were huddled together. Crabbe moved away; and acted swiftly and silently and unerringly as a mother cat. A sluice under the tap of the kitchen sink, a vigorous towelling, and a clean sweater, made a wholesome figure of himself. Boiling water and Bovril generously went into a cup under a saucer. Milk, brought to boiling-point and cooled, went into another cup whipped with a raw egg. Crabbe refreshed himself with an orange; and went over to the bed.

"I want you to shut your eyes and swallow the contents of this cup. It's a raw egg in milk. Just make a mouthful of it, will you? You'll find it frightfully strengthening."

He sat down by Kemp, treating him as one would treat an infant, watching his movements, anticipating, directing, supporting, governing. He brought also the Bovril and some fingers of brown bread; and administered them in the same manner. Kemp's incapacity was something more than amazing. His eyes were closed; and the lovely lashes glittered with unshed tears. His actions were those of one rapt in a trance. There was no effort at all on his part. Only the wonderful expression on his features proved that sentient life and intellect were beating still behind the diaphanous veil of his skin, the pallid mask of his face. He ate and drank what was put to his lips; and let Crabbe arrange his clothes when he lay down again.

"I'm awfully obliged to you," he whispered.

"Please say nothing about that," Crabbe responded. "I'm very glad of the chance of being useful. Now if you'll take a little nap you'll do me a favour. I've got about half-a-dozen more sheets to write before we can get any breakfast; and so quiet will do us both good. Don't mind me. You're not putting me out in the least. All I want is that you should rest a bit and let me do my work."

He lowered the blind near the bed; and deepened the shadow there with a great grey shawl hung upon a clothes-horse. Then he sat down at the table by the far window; and his pen began to fly. In a couple of minutes, his thoughts were far away in the Rome of Giulio de' Medici, Botticelli's favourite model, known to history as Pope Clement the Seventh.

His faculty for abstraction being what it was, cultivated to a pitch which was abnormal and incredible, he wrote with facility for a couple of hours or so. Then, his thoughts began to come back from Italy to Lincoln's Inn Fields. The pace of his pen diminished; and, at length, was still. He scribbled a note to the housekeeper, ordering hot breakfasts for two from the Inns of Court Hotel as early as possible; and placed it on the floor of the hall where she must see it on entering to sweep the offices. When he returned, he tip-toed to the bed; and noted that Kemp was asleep. He was much satisfied by the delicate flush on the cheek which he could see, and the perhaps a little less agonized tension of the corner of the brow. He prepared some more Bovril; and went back to his chair to eat oranges and to meditate on the situation. The splendour of our Lord the Sun flamed in at the open window; and thrilled his veins with the energy and joy of life.[1]

Now he was going to learn secrets. He had no doubt of that.

[1] In February 1904, Rolfe wrote to *Notes & Queries* under the name of Nicholas Crabbe: "I should be glad of the reference in the passage quoted on p. 277 of Henry Harland's *My Friend Prospero*: 'In the spirited phrase of Corvo', 'here came my Lord the Sun' ", and in the issue of 5 March, Frederick Baron Corvo replies: "I think the reference for which Mr Crabbe inquires is to one of my stories of the Abruzzi which appeared in the *Butterfly* for August 1899."

Now he was going to turn over another page of the book of his life; and the gods of his stars alone knew what he would have to write there. The delicious feeling came upon him, which comes upon the swimmer who stands ready to plunge on the brink of a new stream. It is the grand sensation of inquiry, of experiment, of daring discovery; and it is about the most precious sensation which the doctrines of evolution and modernistic and higher criticism have left to us. His thoughts began to run about in all directions: he let them run; and chained them up again. He had been acting in a benevolent way; and he was going to act in a benevolent way; but he was purely selfish all the time. He consistently acted so, because it pleased him; and he inconsistently always made a point of offering any sacrifice, even personal, to give himself pleasure. No one ever pleased him: so he pleased himself. The idea crept into his mind, that he might not have been doing himself justice, that he might have been making a great mistake in keeping at a distance that lonely and mind-delighting little figure on the bed. Kemp was alone; and he was alone; and they had been for nearly a year alone and apart in the same house. Perhaps that was not quite kind to Kemp. And, to be unkind to one who had not injured him, and who had been injured, was unkind to himself. The idea just crept in. Well: the past was the past: it was not yet eight o'clock in the morning; and the whole of the beautiful day was before them. Kemp stirred; and sat up on his bed.

Crabbe went over to him with the fresh Bovril; and made him drink it. Then he brought him across the room; and seated him in the easy chair.

"They're going to give us some breakfast soon," he said. "Can you manage till then with oranges? I've got a case of them."

Kemp made a sign of rejection. He looked frightfully listless and worn.

"I wonder if you'd mind my lighting a cigarette," Crabbe continued. "I always think tobacco the first thing in the morning —'sweet, when the morn is grey,' you know. And may I make one for you too?"

He rolled the cigarette into a cylinder; and handed it to be closed by his guest. Kemp took it; and licked the edge: but, in trying to fold it down, he bungled it with singular clumsiness. The paper broke; and its contents fell shredded to the ground. The pale face became hideously distorted again.

"Oh, can't you see that I'm all but stone-blind?" Kemp gasped; and burst into a passion of pitiful tears.

For the first and only time in his life, Crabbe wished that he had been born an Italian instead of an Englishman. He instantly went to Kemp, gently touching his hand.

"Gracious Powers! My dear man, I'm frightfully sorry to hear that. But don't worry about it. I'm your friend you know. We'll talk things over presently. Do you know, I believe that you are just the man I want." Flotsam and jetsam floated by Crabbe's cave: but the great claws thrust out, tenderly closing in a clutch on the prey.

Quiet knockings sounded outside on the door of the staircase. Waiters entered with breakfast; and then left them alone.

Chapter Fifteen

CRABBE came clean out of his shell; and developed all the maternal side of his nature. The day was too fine to be wasted indoors, he said. He himself wanted to take a holiday and talk. What did Kemp say to going out, and sitting under the trees somewhere by themselves—in Kensington Gardens where one could get glimpses of the Serpentine—"I beg your pardon," he hastened with a wet finger to add. "I ought to have guessed that you don't want to go near the place now. Well: shall we say Hampstead Heath?"

He did not let his guest go out of his clutch: but waited on him hand and foot while he washed himself and arranged his clothes, giving touches of help in intelligent unobtrusiveness during intervals of his own dressing. They turned out at length, a couple of unnotable entities, neat in dark blue and dark grey, specimens of exquisite mediocrity, unnotable, except perhaps for the distinct air and expression of their countenances, 'faces of the world's deliberate refusal,' thoughtful, serene and vivid, trouble-tried. A hansom bore them as far as Jack Straw's Castle; and they wandered away toward Highgate, seeking a nook on a hillside where there were grass and trees and a wide prospect of the sunny world.

"I wonder whether you'll have the patience to listen while I talk about myself," Crabbe said.

"I think you ought rather to ask me to tell you about myself. I owe——."

"Don't. Dear man, if you want to tell me anything, by all means do. But there's no question of owing. Get that idea out of your head before we go any further. I'm sick to death of aseity, of stewing in my own juice. It impedes my psychical and physical growth. I want a friend—one who will be useful to me in my work; and I'm quite sure that you're the very man. If we're going to talk about obligation, that's all to my address, I

can assure you. I'll explain presently. A scheme has come into
my head——."

"It's a great deal more than good of you to put it that way.
But really, I'd rather tell you a few things before you tell me
anything."

"Look here, Kemp. Never force these things. Let them come.
It's far more satisfactory to manipulate than to create. All the
same, I won't deny that there are some things which I would
like to hear you say. I don't think that you'd mind."

"I'll tell you anything. I wish it."

"Yes, yes: but I also wish—to avoid burthening my brain
with a lot of knowledge which doesn't concern me. Let's divide
the subject into two parts: the part which I know I want, and
the part which you think you ought to give. Perhaps these parts
are not two, but one whole. Perhaps the first exhausts the second.
If it does, well and good. If it doesn't—Kemp, may I put
questions?"

"As many as ever you like; and I'll supply deficiencies. I never
felt so brimful of information in all my life."

"Tell me about your eyes. When did you first find it out?"

"At Easter. I woke up one morning quite blind. Everything
was pitch dark. Do you know, I thought it was the middle of the
night; and tried to go to sleep again. But, by and by, I realized
that the traffic in Holborn was roaring; and I knew that it must
be day-time. That gave me a shocker, I can tell you. Well: I just
fumbled about; and bathed my eyes; and blinked them violently;
and, after half an hour or so, very gradually, it was as though a
thick black curtain was being rolled up."

"Go on. I perceive that you are an observer. You don't know
how frightfully interesting you are," Crabbe urged.

"I began to see out of the lower part of one eye: then out of
the lower part of the other. By degrees, the curtain rolled right
up; and I could see. Gad, you know, I was late at the office that
day. A week later, the curtain came bang down over my right
eye when I was crossing Cheapside. I was nearly run over. Then,
all sorts of things began to happen. Sometimes, a blot came in

the middle of my sight: sometimes, on one side: sometimes, on the other. Sometimes, one eye became blind: sometimes, the other: sometimes, both. I was so frightened. I used to look in the glass to try to see if anything was wrong. Of course I couldn't. Then I began to make mistakes at the office."

"It wasn't liver, was it?"

"Not a bit of it. My liver's as right as the mail."

"You know, of course. Did you do anything?"

"Yes, I did. One off-day, I got myself up in civvies; and went to the Eye Department of St Didymus's Hospital. The blighter of an oculist said——. He said something most damnably insolent about my father——."

"I don't want to know——."

"Lucky! For I shouldn't tell you. I wish you to know that the man was a most infernal liar about my father; and that his unwarrantable assumption as to the cause of my disease was totally erroneous."

"I take that for granted. But, did he say that it could be cured?"

"I didn't give him a chance, after that: I just walked out of his clinic. But he gave me a distinct impression."

"How do you mean?"

"Like this. I understood most of the technical words which he used in diagnosis; and it was quite clear that—that I'm to be blind."

"I say, you're not smoking!"

"Oh I can't smoke just now. Let me get this over. It's the kind of blindness which comes on quite suddenly, and takes three to nine months to become complete and final—katapetasmatopia, he called it. Then, a corrupt imagination or a limited experience caused him to advance disgusting theories concerning the cause; and I blundered out of the place."

"Won't you consult someone else?"

"No, never. I'm going to be blind; and that's an end of it. Don't ask me, please."

"Very well—I say, Kemp—I wish—mind, I don't know anything and I promise not to say or to think anything—I do wish you'd let me have a look at your eyes."

"Oh please do." He laid his hat aside; and sat up, turning towards Crabbe his small serious face all white with 'the rare pale light of wonder and of suffering.'

Crabbe came quite close; and gazed into the wide-open eyes. They were most marvellous eyes, of the exact shape of long almonds, each pointed at each end, grandly rounded at the other, set widely apart with the points outward. But the lower lids, being horizontal, gave a singular wistful fullness to the eyes: while the upper lids formed single lines splendidly arched, springing from the pointed paropiai and sweeping in noble peripheries right round to the tear-wells. The dark brown lashes were long, curved, and very fine. But the whites of the eyes had the bluish-white opacity of chalcedonyx, stainless, clear-shining, crystalline, lustrous as wax. The irises shewed that strong smaragdine tint of green, the slightly bluish-green in whose composition there is more blue than yellow, the green of the spectrum which is a simple colour indecomposable into blue and yellow by passage through a prism or in any way whatever, the green of emeralds which have the blaze and the sparkle of fire. But the pupils were small, and of the deep dark black of velvet. They were wonderful eyes—wonderful, because they were so very pure and young, so very hot, so very tired.

Crabbe intently studied them during three or four minutes. Lack of knowledge prevented him from noting any symptom of disease.

"How brave you are," he said, "to bear it all by yourself. I should have yelled. Do they give you any pain?"

"Not a bit," Kemp responded. He lay back on the grass; and brought the brim of his straw hat over the upper part of his face.

"How much can you see now?"

"At this moment, nothing at all. That's because my eyes are shut. I—well the fact is, I keep them shut as much as possible, in case anybody would see that I am diseased——."

"No fear of that. No outsider possibly could see that. I couldn't."

"Do you mean that I'm deceiving you?" Kemp cried with sudden fury.

"No, no, no, I know you're not. Haven't I seen you fall down——."

"Sorry. Do forgive me. I'm so touchy that I'm really not fit to live among men."

"Touchiness is a characteristic of this child too. Let's agree to believe in each other anyhow. But I want to know what happened at the post office."

"I couldn't hide it. I began to blunder: I got reprimanded: got degraded. Then I made a clean breast of it; and resigned. They wanted me to see the doctor: but I wouldn't. I simply took back my uniform; and cut the show."

"When?"

"Is to-day Wednesday? Then it's four weeks and four days ago."

"When's your birthday?"

"The sixteenth of September."

"Good. You know that Wednesday is your important day?"

"I didn't know it: but it seems so. I dined with you once on a Wednesday." He reached for Crabbe's hand.

"We'll dine together on many more Wednesdays, I hope. May I go on? What followed your resignation?"

"At first I was stunned completely. The only clear thing was that I was finished. After a bit I determined to make a tidy end. I had just fifty-five shillings saved; and I resolved to live on that till I could find my way with my eyes shut to—the place where I first met you. I used to practise at night when the streets were empty. The very first thing that happened was the loss of two sovereigns. I think that I was robbed in Shaftesbury Avenue. Then, I gave half a sovereign instead of a sixpence to a police-man, for putting me right one black blind night when I lost my way by St George's Hospital. I spun out the rest; and then, I confess that I funked the next step. In fact—I won't keep anything from you—I behaved like a baby all last night, and started too late———."

"Don't say too late."

"No, not too late. I'm an ungrateful beast, I'm afraid———."

"How long did the five shillings last you?"

"Till last Thursday morning."

"I say, Kemp, don't you think you could tackle some plasmon chocolate now? I've got a packet here."

"Oh how kind you are!"

"I'm not. I'm a voracious cannibal, a gastrimargose anthropophagist; and you're my prey; and I'm going to eat you, and to live on you alive. Just at present, I'm engaged on fattening up my victim. Look here now, it's a silly question to ask, but are you quite sure that there was no other way?"

"I pass you my word of honour that I could find no other way. I hated it. I was desperately frightened of it. I clung to life as long as I could. I say, I think you've been in the wars yourself: but I don't think you ever knew what it feels like when all the lights go out and you're left alone in the dark."

"Pardon me. Psychically I perfectly know the feeling; and physically I know it too, except in the matter of eyesight. I have been left quite alone in the dark, six or seven times, and naked, and with vipers all round me spueing venom. Not that I cared for the last. 'Little men might make a hundred names for me, and tell six hundred tales of me—echoes of their own mean sins writ large'. But I stuck on. It would have been so eminently suitable if only I would have had the goodness to take myself off the earth. So I wouldn't. Also, I couldn't. I'm a coward. I couldn't say to myself, 'This world's no place for me and I'm going somewhere else.' No. I stick on, and clutch what I can. Now you never would ask a beast or a bishop for food. Well: I've done that. I know it's cowardly; and I'm ashamed of myself: but I brazen it out somehow———."

"You don't know the kind of people who offer———."

"Pardon me again. I know the devils perfectly well."

"Then shouldn't you rather get right away out of it all?"

"Infinitely rather: but I haven't the right of choice."

"Isn't death preferable to dishonour?"

"Infinitely preferable: but I'm sure that suicide is wrong——."

"I say, I do hope you're not pious."

"Pious! My worst enemy can't accuse me of that. No. But there's a democratic puritan strain in my blood, and an aristocratic catholic conviction in my brain which I don't practise. I've got a little variable code of instincts of my own: but I assure you that no piety of mine will annoy you, for it doesn't exist. Let's change the subject. I'm dying to propose my scheme to you."

"Fire away. I haven't enjoyed myself so much since—never mind. It's over. I say, isn't the smell of the sun lovely?"

"Well: will you go halves with me in the little I've got? There'll be more by and by: but for the present, I warn you, you'll have to rough it."

"As though I cared for that. But what will I do? I'm not going to be idle."

"I only mention it so that you won't be disappointed in the matter of battels and so on——."

"Tell me, are you a Varsity man or not?"

"Not. I'm an extraordinarily elaborate hypocrite all round. But I'll come to that part of my homologue presently. I'm saying now that, if you can be content to live like an eremite of the Thebaid for the present, there's my cell and half of my beans and greens. What's enough for one is enough for two. You accept. Then now I'll tell you what I am, and all the rest of it. I've got a little treasure in the bank—about a hundred. I write, as you know. Three books of mine are coming out this year; and the publishers promise that they will raise me to plutocracy. Besides, I've a friend-at-court, a publisher's manager in America, who says that he will buy as much as I can write. Besides, I have other irons in the fire, other pots on the boil. You see, I'm a full-blown mystic—I've worked through the bitter noviciate of letters, where many a better man gets choked off——."

"I, for one."

"I guessed it. Well: start again with me."

"Fatten on what you generously give me; and make you no return?"

"Oh dear no. We're going to march arm in arm. You are going to help me in doing all sorts of things which I cannot do alone. You shall know that I had no kind of education to speak of: but I've picked up a little; and I have a natural gift for window-dressing. Most people deem me a terrible philosopher, exquisitely polished, and all that sort of rot. I'm nothing of the kind. I have no fundamental knowledge of anything; and my polish is mere veneer."

"I say, are you pulling my leg? Greek, for instance—your conversation bristles with Greek words——."

"And I don't know my declensions. And I've got a tralation of Kalliphonos of Gadara coming out this very season."

"This is most extraordinary!"

"I concede the consequence. My mental outfit is the most astounding assortment of *tesserae* that ever a miserable mortal was expected to treat. Sometimes, I happen to arrange them in symmetrical patterns; and lo! a mosaic. I can't describe my processes a bit. I work like a freed slave, for the love of the thing; and like a convict in the *ergastulum* for fear of the lash of poverty. If I were pious, as you suspect, I should whine about supernatural intervention and aid. As I'm not, I won't. All the same though, there's something to be said for the theory of obcession: because, when my deeds are done, they are quite new and strange to me. Another characteristic of mine is that I am at once conscious and unconscious of my limitations. I'm unconscious of them in that I, as a matter of course, rush in where angels fear to tread; and, so far, no one in the world of letters has found out what a fool I am. But I'm conscious of them in this way. I feel the lack of that thorough grounding in the rudiments of human letters, which you only get at public schools and universities. This makes me slow. I have no opportunity of acquiring the grounding now: consequently, I waste no end of time rummaging in grammars and lexicons. By which road, I come to you. I want to be able to pick your brains at will. I shall be able to do so much more and so much better work. Think what it will mean to me to be able to say at any hour of the day or night, 'Kemp, what's the genitive of Τυπτο——'."

"Oh you're inimitable," Kemp shrieked, wriggling with joy.

"See? Well then there you are. We'll help each other. You shall sit and knit towels——."

"The very thing! I must do something with my hands— wood-carving I used to be a dab at. I must learn to see with my finger-tips——."

"You shall knit towels—I know how to teach you—and carve wood, and help me with my work, and console me when I'm depressed, and wile away my cantankerous temper, and sweeten my bitter tongue; and we'll exchange ideas and all that sort of rot. The delight of the mere notion makes me frivolous. We both will be the better for each other. We'll be flint and steel; and strike a spark between us. Will you agree? Look here," Crabbe soberly added. "One thing more. We're not out of the wood by a long chalk yet. These devils of publishers are such congenital asses that they may break their promises. Such things —whisper—have been broken. We ought to be prepared for a fight or fights, you know. Do you think yourself able to endure hard times, if they should come? Anyhow, we've got a roof over our heads for three years to come. I mean this, Kemp: when you get miserable and down-hearted—and you've got more to bear than I have—promise me, honour bright, that you won't—do what you meant to do this morning. Lean on me; and, let's see the thing through together. Will you?"

"Oh yes, I'll do whatever you like, for three years."

"Right. We'll be independent of each other by that time. Now let's meander in the direction of Heath Street, and get some lunch at the Express Dairy."

As they ascended the broad brown bicycle track, which leads to the summit of the Heath, Kemp said, "May I ask you a question?"

"Please. Is it not your turn?"

"Tell me what there is in me—leave your own good heart out

of the question—tell me what there is in me besides my helplessness, and my scholastic attainments such as they are, which
attracts you to me. You were very kind to me last year, you
know; and that was before you knew anything about me. You
seemed to take to me from the first. Now why did you do
that?"

"Well: not to beat about the bush—because I thought you
the most exquisitely lovely little person I ever had seen."

Kemp gesticulated disgust.

"Yes, of course you've heard that a million billion times
before. But you haven't heard it from me. I'm giving you a
plain answer to a plain question. I would be bound to tell you
sooner or later; and it's better for both of us to have it over and
be done with it. I admired you, every inch of you, the moment I
set eyes on you. I admired your form because it was as fine as
fine, and your colour because it was as pure as pure—you must
have led a lovely life, and your digestion must be a prize——."

"My body's a machine in splendid order——."

"I admired your gait and comportment, because they told me
of reserved vigour and a brave and daring heart and, incidentally, of your perfect skeleton. And then there was the touch of
mystery which made me admire you more. A youngster, completely self-possessed, and with a mystery! Then—O yes of
course, then there was your infatuating and perplexing and
admirable hair. Do tell me how it came to be white?"

"It used to be a kind of red—Venetian red, like my beard——."

"Beard?"

"Ah yes: you'll have to shave me or to have me shaved every
now and then, I'm such a scrubby little beast about once a
month——."

"But your hair?"

"It went white in the month after I was sent down."

"What did they say about it at the P.O.?"

Kemp chuckled. "Some said I was an albino: others, a Cir-
cassian! And perhaps there was a little head-punching done. Go
on, though."

"Then I admired your swimming. I do adore the breast-stroke when the head is poised superbly."

"So do I. I use no other. I'm sure that our friends the Greek athletes must have used it."

"Because of their magnificent broad chests?"

"Precisely. But do finish the list of my charms."

"I don't think that I shall have occasion to categorize any more of your physical charms. Of course I know a lot more about you since this morning."

"For example."

"You really want to know? Well: why not? I'll tell you. You'll be shocked; and you'll be pleased; and you'll want to punch my head: but it's better that you should know what I think of you. You'll see why, some day, if you don't now. Yes: I'll tell you; and you're not to interrupt me. You're self-contained. You're virgin soil. I think that Ausonius had you in his mind when he tralated *Dum dubitat Natura*——. You're able to make the most of things. Your philosophy is an astonishing mixture of the real with the ideal, with a preponderance of the real. Your faculty of ratiocination is notable. You are hyper-critical, strange to say, not only of everybody and everything, but also of yourself. This gives you an unusual amount of self-knowledge. And you regard your attainments with complacency. You are cautious and methodical and industrious and persevering. You are quite able to supplement your own deficiencies. You are sensitive in all things connected with yourself. Your tendency toward the practical is liable to make you sceptical and selfish. You can be very masterful, very ruthless, very hard. Your predilection is for the pure and perfect in all things, psychical, noetic and physical. You have a fine constitution, and a wonderful faculty of recuperation. Your hypersensitiveness extends to your physique; and you instantly perceive atmospheric changes. It would be quite easy to poison you. I mean that a small dose would suffice. Your weak spot is the solar plexus. You are very modest, not to say squeamish and shy and secretive: you blush readily. You are very intellectual, very discerning in judgment, and as mercurial in mind as you are sprightly in body. You can be very good or very bad, because you are much more clever than most people: you will be one or the other, but never mediocre. You would do well in commerce, or in the commercial department of literature. You are able to take perfect care of Number One; and you are master of yourself: (which is a pregnant paradox, easy for you alone to read.) When you realize that there are one or two other people in the world, you can be an ideal comrade, if you choose: for you are able to adapt yourself to almost any circumstances, I've said it before: but I'll say it again. I think that you are just the man I want———."

"I say you know, this is character-reading with a vengeance. How do you do it?"

"A man named George Arthur Rose, whom I once used to know, taught me."

"Did you ever make a mistake?"

"Never."

"Tell me about George Arthur Rose."

"I've lost touch with him. I suppose he still potters about somewhere. He's just another lonely devil who can't find his proper niche in this world. He wanted to be a priest: but they wouldn't have him—didn't like his auburn hair. Carrots, of course, are admissible: but not rutilant auburn, Ξανθός, the colour of Achilles' hair, the real young nut-colour gleaming like burnished copper in the sun—that's considered unusual and therefore distinct and subtile; and bishops don't like their little priests to be distinct and subtile. However, he stuck to it through thick and thin that that was all he was fit for; and I really believe he was right. I'll tell you a joke about him. Last Leap Year, someone told him that he was a fool to waste his life for a fad; and advised him to settle down and get married. 'Very good', says Rose, 'now I'll make a bargain with my stars. If I get an offer of marriage during this year, from a good-looking charming girl under nineteen with fifty thousand a year, half of which she voluntarily will settle on me, I'll marry her and cultivate the art of husbandry ever after. If I don't get such an offer, I shall know that I am not meant to marry; and I will dismiss the subject for all time, and run for the Popedom.' "

"Oh did he get an offer?"

"Yes: he actually did—an enormous one: but he knew who made it."

"Is he married?"

"No. He jumped at the loophole, which the anonymity of the offer gave him; and escaped."

"What's he doing now?"

"Running for the Popedom, I suppose."

Kemp laughed, and said, "He's a magician, all the same. I say, I suppose you don't want to know what I think of you?"

"No."

"Perhaps it's as well, for I don't know myself. My head's spinning like a top."

"Now will you have a stop or a cheak, or bessed preef, or oached peggs? Poached eggs? Then so will I. And can you stomach cream? I always drink a whole pint of cream whenever I come here."

Chapter Sixteen

KEMP had no intention of being a sleeping partner. He instantly set to work, in the coolest and most systematic manner in the world, to develop his four remaining senses, especially his sense of touch. He wandered, with closed eyes, about the four rooms and the passage, until he instinctively knew every inch of them and the whereabouts of their contents. He announced his intention of acting as housemaid and char-man. His movements were quick and most delicate, and soon became surprisingly accurate. His locomemory was astounding. In the streets, as he was anxious to go unrecognized, he wore a long loose coat like an old man and a big shade over his eyes; and he carried the extended stick of the blind. But he had no longing at all for outdoor life. He slept a great deal; and at other spare times he was quite content to sit alone and knit, reciting choruses of Euripides and long passages from the poems of Robert Bridges. The two agreed that regular exercise was of paramount necessity; and every day, at or before sunrise, they walked to Highgate Ponds, and back after long swimming. Kemp used to touch Crabbe's fingers as far as the spring-board: after that, he set his course by his friend's voice.[1] They were the admiration of the early bathers, from none of whom they would accept a second word. At first, they started on these long walks arm in arm: later, Kemp said that he began to feel and smell the differences of the streets: last, an occasional touch on the coat-sleeve sufficed for guidance. The thick black curtain came down for good. The world continued to revolve: men continued to gyrate in their several important peripheries; and these two lonely ones went on their lonely ways.

[1] Here again Rolfe is writing from personal experience. A friend of his writes in *The Quest*: "His eyes were very weak, and without glasses he was quite helpless . . . When he went to bathe . . . he would enter the water first, and I would stand on the side of the bath, shouting to direct him and tell him when to turn."

116

Crabbe rejoiced in his companion. The look of Kemp was a salve for jaded eyes. 'The youthful face, yet so experienced and calm, was enough; the straight untroubled unseeking eyes resting upon one, giving without ado the one thing needed—it was solace enough.' The sound of him was music to mind and soul; and he had such pretty ways. Crabbe did not take him into the work which he himself was completing. He deemed that to be unfair. But, all the time, he was cogitating new literary ventures, promising himself the assistance of Kemp in their details.

Before the *Medici Book* and the tralation of *Kalliphonos* was finished, Crabbe's thoughts ran on ahead to the future. What next? A livelihood for two must be earned. But how? The money in the bank——. That was plain; and, therefore, some new source of meat and drink must be tapped. This idea hideously worried him. He knew that he durst not reveal it to Kemp, either by word or sign, during these first few months of partnership, before the bonds unbreakably had been welded: otherwise he would have him flying off at a tangent, to smash himself under a pantechnicon van, or a brewer's dray, or something finally flattening and fatal. No. Kemp must not know—until he must know. Crabbe was a suspicious bundle of nerves himself; and he never could trust a friend with his own worst troubles. Those he kept to fester in his shell. In gaining a joy, he had added a new encumbrance, a new responsibility rather, to his life. He began to beat up likely quarters for fresh employment.

Chapter Seventeen

HE went to dine with Thorah; and was disconcerted. Of course they discussed their doings.

"Can you put me in the way of getting anything to do by the time when I shall have finished those things for Schelm and Old-castle?" Crabbe at length bluntly put it.

"My dear chap, what do you think I can do?"

"Influence Schelm."

"I'm sure I've praised you to him over and over again. Haven't I, Eileen?"

"Yes: but I mean make him give me another commission."

Thorah ineptly laughed. He gave the impression of drawing away with a sneer.

"Are you my friend?" Crabbe unwaveringly and most un-diplomatically pursued.

"Do you doubt it?"

"I don't want to doubt it. But there are some things which I cannot understand."

"Eileen, he says that there are some things which he cannot understand. And which be they?"

"Have you any influence with Schelm: or have you none?"

"Oh of course it stands to reason that I have some. But what do you mean?"

"Be frank with me. Tell me definitely what kind of influence you have?"

"What kind? I tell you that I have some."

"I don't believe that you have any."

"Well I have, then: as you'll find out."

"What kind of influence?"

"Why the influence of a partner in the firm, to be sure." The words were rapped out with an irresponsible snarl of annoyance.

"A partner? To what extent?"

"One-sixth, if you must know."

"Thanks very much. Now I'm talking to you as a partner. Do you approve of your principal's action in buying my *Daynian Folk-lore* for £30, and in keeping me waiting eighteen months for publication?"

"I didn't make the bargain. Of course you can't expect me to express disapproval of Schelm's business methods. And as for publication—it's simply delayed because the opportune moment hasn't arrived yet. And look here, while we're talking of *Daynian Folk-lore*, take a word from me as a friend. There's a flavour about that book which I don't like. Cut it out."

"Silly man. The book's in print; and I'm halfway through the first proofs already. But what's this flavour which you've only just discovered?"

Thorah named it. It came upon Crabbe like a clap of thunder, or the blast of some malignant star. His fierce claws quivered. He flamed in the face; and went out, icily and incisively.

"That's quite gratuitous. What a frightfully degenerate imagination you must have. Now mark me: I won't make, or permit to be made, a single alteration——."

"Well, you're a fool for your pains. And all I can say is that, if you persist in publishing that book as it is, I shall have to close my door to you; and all my friends will do the same."

"Let them be closed, here and now." Crabbe sprang up; and went to make his farewell to Mrs Thorah.

"Oh how impossible you are! Come back! I won't have you go. Sit down again; and let's talk sensibly."

"Well I'm sure that I don't want to have a row. But, what am I to understand?"

"Understand what you please, so long as you don't run away and cut your own throat just when we're all trying to help you."

"Oh are you? I'm very glad to hear it. That's just what I want. But why do you keep me in the dark? Let's know exactly where we stand."

"What's your next game, when you've done what you're on now?"

"That's just what I'm asking you. What am I to do?"

"Why don't you write some more Daynian Folk-lore? You said you had heaps."

"So I have. But what about this savour which you've contrived to sniff? And, I say Thorah, what am I to live on while I'm doing it? And what would you say if I told you that I'd found another Daynian who's got a whole heap more stories to tell me?"

"Here? In town? Where did you pick him up? A Daynian like the one who told you the other tales? I should say that you ought to be ashamed of yourself."

Crabbe never knew which kakodaimon had tempted him to the verge of a disclosure of his invention of Kemp. He retrieved his false step with cool but stubborn alacrity.

"How am I to write Daynian Folk-lore, or anything else? These two books which I'm doing for Schelm and Oldcastle have paid my way so far. I want to know what's to come next. I don't say to you now 'Can you use influence?' I say 'will you?' "

"As soon as you've finished the *Kalliphonos*, Schelm's going to bring it out at once. You'll have a book brought out by Old-castle directly after. And then, on top of that, Schelm's going to publish *Daynian Folk-lore*. The last you'll regret: but—there, be calm—I'll say no more—but, anyhow, you've got three books coming out in the next month or so; and you're bound to make a pot on them. I wish I had your prospects instead of my own little book. What can you possibly want more? Oh isn't he unreasonable, Eileen?"

"I want certainty that I'm not going to be stranded again. That's all. Isn't it plain and reasonable? That's what I'm asking you for now. Well: you won't give it to me."

"Because I haven't got it to give!" Thorah shrieked at him.

Crabbe appended a grimly contemptuous smile. "No: on the whole I suppose you haven't."

"Oh do-you-do-you-do-you know what he thinks, Eileen? He thinks that, because I'm Schelm's partner, I'm an accomplice in paying him a pittance for his work; and he thinks that, now that I and Schelm have got a lot of his work in hand, cheap, we're going to wait until he's in the workhouse again before we offer him any more. Now isn't that what you think, Crabbe?"

"Well: I'm bound to admit that you've given me a form of words in which to cast my thoughts."

"There! He admits it, Eileen! And yet you think me your friend, Crabbe."

"Oh I don't think I could take such a liberty as to think that. Things clash somehow. Wait a minute, while I sort them out. Remember, I admit that I'm a savage. I haven't half your culture and exquisite breadth of vices and all that sort of rot. I'm a savage pure and unadulterate. And my hard obtuse untutored savage mind argues like this. I believe that acts speak louder than words. If you are my friend, then my interests are yours. But you are my publisher's partner; and his interests are opposed to mine. Therefore, your interests also are opposed to mine; and therefore again, you are not in reality my friend."

"And that's what you think?"

"Yes. That's what you force me against my will to think. If I am wrong, correct me. I want to be corrected."

"And you really think me capable of that?"

"Yes I do: unless you show me that you're not."

Thorah made a gesture which had been French.

Crabbe sprang up again, fully cancerous; and went over to Mrs Thorah. "Don't mock me any more. I'm bitterly deceived; and I'm furiously angry. Of course I can't tell the blighter here what I think of him. Oh I'm really frightfully sorry," he said.

"Dear savage, far far be it from me to mock at anyone—least of all, you," she responded. "Neither Sidney nor I have anything at heart more than your success. I think you are naughty, and a goose—not a savage. Now you will have to make a new volume to dedicate to us: though of course I dare say you don't care about doing anything nice for me. Now don't be cross. And Heaven bless you."

Crabbe dumbly blundered out into the dark night, eyes protruded and glaring, claws snapping, carapax deeply dented. Oh, clearly the Thorahs were his enemies. The threat of the closed door, the refusal to use influence for getting him employment, the declined dedication of his book, all indicated determination to keep him in the mire of poverty. He not only was not to be helped, but was not to be permitted to emancipate himself.

For the sake of making no mistake, he applied further tests. After sufficient lapse of time, he paid a visit to the bugled satin mother of the lovely Florentine; and was rebuffed by a curt "Notatome." The Florentine and the mouse-mannered sub-editor cut him in the Park. He wrote to Annaly, saying that the Thorahs had declined the dedication of *Daynian Folk-lore*: and inquired his pleasure. He had not the slightest notion of any kind of compromise, of any kind of attempt at justifying himself or pleading for his own interests. He presented facts barely and austerely, as a matter of duty.

Annaly replied that he hardly knew what to say: but perhaps it was best to be frank. He had gathered that there was some element, more or less latent in *Daynian Folk-lore*, of a character which usually was thought objectionable. Crabbe had been good enough to mention that the Thorahs had withdrawn their acceptance of the dedication. If this should be their reason, Annaly naturally would be guided by the course which they had adopted: though he also had heard that the new stories had all the charm and quality which had attracted him so much to Crabbe's first volume.

That letter was conclusive. Thorah had carried out his threat by detrimental (not to say libellous) depreciation of Crabbe and his work. And so the doors were closed.

Crabbe fiercely damned the duplicity which had assailed him so below the belt, in a manner which prevented instant retaliation—in a manner which precluded even justice. He struck off the names of Thorah and Annaly: dedicated *Daynian Folk-lore* "To the Divine Friend, Much Desired"[1]: went on correcting the proofs; and directed his thoughts to the future.

[1] Rolfe dedicated *In His Own Image*, "Divo Amico Desideratissimo. D. D. D. Fridericus."

Chapter Eighteen

H E made the overture of a suggestion to Doron Oldcastle. The notion had occurred to him: he deemed himself to be at present Oldcastle's man, and (as such) bound in a way to give him his opinions.

"I immensely appreciate what you are good enough to courteously specify about feeling bound to first offer your books to me, Mr Crabbe," that publisher responded; "and I hope that I will continue to always deserve such consideration. But I'm afraid I don't think that there would be a large enough public for the book that you name. Don't let me stand in your way though. Try someone else. If you don't succeed, and will raise the matter again, I will be glad. Pardon me a moment." He deliberately smashed his monocle; and called into the outer office, "Syren, please will you have the courtesy to at once go and purchase me a new eye-glass and charge it to Petty Cash." He returned; and continued, "In any case, if we can hit on a good enough idea, I should like to without delay follow the *Medici Book* with somewhat else from your pen."

"That would suit me very well: because I detest being idle. What sort of work would you like?"

"Well now; suggestions must come from you, as nothing for the moment occurs to me, Mr Crabbe. Let me hear you specify some possible suggestions, and the length to which books founded on such would run, and how long it would take to actually produce them; and then I will see whether I cannot start you on the work immediately."

"That's rather a difficult task. You see I don't know the direction in which your taste lies, or the kind of work which you think me capable of producing with success. If you want something after the manner of the *Medici Book*, I could give you Annals of Colonna, or of Sforza, or of Santacroce. They are very important families—quite as important as the Medici. You

123

could have a book, or books about them, compiled from previously printed histories like the *Medici Book*, or compiled from original archives if you give me proper opportunities for research. The last, of course, would be Standard Works———."

"That sounds very feasible, Mr Crabbe: but it requires considering. Can you specify something else?"

"Any amount. I can give you historic romances—about Filibert the Fair, or Umberto the White-handed, Dukes of Savoy, early Sixteenth Century, or about Sigismondo Pandolfo Malatesta, Tyrant of Rimini, beast, brigand, patron of art, pious church-builder: or about Pope John the Twelfth, aged eighteen, Tenth Century: or about Pope Benedict the Ninth, aged ten, Eleventh Century: or you can have the remaining seventeen stories of *Daynian Folk-lore*."

"You give me food for thought, Mr Crabbe. I perceive that you are a gentleman with ideas. Well now: courteously let me have some space to think over what you have specified; and I'll write to you. I'll write to you within a fortnight after you send me the *Medici Book*."

Things seemed to promise well in this quarter. Crabbe finished both his books; and sent them in: taking the precaution to mail a duplicate of the *Kalliphonos* to his well-wisher Welbeck, in America. That person howled with delight across the ocean at so dainty an attention. He had the MS. bound; touched it occasionally, and wondered at the days and nights spent in its realization; and would read it only in that copy. He begged for a duplicate MS. of the *Medici Book* and of all Crabbe's writings, promising to treasure them in remembrance of the one lonely heart which he had found in Modern Babylon, and of the one soul touched by him which nobly had responded to his spirit's call. Further, he sent a definite commission for a story on fashionable life in Italy of the period which Crabbe knew so well. He wanted a tale embodying every act of a man of fashion of that era during a certain four-and-twenty consecutive hours. It was to be written brilliantly, giving the life and atmosphere of the time so that any modern (reading it) could live it for himself.[1] And he offered very decent terms. He said that "Church Welbeck (stick it as much as it will—it must go)" was to be the little man of the future: that he was finding himself in America; and, in the finding, others would find him also: that he had griping pains in the stomach, and was sweltering in sweat, the weather being very hot—"God forgive me, but I am a hard taskmaster when I am like this"—that the New York office was a chaos, preparatory to the cosmic forces which he had set in operation, and it soon would emerge as a thing of beauty. Crabbe read parts of this letter to Kemp.

"Are you consulting me?" Kemp inquired. Crabbe was.

"I am of opinion that the man wants your work. He would like to have the credit of 'making you'. I don't place any value on his rhodomontade: but I think that he has 'push' and will get on after he has got off. I suppose you'll write that tale for him. I think I would, if I were you. But—a word in your ear—don't let him have your original MSS. He thinks that they are going to be valuable, some day."

Crabbe recognized the practical sanity of this: dismissed gloomy forebodings; and seized the flotsam floating by. He began a tale which he called *Four Fine Gentlemen of 1495*. This was easy; and, as the order was definite and the pay certain and good, he paid out rope to Oldcastle in the matter of the successor of the *Medici Book*. There was no pause for him; and he worked at the work which was nearest.

[1] Rolfe's novel *Don Tarquinio*, which records the history of one day in the life of a man of fashion in the era of the Borgia, is based on this story.

Chapter Nineteen

ONE evening, he espied Neddy on a Baker St bus at Piccadilly Circus, looking opulent but glum. He mounted; and inquired what was the matter.

"I'm a rotten owl," Neddy confessed. "There's a very lady-like bit, what I mean to say is dyeuced well-dressed you know, who passes the office sometimes; and I've been tryin to find out who she is. Just now, I came up from the Strand on a white bus; and saw her sittin on this one, begad. So I nipped off mine and climbed up hers. The moment she set eyes on me, up she gets and down she goes lookin knives and vinegar cruets."

"Evidently she saw you see her from the white bus. Evidently a good girl, you goat. And what about petroleum?"

"Nothin. That rotter Bainbrigge's away. But damitall, Crabbe, if you mean that I——."

"But I don't mean. I've known you for fifteen years; and I know that your intentions are irreproachable. I also know that you're the most incapable man in the world for managing your own intrigues. If you weren't, I should let you manage mine. But where is that blighter Bainbrigge?"

"Dunno. He disappears sometimes."

"Have you paid him anything?"

"The guvner tips him a fiver now and then. You needn't look like that, Crabbe! Of course the rotter's poor: but that doesn't make him a scoundrel. Why you're poor yourself!"

"Yes. Thanks for reminding me so delicately. It's my un-pardonable crime and sempiternal coronal."

"Cynical devil!"

"When are you going to Athens?"

"Directly Bainbrigge comes back. Are you comin?"

"Not if I know it. There's a saucy little tagwail for you—there, you owl, over there, in the mauve toque by the lamp-shop. Now just be good enough to listen to my news about myself."

CHAPTER NINETEEN

Neddy listened; and didn't quite see where he came in, begad. Crabbe soothed him. His time would come when Oldcastle should split the infinitives of an agreement for a successor to the *Medici Book*, if not before. As for the commission from America, there was nothing legal about it. It merely was a promise to pay so much for so much, addressed by one man of honour to another.

"Business is business," said Neddy, looking laughingly rueful.

Chapter Twenty

WELBECK proceeded to get on Crabbe's nerves in a Marcus-aurelian letter dealing with the Inevitable, Dreams Sweet Dreams, Powers of Cognition, Epics, Money and Power, Materialized Churches, Troglodytes, Carnal Lust, the Not-yourself, the Extra-thing, and all the mumbo-jumbo of the pseudotheological sophist. It's the pit into which your emancipated Jew falls as easily as a blackbeetle into a basin. Thorah himself (on the whole) talked very much in the same key. Incidentally, Welbeck announced that the final proofs of *Daynian Folk-lore* were gone to press. He said nothing at all about *Kalliphonos*: but he iterated, "Do the *Four Fine Gentlemen*, and I will find you the money." Also, he promised more commissions: he begged Crabbe to come to the Future which awaited him in America: proffered help if he came and if he himself stayed there, but he was uncertain about the last.

"Just now I'm giving hell to Schelm," he wrote: "and I should not be at all surprised that, if he does not give me satisfaction, I shall have occasion to come and tell him what I really think of him. New York is a great city; and I think I shall amass wealth. But not through Schelm. There are other opportunities; and already I am being talked about as a person to be reckoned with." He added that Thorah's book, *Red Rappee*[1] was selling well, being gaily advertised and expected to reach its tenth thousand before Christmas.

The next letter was even more annoying. Welbeck announced his arrival in England in October; "and then I must see you. My seeing you may result in some important step being taken by you. How or where or when, I may not at present say:

[1] This alludes to Harland's most popular novel, *The Cardinal's Snuff-Box*. Published by John Lane in 1900, it put Harland among the very few highly successful novelists of his time.

but you will do wisely if you keep up heart a little longer." And then he presented a nasty dilemma. "By the way, to whom is this dedication ('To the Divine Friend, Much Desired') of *Daynian Folk-lore* intended? Yourself?" (Crabbe yelled.) "If so, I think you had better change it. If you have no one individual in your mind to whom you think worthy of having the book dedicated, leave it out entirely; but, if you are in search of someone who has appreciated and does appreciate your work, I think you need not go a hundred miles to seek him. I should esteem it an honour: but I merely throw this out as a suggestion. If it does not meet with your approval, by all means please yourself."

Crabbe preferred to keep the dedication as it stood. He wanted to see the bodily shape in which the Divine Friend Much Desired would manifest Himself: so he put out his little card of Lodgings to Let. Notwithstanding all the stuff which he called flattery and the indignant Welbeck's 'honest appreciation'— whatever it was, it left him cold and crusty—he was quite certain that he did not respond nobly to Welbeck's or anyone else's spirit call—no: not even to Kemp's, although Kemp never had called or would call. Crabbe knew himself to be a purely personal individual. The word friend meant the whole bag of its intentions to him. He was unable to 'show himself friendly'; and so he denied himself what men are content to call friends. He did this in fairness to them: for, as one who lived on raw oatmeal and oranges, he was not able to offer whiskies and ham sandwiches and seltzers. Had he been able, he perhaps would have permitted himself to feed friends. That he wished to be able, he proved to himself by his assiduity in working to extricate himself from the web of poverty. And, to all those people who came professing admiration and friendship, he grimly said, "Actions before words. If you wish me well, employ me: or help me to get a proper price for my work, and to become your social equal; and then we will begin to ponder the matter of friendship." For he failed to understand how anyone could be friendly, who did not act wholeheartedly on his behalf. He could

129

not understand the friendship which does not give as well as take. Further, he knew that real friendship can stand any test. Here was a grand chance of testing Welbeck's. If the man were in earnest, he would understand and take no offence. If not, his friendship was not worth having. Crabbe replied that the dedication was to stand as it was.

He told Neddy: who said, "Oh, you rotten rotter! Don't you know that the little Jew will circumvent your book?"

He told Kemp: who said nothing—but his smile was an illumination.

And then he went on writing *Four Fine Gentlemen*, wondering when the proofs of *Kalliphonos* would arrive and when *Daynian Folk-lore* would appear, and worrying a little because six weeks had passed and he had no news of the *Medici Book* and its successor.

Toward the end of September, exciting events began to occur. Oldcastle sent a couple of typescribed sheets called *Reader's Report*. Crabbe read it; and was flabbergasted by its portentous pretentious incapacity. Passages of the *Medici Book* were denounced (as acrostics and effeminacies of intellect and strange clumsiness of thought and style) which actually were quoted verbatim from the Bible, Shakespeare, Milton, Evelyn, John Addington Symonds. Crabbe was credited with blunders which were nowhere to be found in his MS. Exception was taken to statements of fact which he had cited from historians of the calibre of Creighton and Pastor. In the inaccurate reading of certain passages, which had been left in the original Italian and French *'quo minus erubescamus'*, the Reader, (whoever she or he was) displayed ignorance amounting to positive genius; and the book was condemned as scurrilous on the evidence of her (or his) own diseased imagination and inability to understand. At the same time, condemnation was chastened by:—

"The mode of treatment, the spirit of the narrative, is just, living, and true. The old wooden myths fall at his (Crabbe's) touch, and new personalities take their place, play their part in

130

the drama, and at the will of God disappear. The survivors inherit the stage and the tradition of the play."

The great claws clutched this screed; and scathed it with *Author's Remarks on Reader's Report.*

The Reader spat a *Second Report*, alleging that the intention of the first had been merely to correct the trivial lapses of one who possesses knowledge superior to one's own; and whimpering, "My work is like the work of a printer's devil": which was altogether charming in a person who was posing as a Judge of Literature and a Publisher's Protoboylcytes. But she (or he) adhered to all former opinions; and exuded spiteful spleen by fearing that Crabbe showed signs of an incurable mania for self-justification. Oldcastle also expressed his own agreement with his Reader; and demanded that Crabbe should make a third copy of the work including a whole posse of alterations in matter and form. Crabbe then very grimly deemed it due to himself to write an unassisted letter.

"I had taken the trouble," he told Oldcastle, "to think out a method and a style of writing. I believe that you gave me this commission: because you liked my previous work. Therefore, it appears to me perfectly amazing that you should agree with your Reader when she (or he) alleges that my style is 'clumsy'. I incontinently and utterly abjure the 'incurable mania for self-justification' (a phrase which I should not have expected to find in a *Reader's Report*) now that I have seen the futility of the same. And, concerning these *Reports* and your decision, I have no more to say. When, seven weeks ago, I delivered the MS. to you for a fortnight's consideration, I expressed my regret that the time named in our contract did not permit me to make a third fair copy. Now, the 143,550 words shall be gelded, re-vised, re-copied, in accordance with your instructions. I estimate that this task will occupy two months. Of course, I need hardly say that on no account will I permit myself to be connected publicly with the new *Medici Book*. I only can accept responsibility for things of which my own judgement approves. So kindly invent a man of straw, John Brown or James Black; and put him as the author of the book. Understand that you shall have exactly what you want, without any reference whatever to my natural rights or sentiments or future commissions."[1]

Kemp said that it was a proper heroic quixotic letter written with a poignard. Crabbe put aside the *Four Fine Gentlemen*; and addressed himself to his ungrateful task.

Oldcastle was frightfully alarmed. Although the bumptious young thing did not quite know what he wanted, he was certain that he did not want to have his book damned by its author. He wanted Crabbe for a tool, not an enemy. The fact was that his paper-maker again was insisting on having something on account, which was not convenient: and, without paper or credit, he was unable to publish the *Medici Book* at the appointed time. Delay was inevitable, said Church Welbeck when consulted. Dust must be thrown into eyes. To save his own face, to evade the necessity for explanation, Oldcastle was trying to arrange that the delay should appear to be caused by Crabbe. So he asked for a fresh copy of the book. He had not contemplated the probability of Crabbe's taking his petition as he had taken it. He simply thought to keep the drudge occupied for a month or two, and to save the expense of a typescribe, until the difficulty with the paper-maker should have been obviated. The idea that a poor author could be so temerarious as to scorn him and all his works, never entered his silly noddle. And so, when he had read Crabbe's letter and withered under the contemptuous withdrawal of the name, he saw that he must make an effort, in the book's interest, to reconstitute amicable relations with its author. He tore off to Crabbe's friend Neddy: thus accentedly putting his fat foot further into everything.

Crabbe met the news with resentful ferocity. "Now listen to me!" he said to Neddy. "This game is not being played properly. When you intervene between me and Oldcastle, you'll do so at my request: not at his. I'll tell you why. A long time ago,

---

[1] This and the subsequent acrimonious correspondence with Oldcastle is an almost exact transcription of the original. See Rolfe's *Letters to Grant Richards* (1952).

I told him that you were going to undertake my business arrangements. The blighter shied: because you're a solicitor; and said that he preferred to personally deal (I'm quoting) with his authors. I conceded the point at great inconvenience: for you know how he kept on interrupting me all the time when I was doing his frightful book. Very well. On these grounds, I decline to take cognizance of any communications, except those which he makes directly to me. Neddy, tell him all this. And add that you find me frightfully irritated at the offensive terms applied and the insufficient attention paid to the work which cost me such enormous and prolonged trouble."

Neddy did his job delightfully. Oldcastle promptly skipped into line, inviting Crabbe to come and see him, "to quietly have a talk and settle any difficulties that I fancy rest largely on mutual misconception."

Crabbe said that there were no misconceptions on his side: as Oldcastle might see by referring to his last letter, where it plainly was stated that he was going to have exactly what his printer's devil had desiderated. And Crabbe declined further discussion. Oldcastle persisted. Crabbe withstood him; and steadily went on writing. Oldcastle was quite sure that, if Crabbe only would come, "they would be able to pleasantly arrange things." Crabbe knew of no things needing arrangement: but, if Oldcastle would name the object of the proposed interview, he would prepare himself and come. The object, according to the publisher, was that he wanted to himself see Crabbe, and to as it were get more thoroughly to an understanding as to what they were going to really do. Crabbe said that that all had been settled by letter. Oldcastle knew all about the letters: but they left nothing clear in his mind. Would Crabbe bring the whole correspondence and have a talk. Crabbe re-iterated four points, viz., he would not discuss the *Reader's Reports*: he would rewrite the book according to instructions: he would do it in two months: he withdrew his name from it. And he would not produce Oldcastle's letters (he saw the dodge): because they were covered with commentaries which, at present, were for his own private eye. To this he added (at Neddy's dictation), "Consciousness of my own inability to do justice to myself, when conducting my affairs by personal interviews, has proved to me the absolute necessity of adhering to written communications for the reason that this course alone enables me to benefit by mature consideration and advice."

The thought, that it would be well (if possible) to avoid a final and formal rupture from Oldcastle, was prominent in his mind all the time. Neddy brayed it at him. Kemp tacitly indicated a like notion. So, when he had solaced his sore self with all these martial demonstrations and had reduced his publisher to (what he deemed to be) a fitting state of mind, Crabbe went to see him. By request, he reached the tradesman's shop at three-quarters after noon. Oldcastle, semi-blind in a brand-new monocle, invited him to courteously step a little way. The two set out; and the publisher was affable. He regretted; and nothing could be farther from his thoughts; and he would not or the world; and he sincerely trusted.

Crabbe displayed a mood which might be melting. "It's a very serious thing for me to find that I'm no further advanced than I was last July, when you told me that you'd take a week or two to read the MS., and start me on a new work immediately. Now, why don't you throw over your Reader altogether, and let me burn those fatuous *Reports* and all the letters which you've written to me since August, and consider that they never were. I say this, because I believe that a blunder has been made and that you know it. I don't want to rub that in."

"There's nothing I would like better," Oldcastle pranced to say. "Let's cancel the past and begin again; and I'll personally see that you gain largely by the book. When did you specify you could let me have it?"

"On the twelfth of November."

"Then that's a bargain. Well now: which way are you going? This turning leads to Regent Street, and that to Oxford Street. You'll courteously excuse me, I know, because I turn in here to usually have my luncheon."

CHAPTER TWENTY

And Crabbe found himself alone on the pavement. He said what the situation demanded; and thanked his stars that he had not written his name to anything.

Oldcastle got the new *Medici Book* on the twelfth of November.

Chapter Twenty-one

CHURCH WELBECK ESQUIRE dawned on London. His advent was announced to Crabbe by a clerk's card from Schelm's London office, which stated that he could be seen at certain hours at a given place. Crabbe acknowledged receipt of this missive, with deep gratitude for the proffer of so Beatific a Vision, which (he feared) was not for the likes of him. That brought Welbeck to reason and to Crabbe *instanter*. Kemp secluded himself in his own den. Neddy came to meet the New York manager.

Welbeck was all glorious without. His pose was *Americanorum Americanissimus*. The tobacco, of which he made gargantuan cigarettes, cost him a pound a pound. His socks were silk and open-worked; and his gold fountain-pen really did hold half a pint. They let him recite his very glorious acts. There were no flies on him. He had a cinch on things. Back-numbers made him tired. He had squelched Schelm to his face, and to Mrs Schelm. "Has not my husband got one good point?" the latter plaintively had inquired. He had dined Oldcastle and his wife at the Carlton. "She wath a thhowy bit," in Welbeck's opinion, "white thatin and pearlth and pink thilk thtockingth." The dinner had cost him fifteen pounds, chiefly because of some mess made of *foie gras* and unlaid peahen's eggs. Oldcastle had sounded him as to a partnership: suggesting that he should manage an American branch of the House of Doron Oldcastle Limited. That, though, was in the air. He might do better for himself by staying with the squelched Schelm for the present.

After handing round the hat for the half-pennies of admiration, Welbeck continued, "And now what'th all thith about thith *Medithi Book?*"

"What have you heard; and from whom?"

"Oldcathle told me at the Carlton that, when your thtuff came in, he found he couldn't pothibly print it. You wrote him a graphic account, he thayth, of a bithop qualifying for prothecution under the Criminal Law Amendment Act."

"Oh did I? Oh did he say that? Well: he didn't tell me it was a bishop. He and his Reader said that it was 'a bestial cardinal subsequently made Pope'."

"But whatever did you do that for?"

"I'm not sure that I did. Wait, please . . . Now this is the original MS. which I sent in. And this is the chapter of which that liar and ignoramus has been bleating to you. Just cast your glittering eye over it."

"M-m-m-m-m-m-m. Well?"

"Well?"

"There'th nothing about that here!"

"No. Nor has there ever been in the whole book."

"Then what did Oldcathle mean?"

"The devils alone can say. I don't know what he meant: unless he was anxious to display the facts that neither he nor his Reader can read Italian, and that they both have very nasty minds."

"Hummh! What wath hith object?"

"The book was due to be published this autumn. Perhaps it wasn't convenient . . ."

"Crabbe, what do you know?"

"Most things."

"About the paper-maker?"

"Yes. Thanks for telling me."

"Hummh! The man'th a fool. He'll make a meth of thith book thomehow. Why don't you buy it back from him; and let Thchelm have it inthtead?"

"That's not by any means half a bad notion. Neddy, what do you say? Neddy's my business manager, I must tell you, Welbeck."

"Yes: and I tell you what I mean to say. I'm not going to let him bally well muck his business any more," Neddy affirmed. "You see the thing's like this, begad. Here's Oldcastle wanting his work and Schelm wanting his work; and I'm going to play those two publishing rotters off against each other for all I'm worth."

The more vigorous and alert mind of Crabbe doubted the advisability of advertising that scheme to Schelm's manager, who was not unlikely to eventuate as Oldcastle's partner, and not slow to acknowledge cognizance with a pregnant and portentous "Hummmh!" He instantly lightly switched the conversation away with a wet finger to Welbeck's own future in New York.

That was going to be Great; forty-five editions of Thorah's *Red Rappee* already were sold. And, as soon as he got back, Crabbe's *Daynian Folk-lore* and *Kalliphonos* would be issued and pushed to a similar altitude.

"What did you mean by saying that your seeing me now would result in an important step being taken by me?" Crabbe said to Welbeck.

"I'm not ready to tell you. You mutht trutht me a little longer; and believe that I keep your betht interethtth very near my heart. I'm thorry that you won't dedicate your *Daynian Folk-lore* to me."

"Well, I won't. You understand my feeling. Let me see you make a success of that and the *Kalliphonos*; and then, when I've got a name and a dedication from me is worth having, I'll write a far better book and dedicate it to you. Make me, first; and then I'll glorify you. Scratch my back; and I'll scratch yours. Understand?"

"Very good. Now what'th the newth about the *Four Fine Gentlemen*?"

It would be ready in a week: meanwhile, here was what was done. Welbeck read it; and howled "Great" incessantly, with demonstrations towards Crabbe's neck. The little man was a rabid enthusiast at heart, undoubtedly. He recrossed the Atlantic with the new MS., vowing to bring out *Daynian Folk-lore* instantly and to delay no longer with the *Kalliphonos*. Proofs of the latter should come at once. All the same, he left no money behind him; and Crabbe did not like to press for the payment promised for the *Four Fine Gentlemen*. In literature the only way of getting any money at all is to pretend that you won't touch it with a pair of tongs if it were offered to you. Then, either you receive voluntary cheques on account of works whose very schemes are only in the shadows of your cerebellum, or you don't get a farthing.

In the middle of December, Oldcastle wrote, begging to specify that he was going to really publish the *Medici Book* at the commencement of the coming season. Crabbe met Neddy pervading Burlington Arcade with a placidly genteel air of condescension: and inquired after Bainbrigge.

"Oh he's all serene: but what I mean to say is he's gettin rather a bore, that rotter."

"In what way?

"Wants to go to Greece, begad."

"Well, why don't you?"

"Oh the guvner's gettin a bit tired. Fact is we've put all our spare cash into this business; and now we want some more."

"I thought that respectable solicitors always had a lot of money waiting for investments."

"So we have. But you don't suppose we can put our clients' money into anythin without their bally consent?"

"Why not ask for their consent?"

"Don't you see we haven't got good security to offer?"

"Of course you haven't. The whole thing's pure speculation. But I should have thought that plenty of your clients would be only too glad to speculate in a thing which commended itself to a sober old firm like yours."

"You're not a man of business, begad."

"I thank my stars I'm not. I don't admire the samples. Don't swear so loudly. But you spoke of an expert's opinion about your oil-island. If that is good enough to start a company on, it ought to be good enough to raise money on."

"So it would be, if we'd got it: but we haven't. Can't you see? The Blackstone rotter said what I told you: but he hasn't written it."

"Why don't you give the man his fee, and get him to write it?"

"He won't, begad!"

"Have you tried him?"

"Yes."

"The dickens you have! And he won't put his words in writing?"

"No he won't. The guvner went to him himself: but he positively declined. He said that he went to Zante for the Scotty-rotters' syndicate; and that what he discovered outside their business on that trip was a thing which he wasn't bound to tell them, but which he might sell to them if they asked him: but he couldn't professionally sell it to anyone else, or even use it himself, because such sale or use would be an unfriendly act toward the syndicate which was the means of his makin a certain discovery. I hope that's clear and categorical. I'm not goin to say it over again. Begad, Crabbe, why will you always make me talk shop, when you know how I hate it?"

"Why don't you get some other expert's opinion?"

"Means sendin another man to Zante. Means beginnin all expenses over again. No, thenks. Besides, there is no other expert."

"Then what are you going to do?"

"Dunno. Talk about somethin else. What are you doin yourself? How's Oldcastle?"

"Playing hide and seek, as usual. Says that he won't part with the *Medici Book* on any account."

"Now look here, Crabbe, if you don't manage to buy that book back you will be a damnrottenrotter!"

"I've asked him to sell: and he says he won't."

"Asked him—yes—as though you were offerin the option of tripes or potato parins to a bear. I know the sort of letter you'd write. Why the devil don't you let me do these things for you?"

"Let you? I only wish you would. But I never can find you when I want you."

"Well, you've got me now."

"Cut in, by all means; and good luck to you. What do you propose?"

"I'll tell him that, bein under the impression that I might be able to assist in the matter of the *Medici Book*, I have with great difficulty persuaded you to courteously acquiesce in my endeavours to in fact remove little unpleasantnesses; and I'll offer to actually go and see him."

"Good!"

Neddy wrote his little offer. Oldcastle smashed a monocle; and bounced at it. (I think that he sniffed a whiff of complacent jackass; and preferred it to the tenacity of indurated crustacean.) Neddy's report of the interview was, that Oldcastle didn't want to sell: but, if Crabbe and his business-manager would come and talk things over, some arrangement might be arrived at.

Crabbe declined, for he had begun a new book: but (by request) he gave Neddy a Power of Attorney irrevocable for six months.

Armed with this, and finding Oldcastle inaccessible by blandishments, Neddy anon proceeded with severity. He was instructed to say that his client demurred to the inaccurate statements which Oldcastle had permitted himself to make concerning the propriety of the original *Medici Book*. Oldcastle retorted he had never at any time or to any person made such statements. That, both Neddy and Crabbe knew to be a gratuitous and stupid lie: because Welbeck had had neither means of nor motive for reporting such statements except by way of Oldcastle at the Carlton. Oldcastle repeated his request for an interview. Neddy now urged Crabbe not to consent; and stated that, with the proviso that his client's position already had been defined, he himself was prepared to give due consideration to proposals which Oldcastle might make in writing. Oldcastle would not make proposals: but invited Crabbe to come and approve of the "format" of the book.

Neddy declined: iterating that Crabbe had expressed his entire disapproval of the publication of the book in its present form, in proof of which he had withdrawn his name from it by two separate letters. He added that Crabbe claimed the right to do this, in view of the fact that the contract did not contain stipulations for the use of his signature or for the submission of his work to any censorship.

Oldcastle thanked Neddy for his kindness in doing what he could from beginning to end to if possible render relations more pleasant; and announced that proofs of the *Medici Book* would be sent to Crabbe in due course.

Neddy feared that he was unable to consider that as being in any way a solution of the difficulty. He had learned, from the voluminous correspondence which had passed between his friend and Oldcastle, that the latter found occasion to be dissatisfied with the MS., and never had expressed thanks for the gratuitous copy made after expiry of contract. Also, Oldcastle still seemed to think that additional revision and further trouble on Crabbe's part was necessary. These circumstances tended to impress Neddy with the notion that Oldcastle could not be anxious, in his own interest, to waste money on the publication of a book which he viewed with such disfavour, and would welcome the opportunity of releasing himself, both from the work itself and from the obligations which he lay under to Crabbe, by gracefully conceding to the latter the option of buying back the *Medici Book*.

And then, Oldcastle delivered a masterly if somewhat dirty *coup-de-jarnac*. He sent Neddy an anonymous letter of personal contempt.

Neddy was infuriated to think that he should be exposed to so gross an affront. The habit of persons of his mental calibre is to wreak revenge on the nearest object, regardless of honour or right or even common sense. He flung back the whole correspondence and the whole affair with violent recriminations upon Crabbe.

Crabbe in a moment realized the fatality of leaving things like that. He went to Neddy; and implored him to write one more letter to Oldcastle, a most severe one, addressing him as "Sir", and saying, "I am in receipt of an anonymous type-scribed document emanating from your office; and I beg to inform you that it is contrary to my practice, in common with that of all respectable solicitors, to entertain correspondence of that description." He urged that, on the one hand, so caustic a reprimand might recall Oldcastle to a sense of ordinary decency, and prevent the complete rupture of negotiations: while on the other hand, if it failed in that, it at least would put and leave the publisher finally and irretrievably in the wrong.

Neddy, still writhing under the insult, sought solace lolling in a lounge chair, gorging himself with chocolate creams, reading erotic novels. His collar and waistcoat and braces were unbuttoned, and his feet comfy in old pumps. He flatly refused to listen to Crabbe: whom he inanely dared to hold responsible for Oldcastle's misbehaviour.

Crabbe resented such injustice; and realized that the moment for splitting brass rags was come. He touched Neddy upon the raw, rancorously denouncing him as a false and treacherous friend, one unable to stand through storm, anxious enough to wear the crown and pitifully eager to avoid bearing the cross.

Neddy put on the wicked glare of a friend in a phrenzy, meditating revenges and slaughters and mind-grieving evils. But, in his tenderest parts, the great claws savagely clutched him, tore off the mask of his manners, and stripped his selfishness naked—flung him, at length, and left him bogged in the swamp of the shameful.

Chapter Twenty-two

BY way of relief, Crabbe betook himself to Kemp, knitting, knitting, knitting, always silent, always ready to speak gently and generously and with virility, always patient and pathetic, 'with a face like a star, so steadfast and clear and true that he felt renewed even by looking on it.' Thence, he returned to his new book. That was going to be something quite out of the common —something which never had been seen or done or even dreamed about before, pleasure-giving, all his own. It was shaping well.

National events occurred, to which no one but a beetle could be blind. On the Festival of the Purification, he gave himself a day's holiday, and the joy of standing ankle-deep in the horse-trough by the Marble Arch, holding Kemp seated on his shoulders while a pageant passed. He described it aloud as it passed; and Kemp said that he saw it by that and smell and taste and touch. When he got back to Lincoln's Inn Fields late in the afternoon, some benefic star moved Crabbe to recall the fact of his existence to the remembrance of the man of New York, by the following letter:

Dear Welbeck,
The Majesty of England, the Great Queen, went through Her capital today to Her exsequies at Windsor, devoid of Cross, devoid of Canopy. Which is to say that the funeral-procession lacked two items of signal importance, viz., the emblem of Christianity—and She was Defender of the Faith, —and the unique emblem of Sovereignty—and She was Ruler of the Seas, Mother and Mistress of Autocrats and Kings, Herself a Prince Incomparable.

I suppose that this incongruous inconsistency may be accounted for by saying that it is English—pretty Fanny's way? Not that we English lack wit, or reverence, or love: but a nation—which babbles of the Queen's "Sarcophagus", meaning thereby the Aberdeen granite tomb which is not

CHAPTER TWENTY-TWO

"flesh-devouring", carnivorous, σαρχοφάγος, in any sense of the word, (not being made of that peculiar limestone quarried at Assos in the Troad, which consumed corpses laid in coffins of it),—is capable of any tops-i'-th'-turfiness!

The fact is, my dear Welbeck, that we English have become inchanted by you dear young noisy unknowing Americans; and we try to imitate you. Look at our newssheets; and mark the tokens. The British—(ridiculous misnomer, when there are no British or Britains any more but only England and the English predominant in all the world!) —Lion has been attempting to fly like the Eagle, rejecting his proper part, grave, ponderous, slow, and sure. Britannia, in this last decade, has been going forth in Uncle Sam's unmentionables, on a "bike" (an' it please you); and (Lord ha' mercy on me!) how silly she does look!

This exposition of the inappropriate and inopportune may be ascribed to the education (pass me the word) of the Masses by the School-board Act of 1870. It has turned a nation of heroes and tradesmen into petty coxcombs and shams; and has swamped (certainly silenced) the scholar and the gentleman. The last, on venturing to emphasize the distinction between Sentiment and Principle, Might and Right, Right and Wrong, promptly (and more or less impolitely) are labelled "back-numbers" in favour of something "Dylymylyte" and "Upterdight" as the Schoolboard's progeny enunciates its shibboleths.

Democracy rampant is all very well in America: for exuberant youth does right to gambol. But, for grave old England to ape Keltogothic America, is as inept as for sober rams and ewes to skip in lamb-fashion. First, it makes the beholder laugh. Secondly, it makes him sick. Thirdly, it makes him vehemently angry. I detest, and denounce as criminal, that finite mortal man who (having found a groove which fits his atrophied brain and hypertrophied organs) screams to Kosmos, 'This is the way, the only way; and, if you won't mutilate yourself to fit it, then be damned to you, you're dotty, balmy on the crumpet, impossible, and you practise the Bulgarian Heresy!' And so on. "But the minds of the prudent are flexible: for the language of mortals is voluble; and the discourses thereof are numerous and varied; and vast is the distribution of words here and there." I hold, with the Primate-Poet, that there is room for all opinions, for all systems, each in its convenient sphere: that the curses of this age are the craving to convert, the fear of individual singularity, the notion that a man (whom you can distinguish in a crowd) must be in mortal sin. I may be wrong. That's for me and my Judge to decide. I call myself 'broad-minded'. Also, I mean what I say—which makes me distinctly singular. I admit that 'broadmindedness', as understood here and there, differs from mine. Different it is. Your American shriekers shriek, 'See what a great nation we are!' (I don't deny it: none but a fool and blind would.) And, in like manner, our English yellers yell as well. If they would be content to have my admiration, without insisting, "Whosoever will be saved, before all things it is necessary that he should howl with us", all then would be well. But they won't. And all is not well. Here, on this side, (if you mark me) we are going to have a change: for we English have gotten a King. You don't lay much store by Kings: but I do, upon conviction —though I know that I'm not rich enough to publish my convictions. To-day, for the first time, I have seen a King of England face to face. Also, I have had an opportunity of comparing him with the finest specimen of an Emperor which the world ever has seen; and, if I know anything of physiognomy, I can say that the Excellent Majesty of Edward is indeed a King. On horse-back, He is the shape of an equilateral triangle, firm-fixed, immoveable, forceful, reserved, *sibi imperiosus, contemnere honores fortis; et in seipso totus teres atque rotundus, externi ne quid valeat per laeve morari.* A man is a very splendid thing when he is a Man: but This is something more than a Man. This also is a King. I think that you know me to have sampled some sorts and conditions of men, not forgetting our Lord the Pope: but I solemnly assure you that I never have received such an impression from a human presence, as this morning in the Presence of England's Edward. I am not overburthened with the vice of obsequious humility: but I felt that, then, my place was on one knee.

I augur the very best. The King's Majesty has the advantage of knowledge of good and evil. "Madcap Hal" became Henry of England and Victor of Azincour under the unction of kingship. And, with the wise, I prefer pure gold which has been tried in the fire. Looking on His royal face, I realized that there *is* a divinity which doth hedge a king. I have seen—therefore I believe—blessed (and you know the rest). The King is a Force. He is the King. The habit of England will change, already is changing, strengthening, passing from flaccidity to stability. Apes that we are, sedulous apes, snobs if you will, we're going now to ape the kingly manliness of the King. And thanks be unto all gods for this signal mercy.

The less said about the English newspapers during this novendial, the better. Barring *Times, Morning Post, Globe, St James' Gazette,* they have chattered and shrieked and squeaked platitudes and shibboleths and stereotyped plates, in a manner which would make the *New York World* and Mr Rudyard Kipling's gibbering monkey-people green with jealousy. Terrified by Death into indecent indignity, the journalist-guttersnipe has treated the Translation of Divine Victoria—(could any poet want a nobler theme? Look how sumptuously Henley has done it in to-day's *Post*) —much as a girls' board-school would treat the expulsion of a senior pupil, tricking out stark phrenetic horror with an access of smugly hypocritical virtue, with well-worn tags, with pretty paganisms. We're all in black, with frightened faces the length of your arm. Also, we're all cock-sure that the Great Queen has gone from a corruptible crown to an incorruptible, from a pain-full old-age here to a joy-full youth unending there. And, to mark our faith in our Christian profession (to say nothing of the fitness of things), we don't go gloriously triumphing in garbs of silver-white and yellow-gold, singing paeans of exsaultation because the Highest among us has gone from what we assert to be 'a vale of woe' to what we are convinced is 'an abode of bliss': but we masquerade in sooty habits hued like the

147

pit, to the canting whine of timid dirges, these being our notion of what we abjectly call "shewing proper respect." (We are a most remarkable people.) This Enormous Event has been defiled by every degenerate degradation known to board-school-nurtured Fleet Street. Stately simplicity was the key in which to have written. There's an epitaph in the Catacombs which would have served—*VICTORIA DORMIT*——. Could anything be more lovely? But tawdry tinsel was Fleet Street's tribute to the gold of Her.

The King's Command, that the funeral-route should be draped with purple, was disobeyed: except in the case of two solitary houses in Park Lane. These used purple, *purpureus*, πορφύριος, i.e. porphyry-colour, i.e. dark glistening brownish-red. All the rest (and I walked all the way) hung themselves with aniline violet, cheap, skimpy, eye-blistering, hideous. Lord Brassey's house by the Marble Arch burst out with a 'Portion' insulting to the firmament, brassy; and howled the obvious to all and sundry, 'Our Bluvvid Sovring as dipartid in something puffick something' or some such insufferably sentimental banality.

I did not see the naval show: but the Navy is the one department of this nation which can be trusted to behave itself seemly. Its style is beyond reproach, above criticism. The military show was magnificent, but (as I have said) perfectly pagan and perfectly unregal, for want of those two things, the Cross and the Canopy. Why there wasn't even the cross-potent gules of Saint George Protector of the Kingdom on the pallium: which simply was a glorified bed-quilt of white satin with armorials at the corners. St Paul's Cathedral possesses a beautiful cross; and used it at Dr Creighton's funeral the other day; and there are a hundred others in the land. I concede the gun-carriage: for that was a daring creation of a precedent; and daring is just now entirely admirable. As for the crown and sceptre on the coffin—they looked splendid, and huge: but they were not enough: for mere kings-of-arms wear crowns (not coronets like peers) and brandish sceptres. But I cannot forgive the omission of the thirty-two-poled canopy (eight poles more than are allotted to any other monarch in the world, including the Father of Princes and Kings) which is the unique symbol of English sovereignty. This blunder may be ascribed to the egregious effete Earl Marshal.

And, talking of him, please note the Cardinal Archbishop's latest attempt to push forward, latest exposition of tact. I'm not going to embarrass you with my opinions: because you can't do me the justice of believing me capable of taking a judicial view of people who so atrociously and inhumanly have man-handled me and ruined my not abnormally blameful life: but I simply will compile from the newspapers; and you may furnish your own commentary. First, Queen Victoria dies. Secondly, from Rome by wire comes news that God's Vicegerent, on hearing, dropped on His knees, prayed for half-an-hour, said Mass for the repose of Her soul: and was sending back the Cardinal Archbishop, hot-foot, stomach-to-earth, to England as His representative at the exsequies. Thirdly, the days roll by. Fourthly, the Cardinal Archbishop, still in Rome, issues an elaborate pastoral, formally forbidding public prayers for the Queen, at Whom he sneers as an Heresiarch and Archschismatic: but contemptuously and superciliously laying no embargo on private prayers, which the few loyal English Catholics (as distinguished from the hordes of Fenians) can say in secret (at their peril), while the Catholic Archbishops of France and Canada and the Holiness of the Pope Himself are singing solemn requiems. Fifthly, on the ninth day, more telegraphs from Rome announce that His Eminency of Westminster is detained in Rome by a cold: (O commodious cold) that he will leave shortly; and travel to England by Feb. 24th by slow stages. And the *Pall Mall Gazette* has an interview:—

Interviewer. Can His Holiness be represented at the funeral of a non-Catholic sovereign?

Cardinal Archbishop. Has the Pope been invited?

Interviewer. If He were invited, would He accept?

Cardinal Archbishop. At the funeral of the Emperor William I and the coronation of Tzar Nicholas II He did accept; and the Papal Envoys arrived too late.

Interviewer perfectly understood that the Holy See would
have liked to have received an invitation, as a recognition
of the supreme rank of the Roman Pontiff; and that, in such
a case, a pontifical ablegate would have been sent, and
would have arrived after the funeral. O filthy paltry unholy
subterfuge by which degenerate Rome would play with
rejuvenescent England! The invitation was not sent. *Io
paean!* You remember with what ostentatious vulgarity
Vaughan qualified himself for a snub from the Prince of
Wales at the Academy banquet some years ago. You know
that, since then, he has been *persona ingratissima*, completely out of court. Now note another bid for a nod. He was
coming to represent the Pope at the funeral. The nod was
delayed. He would have revenge. (Oh I know my Catholics!) He denounces Queen Victoria as being beyond the
pale of Christian charity. (Oh I do think it deliciously
Christian to forbid intercession for one's worst enemy;
and She never was that!) And so His Eminency sets back
the Catholic clock for fifty years: saturates his spleen; and
wins the adulation of the Fenian Irish.

Well: it is now a quarter-past-two to-morrow morning;
and I am tired of criticizing other people; and I have my
own conscience to criticize before I dare to go to bed. So I
will say no more than that I have written this impromptu
solely as a literary exercise, to let you see how much my
style has deteriorated under my present dismal circumstances. For I've got no (paying) work to do.

Faithfully yours,
Nicholas Crabbe.

P.S. By the by, will you do me the honour of accepting the
dedication of the tralation of *Kalliphonos*.

This letter accurately served its purpose of being a tremendous
jog to the elbow. Welbeck instantly emitted a couple of thousand
words on America *v.* England, school-boards, catholics, and
kings. He called it an "elaborate dialectic", presumably because
it did not contain a single question. He went on to say:—

"Frankly, your style has improved. I do not know when I
enjoyed reading a description of any function so much. I wish

to have you do more of this kind of thing. Deterioration be hanged. You were cut out for the New Journalist. By 'new' I mean the true journalist of the future, who is the scholar and not the skimmer." (Crabbe yelled again.) "Look to it, you son of earth, you dreamer of dreams! My silence has been none of my seeking, or of any lack of desire to communicate with you. Since I arrived, I have had nothing but work and weariness. However, here I am again, at the bidding of your letter and in response to my own feelings. Your *Daynian Folk-lore* is actually ready, bound and all, and only awaits the publisher's work in London, which is to copyright the book there and let me know in advance date on which copyright takes place, so that I can make simultaneous publication. I think without vanity that I have made as pretty a book of it as you have ever seen. By the same mail with this goes a copy. Show it to no one: because it is not yet published; and let me know what you think of it. Find out from Schelm whether he is going to publish this book first or the *Kalliphonos.* I accept the dedication of the last with thanks, and keenly appreciate the honor. I will write a very learned introduction with all my heart and all my skill such as it is. Pray tell me what you are doing, and what new things you are meditating. Send me all you write. I can get good money for your work quite easily."

Crabbe instantly sat down and read his own book. It was a frightfully pretty witty subtile violet-and-white book, full of pathos and laughter and good sense and wild absurdity and real beauty and damnably persistent printer's errors; and he never had seen it before. He had a delightful morning in the easy chair, reading and roaring and raving and ramping over his own work.

On going back to his writing table, he was not satisfied. He had displayed his literary ability to Welbeck in various directions. He had shewn him imagination on the one hand, and (what fools take for) scholarship on the other. He had shewn the power of reproducing the past, of manipulating the present, of foreseeing the future. He also had shewn indefatigable readiness and energy. And, if words meant things, he had convinced Welbeck of his value. "Let me have all your work, send me all you write. I can get good money for your work quite easily:"— could anything be plainer? Welbeck (for Schelm) had two books of his in print. These had been paid for by Schelm. Besides, Welbeck had the *Four Fine Gentlemen* and a pile of essays and stories. Yet he sent no money. Was it possible that he had not realized that Crabbe must live, must have the certainty of being able to live, or he could not write. What was the good of trying to continue to write for people who paid nothing? If it was quite easy to get good money for Crabbe's work, Crabbe himself would like to see some. He wrote his mind to Welbeck.

Welbeck replied that no man on earth, except perhaps Crabbe, was more enthusiastic about his work than he was: begged him, for God's sake, not to despair: things must come round some day. To hell with Oldcastle, who made him tired. To hell with anybody who wanted to swindle or to use Crabbe for private gain. *Kalliphonos* was not to appear this spring: but it should come out in September. Welbeck wanted to give *Daynian Folk-lore* all the shove he could. It was being advertised as an Easter offering to the people of America. From what his correspondents told him, Welbeck opined that the English book-trade was at a pretty low ebb. Oldcastle actually was issuing sixpenny novels. Ah, what a fall was there! Welbeck suspected that the mule was kicking. It had tried to snort like a horse: but the last snort seemed to have been promulged. Oldcastle must find it hard to keep the skin on his asinine corpus and preserve even the appearance of the nobler animal. Welbeck knew that Crabbe could do stuff like the Exsequies letter on his head. What he didn't know was why he did not do it. That sort of thing earned money. Welbeck could sell it. He prayed Crabbe to do it until he could afford not to do it. He praised it, knowing it to be saleable: not because it was the best which Crabbe could do. He knew that it was not. But he wanted Crabbe to get to that state of body and mind in which he could do what his soul impelled him to do. He wished him to take any current event *'in transitu'*; and to write of it as he had written of the Exsequies; and to send it to him, and he would send back sums of money. Crabbe then would earn a handsome competency; and be better able to turn to his other work. "Take the journalist's point of view. That's all I ask. I'll get the rest for you, meaning by rest—money." He longed to drag Crabbe out of the Slough of Despond. He would do the workaday thing: Crabbe should do the Everlasting. Welbeck also announced that he was engaged in great schemes not connected with Schelm. He was returning to England in July; and begged Crabbe to see him then.

Crabbe said everything all over again. As long as he was kept in the background, out of the world, he could not write of what went on in the foreground of the world. Just that once, at the funeral of Queen Victoria, the gods of his stars had permitted him to see an Event; and he had shewn that he could describe what he saw. When he was paid for the work which had been in Welbeck's hands for a year, he would be able to come to the front and to inspect other events which, in turn, he would describe. He did not shy at journalism, or at any honest work. He craved it with shouts. He always had been craving it. But he expected pay for it. And he was not paid. And he was not going to write at random. He asked Welbeck to let him have something definite.

Welbeck offered him a pound a week for ten hours' work a day, six days a week, in ungermane research at the British Museum, just to pass the time.

Crabbe refused it. He wanted payment for work already done.

Welbeck evaded the point. It was very difficult to do anything so far away from England. He was harassed twice a week by mails from Schelm in London; and the many things which required attention just made his head ache—they came in such battalions. He wished that he could relieve Crabbe of financial troubles: but it was quite beyond him. The case was a very peculiar one. It was a terrible big fight, the game of life in America. Crabbe could have no idea of the pace. It was simply killing to the man of poor physique. Welbeck was beginning to feel the effects of it. Not only had he to fight the game there: but he also had to contend against ill feeling in the London house. Schelm did not make things pleasant for him. Schelm liked to rub it in whenever he found an opening; and he made openings when they were not ready-made for him. The poetical grain-and-green-eating aesthete with long hair and a flourishing mess for a necktie, whom Welbeck had raised from clerkship to the managership, was sly, sir, sly, and hand-in-glove with Schelm. Altogether Welbeck's office was no sinecure. Oldcastle was announcing publication of the *Medici Book* in America. *Daynian Folk-lore* was getting quite good notices; and Welbeck was pushing it to the utmost of his power. "It's a sad world, is it not? And yet, what a bright place it is, after all. Now I must wrestle with that demon of a Schelm," Welbeck concluded.

The dishonesty of all this palaver set the claws a-snapping. Where was that "good money" which was "quite easy to get"? Crabbe's abominable habit, of reading rigidly on (instead of between) the lines, quite prevented him from realizing that his correspondent himself was in dire difficulties. He replied austerely, regretting that Welbeck continued to belie the promises on which he had obtained confidence, obedience, and (say) 250,000 words of literature. Finding himself materially injured by following Welbeck's directions, Crabbe thought that he now would withdraw. He would have been pleased to let Welbeck make him a successful writer: but he could not afford neglect. If due attention had been paid to his letters—if the obligations voluntarily undertaken had been fulfilled—he would not complain: but evasion and superficiality were displeasing. He of course would regret rupture: because he had a personal regard for Welbeck; and, hence, had been willing to owe success to him. But he perceived that Welbeck could not be both publisher and friend. Therefore, he preferred to owe success to himself. If Welbeck had kept one part of the bargain, Crabbe would not object to continue to keep the other: but, under the circumstances, he felt free to look after his own interests. He asked for the return of the book called *Four Fine Gentlemen of 1495*, and of all the other MSS. which Welbeck had obtained from him; and he cancelled the dedication of the *Kalliphonos*, if Welbeck should decide to break with him.

Welbeck did not understand.

Crabbe could not provide him with an understanding. Welbeck retained the MSS.: and they never were paid for. So, once more, Crabbe fell in the toils of a friend and despoiler.

Chapter Twenty-three

Daynian Folk-lore received genial and rather intelligent appreciation from English as well as from American reviewers. The *Spectator* and the *Largest Circulation*[1] were particularly laudatory. A publisher, who wanted to make the book successful, could have found plenty of literary praise of it for the embellishment of advertisements.

But Slim Schelm played the waiting game. He did not want to succeed with Crabbe's one book, nor with his next: because, in that case, the author's literary value would have risen, and a fourth book would not be obtainable outright for five-and-twenty or thirty pounds. But, when Schelm should have issued half a dozen books by Crabbe, getting them cheap and keeping them in first editions, then, he might make a success of the seventh, to Crabbe's benefit (if he should live so long); and the success of the seventh would arouse public interest in its six predecessors. Then, all of this writer's works would be boomed; and Schelm would net the profits of the seven: but Crabbe, of the seventh only. It's the trick of tricksters of the trade.

Crabbe looked on *Daynian folk-lore* and *Kalliphonos* as part of the price which the unknown writer pays for the privilege of publication. The weary years of working and waiting, the sweat of brain which he had spent on them, were just as much lost to him as were the MSS. which Welbeck had wheedled from him. So he looked not back: but forward; and went on with his new lovely book, which he had called *Necessary Propositions*.[2]

He heard that Neddy had been stung acutely into action by his means. He thought it excellent. That hebete exhausted creature cumbered the earth; and now knew it. He was not capable of doing—doing anything. No one liked him. No one admired him. His life was continual dismal mediocre monotony: simply because he (the last of an intermarried sapless race of

[1] *The Daily Telegraph.* [2] *Hadrian the Seventh.*

aboriginal Catholics) had not ability to make a life for himself on his certain £250 a year and fine prospects. The row with Crabbe stung him to one of two aims—to die, or to do. He was pious to ostentation: his religion prevented suicide. He bought a sumptuous 'trousseau'—six dozen tooth-brushes gives the scale—and sailed to South Africa as an Imperial Yeoman determined on death or decoration. Incidentally as a matter of revenge, he absconded with all Crabbe's private papers, which had been for several years in his solicitorial care. Crabbe asked for them before his departure: but he waited to get beyond the Bay of Biscay before sneering a refusal. Crabbe cursed a little at the loss, which was serious; and let them go. He taught himself to learn that it is quite the fashion of piety to plunder the defenceless poor.

The money difficulty became a Horror.

Crabbe constituted a simply elaborate scheme for obtaining credit when necessary. Hitherto he had bought his small assortment of goods in large quantities, for cash on delivery, and always from the same tradesmen. He was known to these people, as an eccentric, full of genial chat, and as safe as the bank. Now, while he still was able to pay cash, he did not pay until after the bills had been delivered twice. He excused himself on the score of absent-mindedness, gradually habituating his purveyors to longer delays, maintaining a high-handed demeanour and giving no ground for suspicion as to the state of his finances. So, he built up confidence against an evil day; and, at the same time augmented his stores. But he reduced his rate of consumption: he cut down his ration of oatmeal and oranges to the minimum.

Kemp fed like a sparrow at all times, chiefly on apples and nuts and an occasional egg. This was his choice: for Crabbe gave him no sign of scarcity. He lived nearly entirely on his thoughts, sitting almost always alone with his knitting: but his pure sightless face and quiet voice and splendid intellect always were at Crabbe's disposal, and a joy. Perhaps they talked together during three hours a week in all. Still the time did not

seem to have come when they would write in collaboration: that
was shaping itself.

Crabbe coolly wrote in his own new lovely book. From time
to time, when fear (of having to broach the last banked £100)
became insuperable, he invented a posse of pseudonyms and
furiously wrote frightful rot which he sold to monthlies and
weeklies. Once, in a tight corner, he grabbed a pair of Kemp's
knitting-needles, a ball of Strutt's No. 2 Knitting-Cotton, and
half a dozen completed towels: dressed himself in very old
clothes; and sat all day on the pavement of Finchley Road by the
Swimming Baths, where no one would know him, knitting a
towel and exposing the others for sale. They fetched three half-
crowns a-piece: for the luxurious novelty of thick soft absorbent
hand-made bath-towels recommended itself to fingerers; and he
cleared nine-and-twenty shillings of clear profit. Light, fire,
cleanliness, materials, food, and tobacco, must be had; and he
remembered this way of procuring them, frequently using it.
These days in the open air, too, gave space to his active mind.
He suffered acutely sometimes from the aspect of the people
whom he saw—females an-hungered for a man—triplets of little
clerics, (novices from some neighbouring noviciate), rustics
frightfully garbed in ill-fitting canonicals, thrashing among the
crowds, gazing with ignorant unseeing eyes, good, narrow, on-
the-make. But now and then he was gladdened by the proud
secure carriage of some unknown boy, noncurant, saucy, shrilly
whistling. It was at this time when he first noted (and began to
elaborate his subsequent thesis on) the perfectly astounding
likeness of the young King of Spain to the portraits of the
juvenile cleric who at the time was Pope Leo the Thirteenth.

At a proper moment, he stiffly announced to Oldcastle that he
was managing his own affairs; and instantly was invited to an
interview "in reference to your courteously specifying the illustrations for your book and finally approving of its final format."

Crabbe repeated his refusal to be connected with the *Medici
Book* as it stood: stated that his list of illustrations had been in
Oldcastle's hands for more than a year: and, as a salve to any

wound which his aloofness might cause, presented a rubbing of an unique Medici coin in his possession. Oldcastle would borrow that coin for a week; and reproduce its reverse as a cover-design. Crabbe saw no reason why he should not lend it: such a little concession did not involve approval of the frightful book; and perhaps might soften the heart of Oldcastle. He sent it. The publisher asked him to come to lunch in a week's time, to fetch the coin: he would be glad to discuss one or two matters with Crabbe.

Crabbe did not want to appear ungracious: he never ate luncheons: interruption of his work, even for a couple of hours, was grave inconvenience: but, something was due to Oldcastle on account of exasperation received through the idiomata of Neddy; and, therefore, if he would agree to consider conversation privileged, Crabbe would come and see him have his lunch and talk to him.

Oldcastle was sorry if Crabbe never ate luncheon; and stupidly reminded him of a lunch which he had enjoyed in the dim past; but he vaulted at the chance of a meeting, naming one-fifteen p.m. as its hour, and looking forward to it with unfeigned pleasure. Was he going to have his own way, after all?

In order to make Oldcastle quite happy and comfortable in his mind, Crabbe stripped him stark of all delusions by explaining that it only was publishers' lunches which he did not eat. Then he put on a pair of black spectacles, so that his loquent eyes might not bewray him; and, at the appointed time, he entered the office. Instantly a fight about lunch began, Oldcastle remonstratingly proffering, Crabbe with firm fastidy refusing. They strolled out-of-doors toward Romano's. Crabbe would go anywhere and talk: but he would not eat. A lunch at Romano's? No. Then the Grand Hotel? No. Then Prince's? No. Crabbe began to sniff danger; and his feelers vibrated very cautiously. Then they would go the Tivoli Bar: Oldcastle would take a leaf out of Crabbe's book for once: a publisher's life was not a happy one— he had to eat far too many lunches: as a matter of fact he was starving, but he nobly would mortify carnal lust and have a sandwich. He smashed a monocle, and asked pardon for a moment while he went into Aitchison's and purchased a new one and charged it to—"well never mind that now," he added.

They entered the Tivoli Bar. Oldcastle commanded a sandwich and a whiskied seltzer; and Crabbe—Crabbe folded his claws and consented to black coffee. Oldcastle stared at a writer, wan, cold, emaciated, obviously in want, who could refuse the lunch of a publisher bent upon swindling him. The meeting opened inauspiciously.

Oldcastle produced proofs of the first thirty-two pages of the *Medici Book*. Crabbe clutched; and was for reading them then and there: but other things claimed his attention. The publisher at last was conscious that he hitherto had been playing the jackass, and that that diversion had landed him in difficulties. Here he was, with a big book on his hands, which already had cost him £60 odd. He had refused to sell it; and the author had withdrawn his name and countenance. In fact, he had said that the book in its present form was a tissue of falsehood. Oldcastle could not hope to recoup the outlay on a book like that. He did not indicate these thoughts in words: but they inspired his actions; and Crabbe (unknown to him) fully perceived the situation.

Oldcastle set himself to try to get the author's approval of, and permission to connect him with, the *Medici Book*. He proposed that, if Crabbe would assist (by advice, consent, and proof-reading) in getting out the book at once, the first thousand should be sold off immediately; and then he would give a commission for complete revision on Crabbe's own model, which he would issue as the second edition. Further, as the contract had expired nine months ago, and as Crabbe had taken the trouble (since) of rewriting the book, the correction of proofs (at this date) became extra work which would be paid for; and £10 ("a typescribe's fee") would be given for the fair copy now in hand. There was his offer; and he dressed it up in all imaginable compliments and graces.

Crabbe informed him that the book (in its present state) was an insult to the public intelligence: promised to ponder his proposals; and took away the bundle of proofs to read. Study of these first thirty-two pages told him strange tales. Meditation on the proposals shewed him a pitfall. He wrote to Oldcastle, requesting that imperative instructions should be given to the printer to adhere to the MS. and refrain from illegitimate omissions. "It is quite enough to correct errors, without having to deal with those gratuitously intercalated by compositors' indiscretions." Secondly, he said that the proviso in the former contract (giving the author £25 when the book should go into a second edition) would be annulled, if the proposal (for complete reconstruction of the book at that stage) were to be adopted. Such reconstruction would need months and months of labour and research in three countries; and £25 was not to be thought of in connection with it. Thirdly, he asked Oldcastle to write to him on the subject of this new arrangement, and regarding the promised payment for proof-reading and the fee for the fair copy. He also asked for the return of the Medici coin.

Oldcastle fenced for a fortnight, demanding fresh interviews, and pouring in proofs up to page 112.

Crabbe kept at a distance, shooting out both eyes, waving his feelers in search for sensations, soliciting a draft of proposals as a basis for discussion. He continued to beg for the Medici coin.

Oldcastle pretended that Crabbe laboured under delusions as to his rights; and committed himself to a mis-statement of the contract, threatening that he legally was entitled to keep the *Medici Book* in type, and to go on selling it, paying the author no further sums of any kind. And he attempted to retract his Tivoli proposals. He could not see, now, that proof-reading was extra work; and he found it impossible to make a definite proposal concerning the rewriting of the second edition.

Crabbe was vexed by Oldcastle's vacillation, dishonesty, crooked running, and by the frightful new mutilation which the MS. was suffering in the press. It was being deprived of its only redeeming features, and becoming utterly impossible. And he said so.

The publisher refused to admit the author's corrections of divergencies from the MS., as he wished to avoid over-running and expense. The book was to be done on the cheap; and full advantage would be taken of Crabbe's inexperience and forebearance and helplessness.

Crabbe was furious, when he once more contemplated the whole series of Oldcastle's scurvy tricks. He was but a novice yet. It is not necessary for the noviciate to know anything; but only to sacrifice his pig. He was about to sacrifice. He was about to become initiate. Many are the thyrsos-bearers: few indeed are the mystics.

Chapter Twenty-four

W H E N Crabbe was at these loggerheads with Oldcastle, a letter arrived at Schelm's addressed to the author of *Daynian Folk-lore*. It came from a complete outsider, of whom Crabbe never even had heard. The man was a painter. He wrote rather tackily, with wonderment, appreciation, protest, praising the book to the skies, not without taste and discrimination. He called it an achievement; and sympathized with the personal temperamental trouble which it portrayed. He offered his hand, with his heart in it; and willingly would be a friend.

Was the Divine Friend, then, really an applicant for lodgings —the Much Desired, always young, always lovely, always faithful? Crabbe crept into his crevice to ponder.

In dedicating his book, he had been actuated by no motive but a superstitious one. At the same time, he was utterly squeamish of all men; and he had flung the thing at random to the gods (who dwell in Olympian mansions), naming one, without the slightest real belief in His Divinity's existence. And Crabbe was not old enough an author to know the propensities of the 'gentle reader' with a pen. This letter literally sang songs to him out of a clear blue heaven. Then he felt fear. The writer betrayed connection, slight, distant, unpromising of danger—but a connection —with the friends of the bitter foes of Crabbe's past life. He suspected traps, and complots; and began to be desperately afraid.

The question of Kemp assailed him. But he knew little or nothing of Kemp. That pale martyr was to him a saint in a shrine, a gem in a ring. He did not belong. He was something to be looked at, cared for, invoked, guarded. He bestowed the help of his presence: he shed his rays—but he was not near. He was a pattern and a guide, a treasure and a joy—but he was apart. Besides——. Then it would be no disloyalty to Kemp for Crabbe to accept the heart and hand of the Divine Friend, Who was able to give life to them both. As they were, they would be better (and much more comfortable) in two graves. And the letter came fortuitously out of the vast void. Who was he, that he should refuse to hear a Message?

He perpended during a week; and deliberately responded:—

"I do not know whether to thank you for your letter: or to exsecrate you. I do not know whether to thank you for Hope: or to exsecrate you for another illusion dispelled, for additional matter for Despair. I rejoice that my book has delighted you. But you terrify me when you tell me your connections. Then what have you to do with me? Do you not already know me? If you do not, I beg you to ask all or any of my thirteen worst enemies, whose names and addresses I have written here, to tell you about me. Till you have read this, I have no more to say. In secret I am fled away; and I will live alone, until——. I dedicated my book to the Divine Friend, Much Desired. I do not know whether you are he—or another."[1]

Proof of divinity was given by inability to be rebuffed. (Crabbe's willingness to be taken-advantage-of was too evident not to be taken-advantage-of.) The painter would not shew cause for cursing, but for blessing. He refused to inquire of the thirteen enemies, saying that he probably would find them hateful, egotistical, wishful to chain divine things down to petty personal limitations. He denied that he was under any influence but his own. He wished to take Crabbe as he was, in spite of enemies. He had had almost unique tests of his power of affording friendship. The mystery of personal magnetism was all-wonderful. If (in the present case) it were propitious, then he was the Divine Friend—he claimed the title—to the death. He begged Crabbe to confide in his honour.

Crabbe rushed to try the *sors* in a Book of Hours. The first was "*Behold, I send Mine Angel*": the second, "*for the mouth of those speaking iniquity has been obstructed*". He went no further: but wrote, "Let us meet."

He went and found the painter to be a man who (in a previous incarnation) must have sat for Moroni's celebrated Portrait of a

[1] This is a transcription of Rolfe's letter to Trevor Haddon.

Tailor. A wife and three children were presented. Conversation travelled, not very swiftly: but it travelled. Ideas were exchanged; and sympathy seemed to be in the air. Crabbe was desperately frightened, horribly afraid of blundering: he poked out both eyes, and waved his feelers, being violently anxious not to miss any sympathetic sensations. He made a clean breast of his frightful (but not abnormally blameful) past. The painter said, "If I had suffered what you have suffered, I should have gone out of my mind." Omitting mention of his charge, (that being a subject proper to himself and Kemp alone), Crabbe described his present life, acts, hopes, fears. Indeed, in the knowledge that a friend is one soul in two bodies, he made the wildest and most frantic efforts to correspond with the graces which were offered to him.

(I fear that, here, I must diverge a little from my narration, in order to make you understand this difficult and complex but not really impossible person.)

Once a year, the Fenians of Proud Preston are wont to make a show of themselves, pervading the streets in garbs of gimp and tinsel with top hats. Part of the show is a waggon containing a mummer disguised as Saint Luke Evangelist, Physician, Painter, and Chancellor of Our Lady the Virgin. Before him, in a waggon, is an easel bearing a canvas on which he seems to paint God's Mother's wistful face. It is a dodge. The portrait already is there, covered by a coat of whitewash. As the waggon moves, the mummer dips his brushes in clear water; and, little by little, washes off the whitewash, causing the painted features gradually to appear.

Crabbe's method of revealing himself was the reverse of this. The gods of his stars and his angel-guardian alone knew what his psychical features really were: for, out of timidity, out of a paramount desire not to do wrong, he blackened his tints and blurred his contours as assiduously as possible, so that the beholder should win the merit of finding him for himself. He was not anxious to hide: but he was vehemently anxious not to miss a chance of being unmistakably and finally found.

The painter seemed to find him: he said that he could guess at and apprehend, in Crabbe's spiritual essence, a good for every ill alleged. He perceived that Crabbe's misease was physical rather than psychical; and addressed himself (so he said) to the solution of temporal difficulty. (The policy of promising much and performing little is as old as Brother Guido da Montefeltro of the Friars Minor, branded with imperishable infamy by Dante.) He secretly wrote to a friend of his, a literary agent, as follows:—

Dear Mr Vere Perkins,
I recently read a book called *Daynian Folk-lore* by Nicholas Crabbe that I had seen noticed. Some small parts of the book were published in the *Blue Volume* some years ago. It is about a part of Europe and the sort of stories the people of Daynia are supposed to be familiar with. This may not sound very attractive to you, but to me who have been there the book was entrancing, and the literary quality most liquid flexible and expressive of an attractive personality. I have said quite enough in this sentence if you have the hearing ear. If you are on the look out for something of which a great success can be made by skilled manipulation here is an opening. On the strength of this book I sought acquaintance with the author, and found a man who lives in his work and who is not a business man able to fight his own battles. I read also that you were intending to run a few select authors. In case you want to associate yourself with a rising name, I take the liberty of asking you to read this book and judge for yourself of the author's quality. And I am writing this without his knowledge.

When the deed was done, Crabbe received a copy of this letter with a packet of printed matters. The latter advised him of Literary Agency on a New System. Mr Vere Perkins, late of certain newspapers Literary Staves, Founder and First Editor of a Monthly, begged to proclaim that he had Now set up in business as a Literary Agent within a sabbath-day's journey from Fleet Street, Where he had made arrangements to deal with all forms of Literary Property and Rights. He was Now agonizing to obtain the Representation of a limited number of Authors, and to give to the interests of Each his own close and continued Personal Attention. Experience in some of the best publishing Houses had taught him that there was Now an Opening for an agent who would Study the Drift of the book-market, who would seriously attempt to limit the Task of the author to that of writing, who would promptly advise clients of changes which Might affect their efforts, and who would Go to the Trouble to Read the MSS. that were submitted to him with a view to Selecting the best Channel for them without any weary or irritating Delays. Communications from Authors were Now invited in Strict Confidence. Mr P. was desirous to undertake no representation to which he could not Render good and useful service. Terms by Arrangement.

Apart from the blood-curdling vulgarity of its style, this scheme sounded most delectable. The idea, of having nothing to do except to sit on chairs and make books while one's agent rolled in a modest income, fascinated a writer who took his trade seriously and was rather nauseated by the imbecility and in-urbanity of Bar-Abbas. Crabbe was on tenter-hooks, till he knew that the painter's recommendation had induced Mr Vere Perkins to include him among that strictly limited number of authors.

The Literary Agent instantly asked for the loan of *Daynian Folk-lore* and the favour of a visit. Crabbe sent the book; and followed it, a few days later. He explained his literary situation in general; and made particular reference to the deadlock existing between himself and the publisher of the *Medici Book*. That thing was mere hack-work, written to contract. The contract had expired in July; and Oldcastle twice had failed to issue the book at the times arranged, viz., November and February. Now, nine months after expiry of contract, Oldcastle was howling for him to correct proofs, select illustrations, and supervise production of a picturesque farrago which he despised, from which he had withdrawn his name, which was being mangled in proof till it totally misrepresented its author who had ceased to take any interest at all in the frightful thing. He made a great point of the fact that Oldcastle had refused to sell it back to him.

Perkins pronounced the case lovely and quite in accord with that publisher's usual methods. Had Crabbe corrected any proofs? Like a good-natured fool he had corrected 112 pages. Perkins wished to have these pages; and the affair must be left entirely in his hands. Crabbe desired nothing better. On no account was Crabbe to answer any letters which Oldcastle might write. Agreed: for he detested writing letters at all times, especially to an incorrigible splitter of infinitives: *"chi pratica lo zoppo impara a zoppicare,"* he asserted. Having read and pigeon-holed the contract, Perkins stated that all the work now demanded was extra, and ought to be paid for; and he would undertake to bring the publisher to reason. And what was Crabbe doing now?

He had a book called *Necessary Propositions* on toward completion. Any short stories? Heaps: but would not Mr Perkins come to tea at the painter's studio, and see some of Crabbe's odds and ends? He would, with pleasure; and, meanwhile, let him have those 112 pages of Oldcastle's proofs.

The proofs were sent; and Perkins brought his lovely porcelain teeth to tea. Crabbe and the painter discussed him before he arrived. Crabbe said that he seemed mild and amiable enough—cooed like any sucking dove: but he deemed him hebete, worn-out, anything but a vigorous personality. Asked for his exquisite reason, Crabbe said that inability to be attentive accompanied all forms of exhaustion; and he added that he was frightfully afraid of Perkins, who had let slip the fact that he also was a client of the friends of the rascal who swore to prevent Crabbe from earning a living ever. The painter laughed. This was not the Dark Ages, but England and the Twentieth Century. He hoped that Crabbe was not going to let his little prejudices cause him to stand in his own light. Crabbe denied the thing. He cited R.L.S., saying that a habit of solitude tended to perpetuate itself; and that an austerity (of which he was quite unconscious) and a pride (which seemed arrogance and perhaps was chiefly shyness) appeared hitherto to have discouraged and offended men with whom he had had to do. But his pose was to take things as they came and on their merits. Perkins was no invention of his: but merely a fortuitous occurrence, apparently. Farm Street or not, if he chose to earn an honest 10% by selling Crabbe's writings, Crabbe was not the man to obstruct him.

And, at that, Perkins glided in grinning weakly. He chose *crème de menthe* and a meringue. His conversation consisted of the recitation of *ut-diciturs* concerning the pasts and private peccadillos of publishers. At an early opportunity, Crabbe shewed him the MS. of *Necessary Propositions*; and read some of the tid-bits. He raved in their praise. Could not Crabbe let him have a few pages to shew to publishers?

No: because of the futility of shewing incomplete work to publishers and children. Perkins could get advances—large advances of cash—if Crabbe only would entrust a few pages to him: but short stories he could sell on sight. And he made such pathetic old mouths over china teeth, that Crabbe gave him a sheaf of short stories and a parcel of essays, and the sixty-page skeleton of a romance called *The Kataleptic Phantasm*.[1] His extreme eagerness caused Crabbe to believe that the gods of his stars were about to be propitious after all those frightful years. As for the little difficulty with young Oldcastle (Perkins invected) Crabbe might consider himself master of the situation. The *Medici Book* could not be produced without him. His course was to lie low. Presently, Oldcastle would want to publish; and would be obliged to come to terms. Of course Crabbe must not do any work at this date without a new agreement about payment. Perkins himself would go and see the Archsplitter of Infinitives (goo-goo!) and put the case fairly and squarely before him.

That spring evening faded in rose-coloured flushes and golden.

[1] *Don Tarquinio*, subtitled *A Kataleptic Phantasmatic Romance.*

Chapter Twenty-five

THE Literary Agent's method of doing business was by correspondence. This was always weird, sometimes terrible, generally comical. He got to work at once; and, on the seventh of May, wrote:—

"I have just seen Oldcastle and he declines to make any payment for correction of proofs. He says however oddly enough if you and I go over together to-morrow morning he might come to some arrangement of a working character. I now think it is a pity you don't cultivate friendly relations with your publisher and I begin to doubt whether I can now be of any further service to you, there are agents older than myself. Would you care to put the matter into their hands?"

That was pretty ghastly for a beginning. Crabbe instantly precipitated himself upon the painter, demanding what game his man was up to. That Divine Friend alleged that Perkins was a martyr to neuralgia: that his letter merely marked a twinge; and he besought Crabbe not to be a fool. After much argument and many promises he persuaded him to soothe Perkins with these words.

"I trust absolutely in your discretion as my Literary Agent. In obedience to your directions, I decline to waste any more time in running after Oldcastle, until he pays or promises to pay, for the extra work outside the contract which he wishes me to do. In March, he verbally promised, in the Tivoli Bar (where I drank black coffee), to pay for the proof corrections."

The very next day brought a card of complete face-turn from Perkins:—

"Wednesday late. Thanks for your letter the gist of which I have communicated to Oldcastle. I am now dealing with your short stories and essays and hope to have good news to report thereon very soon, I quite agree with your latest attitude to Oldcastle."

The next day, Perkins wrote:—

"Herewith I now send you a letter I have just received from O. and a copy of my reply thereto please give me a call so as we can now deal with proofs and MSS. say early next week."

"(Enclosure I) 'Dear Mr Perkins, Many thanks for your post-card, but please specify if I am to virtually understand that your client refuses to as is only usual correct any more proofs for me. If *this* is the position that he takes up may I ask that he will have the goodness to immediately return whatever proofs he has by him, and whatever manuscript? Sincerely yours, Doron Old-castle.'

"(Enclosure II) 'Dear Mr Oldcastle, In reply to favour of even date you may now take it that my client refuses to correct any proofs unless payment is made for work involved. I will now ask him to return proofs and MSS. as requested and regret you have not seen your way to meet an admittedly difficult position, Thanking you for your courtesy and consideration, Yours sincerely, V. Perkins.' "

Crabbe thought the incapacity (here shewn) to be rather comical; and noted the abject oleaginous celerity with which his Literary Agent hastened to abase himself before a publisher. It seemed to him that Perkins might have complimented Old-castle just as aptly on his corsets and complexion as upon his courtesy and consideration. He was moved to compile parallel tables of the advantages derivable by a literary agent (a) from the author (β) from the publisher. The result was so quaint and weird that he shewed it to the painter; and Perkins once more was invited to tea. He replied, on the eleventh of May:—

"Thank you very much but I am afraid you must not now ask me to tea, I have so much to do. I have heard no more from O. oddly enough so suggest you now sit quite tight and say nothing at this point, business has its own code and method and with this O. has honourably complied. Indeed I now think I must now tell you that if you name personal matters again I must decline to represent you in any sense and shall have to return all your

MSS. forthwith, just do your work and let me sell it to the best advantage."

Crabbe was flabbergasted. Perkins certainly had what Harold Frederic calls "a talent for the inopportune amounting to positive genius." The bulk of his letter was in response to nothing, and quite gratuitous. What else was Crabbe doing— what else did he desire to do but to mind his own business! The only personal matters which ever had been named between the two, had been named by Perkins himself, in the painter's studio, on the occasion of the first meeting. He had asked Crabbe whether there was any truth in the rumour (which he had on good authority) that Slim Schelm recently had been confined in a lunatic asylum.

Crabbe laughingly had responded that Perkins' good authority was (he feared) some evilly disposed person anxious to gratify a little private malice; and he begged leave to indicate a few trifling inaccuracies. If 'inebriates' home' were substituted for 'lunatic asylum', and 'stayed a few days' for 'confined', (he said), then the rumour might be taken as true: for (he added) 'Schelm's father is a doctor who keeps one of the biggest private institutions of that kind in the country; and Schelm, being a very dutiful son as well as a very undutiful publisher occasionally pays a filial visit to his parents.' Perkins had choked prepared chuckles at that. So, Crabbe utterly failed to understand the object of the present letter. It did not occur to him that a professed business man could write a letter without any object at all. His instinct told him to sever his connection with so very tiresome an old totterer on the spot. But the painter (whom he again consulted) again alleged neuralgia; and, being unwilling to treat any man unmercifully, Crabbe frigidly replied to Perkins that he asked nothing better than to be permitted to do his work while his literary agent disposed of it to their mutual advantage. He reminded Perkins that he had had all Oldcastle's proofs and MSS. in his own hands since the twenty-eighth of April, with freedom to deal with them as he deemed best. He also presented a copy of the violet American edition of *Daynian*

172

Folk-lore, and asked for return of copy of the grey English edition lent on the twenty-second of April, which he required for another purpose.

On the thirteenth of May, Perkins sent a letter from Oldcastle, with a copy of his response:—

"I. I shall be glad if you will let me have proofs and MS. at your earliest convenience.

"II. I have now sent your letter on to my client asking him to give the matter his earliest attention."

The next day, Perkins wrote again:—

"I am now very grateful for the American edition of your book, I have been rather upset lately because the London editor of a New York Firm to whom I lent it has been sticking rather closer to the other volume than becometh a literary brother oddly enough but good may come out of evil,"—("*O vilissime haeretice*," Crabbe ejaculated; "*Anathema sis!*")—"I have now had one very strong nibble for you from the *Dylymyle* oddly enough, thanking you again."

And the same day he also sent a letter from Oldcastle, with a copy of his response:—

"I. I am obliged for your letter to hand concerning your client's proofs and MS. I take it that you will courteously see that they are returned to me within a few days.

"II. I will now send your letter to my client and hope you will come to some terms with him, but the matter will now pass out of my hands. I have done my best to bring it to an amiable solution, but have now failed and so cannot undertake any farther trouble."

On the fifteenth of May, Perkins sent another letter from Oldcastle, appending to it a note written with the paw of a timid terrier to whom his master has said "Bad Dog!":—

"I. 'In reply to letter to hand I am sorry that you have sent on my letters to your client without first courteously consulting me, especially as you gave me to distinctly understand that you were acting as his literary agent.'

"II. (Note) I do not propose to reply to this it is a pity, but O. seems to be a little annoyed with me oddly enough."

Crabbe called the painter's attention to Perkins' abderitic adhesion to these confounded 112 pages of proofs and MS., which had been in his possession during three weeks with discretionary powers. Whereupon the Divine One (and mentor) struck him into frantic silence with the following post-card:—

"Perkins says it is a great pity you didn't go with him to see O. before he went to Monte Carlo. Meanwhile he is trying to interest the *Dylymyle* and others."

Crabbe pondered this: for Perkins emphatically had approved of his refusal to visit Oldcastle on the eighth of May, and had made no mention of the latter's latest jaunt to Monte Carlo. He, too, was not quite satisfied with the painter: for he did not want arguments (from a man who posed as the Divine Friend) but sympathy, sensibility, emotional bonds. And he began to esteem the painter almost as amazing and annoying as the literary agent. But when, on the seventeenth of May, Perkins triumphantly sent him a package and certain letters dismissory, he felt as though he really must do something violent. His literary agent wrote:—

"I now return you proofs and MS. of Mr Doron Oldcastle's book but hope the matter may soon be amiably settled."

The effect, upon Crabbe, of that idiotic old dodderer's reiterate "now", was one of the wildest exasperation. He only contrived to keep the King's Peace by strenuous effort: but, as he made a duty of cultivating his keen sense of the ridiculous, after a few days he placed the queer old thing's oscillations in the category of the immensurably inconceivably comical; and deliberated to let him have as much rope as he wanted.

Also, when he detested a thing, Crabbe never cared to exhaust his detestation before he could pinch to pieces. Nothing—and he said it without hesitation—could make his position worse than it was: therefore, he was as negligent as possible of all consequences. He who comes from Awizi fears not hot ashes. Not one of the literary crew (with whom he had dealings) ever realized that. Life, says Horace Walpole, is a comedy for those who think, a tragedy to those who feel. Crabbe both thought and felt. Anyhow, he would permit himself the pleasure of contem-

174

plating the gyrations and the contortuplications of his literary agent.

He returned the package to Perkins: remarking that he was going to take his house-boat into a backwater above Abingdon for a couple of months, and that he deemed it right for Old-castle's proofs to be in safe custody and to be dealt with fitly.

On the twenty-ninth of May, Perkins wrote:—

"As you sent the proofs to me to be dealt with as I thought fit I have now sent them to O. with a note expressing hope that as the work is now done he will see his way to make you a suitable payment. I have also warmly repudiated his insinuendo that I was not your agent or his claim to say how I should deal with my principals and hope good will ensue in consequence, with all good wishes."

Neuralgia, Crabbe knew—oh, jolly well he knew—to be no joke. But, wasn't it wonderful what an effect it had upon a literary agent's letters! One could mark the throbs, the paroxysms, the spells of ease, all quite distinctly.

On the fifth of June, Perkins announced the sale of a short story:—

"The editor of *The Mohawk* will take *A Debt Paid* at price of a guinea per 1,000 words single use but stipulates you send photo for reproduction therewith oddly enough, please send one and oblige. O.'s manager came round and saw me *re* proofs and said he'd consult O. on his return from Monte Carlo in course of a fortnight, *re* payment."

Crabbe sent the photograph; and the story appeared. During the ensuing weeks, it came into his mind that Perkins had done a lot of work for nothing, (futile and agitating old silly though he was); and that 10% commission on *The Mohawk*'s couple of guineas would be a very absurd and unhandsome tip to offer him. Also, the thought occurred that it would be singularly horrid to be vituperated as being stingy to a brother in the Faith—Crabbe knew the propensities of his brothers in the Faith; and that his own prospects perhaps might be improved by giving a certain kind of nudge to Perkins. So, he indited an urbane epistle, thanking his literary agent for his exertions; and, (beating his bosom thrice), he committed the impropriety of raising the commission from 10% to 25%.

On the twenty-sixth of June, Perkins wrote:—

"I am very touched by the kind tone of your letter the offer in which I now cordially endorse, but am very annoyed I have not been able to do more for you up to the present I will go and see O. to-morrow. He returned on Monday oddly enough, but meanwhile please understand a New York Firm are quite willing to make you a substantial advance if they find the amount you have written of *Necessary Propositions* as good as they expect and believe it to be so hadn't you better send the stuff on to me? In fact I promised their editor he should see it in ten days, have written *Mohawk* for money, sixty-page skeleton of *The Kataleptic Phantasm* is now before another firm from whom I have apprehensions."

The darkness of Crabbe's life suddenly and unexpectedly was illuminated. The King of Allobroga and Daynia deigned to send him a letter of thanks for *Daynian Folk-lore* which His Majesty had read. Crabbe passed the missive to Perkins; and mentioned that he was extremely hard up.

On the sixth of July, Perkins wrote:—

"The Only Way to raise some cash is to get some firm like the New York one to make an advance and a house will only do that after they have seen the approved part of the MSS. I have now sent the King's letter to *The Minervium* from which quarter it will be widely copied."

Crabbe responded that he hardly thought *The Minervium* likely to note him: but that *Letters*[1] always had shewn comity toward him. He asked when *The Mohawk* was going to pay; and what had resulted from the interview with Oldcastle. He hoped for good news of *The Kataleptic Phantasm* and repeated, in regard to the New York firm and *Necessary Propositions* that he would not let publishers or children see unfinished work. The fact was that his working power was becoming diminished. His fright-

[1] *Literature.*

fully meagre diet no longer provided him with that swift inerrant touch which had been his a year ago. Consequently, his production was slow and painful: alterations and revisions almost obliterated the text of his MS. Nevertheless, he was determined that nothing should prevent *Necessary Propositions* from being a deliberate masterpiece; and he spared himself not at all. But he had broken into his balance at the bank.

On the eighth of July, Perkins wrote:—

"I have seen O. this afternoon and cannot get to a point beyond this that if you will correct the balance of the proofs, he will be prepared to pay you something but will not state the amount oddly enough. Later he would be willing to do other business with you through an agent if you so wished, don't you think therefore that it would be a good move to patch up the quarrel with him? It seems to me a pity that the matter should end with friction and if you will do the proofs on those terms, I will send them on at once. I will write *The Mohawk* again and now return the American *Daynian Folk-lore* you lent me last April."

Crabbe had expected that Oldcastle would evade the argument *Ad Crumenam*. He was not one of the queens of Aix or Monte Carlo. And he was prepared for vacillation on the part of Perkins. He did not approve of 'moves', good or bad. Take a line and stick to it, he said. So, he sent no response to Perkins' letter: but waited for the next variation of the vane. Then Oldcastle, suddenly and on his own initiative, began to bombard him with letters. Needless to say that he did not open them: but sent them to his literary agent early in August.

On the seventh of that month, Perkins wrote:—

"I have now been several times to *The Mohawk* without effect and yesterday wrote a private letter to the editor, and asked him as a personal favour to pay up. *The Minervium* has not inserted the King's letter oddly enough and I can do nothing more, will you therefore send it to *Letters* or *World of Letters*[1] yourself, as to O. I returned another letter of his and told him I had not your address, I also sent him his letters those you sent me and

[1] *Literary World.*

explained you had forwarded them, without comment. In its present form I can now do nothing with *The Kataleptic Phantasm* and so return it for expansion herewith."

Crabbe responded:—

"I entirely approve of your action in regard to Oldcastle. What you have said is another matter—an example of the Lie Officiose, which is told to excuse oneself or another, and merely a Venial Sin according to your Jesuit catechism—(for you perfectly know that I go to Schelm's for my letters every other day). That I cannot approve. But please make it quite plain to Oldcastle that I refuse to communicate with him, or to undertake any work for him, till he confirms his verbal promises by a written agreement."

Chapter Twenty-six

O n the thirteenth of August, Perkins wrote:—

"I am now sorry to say I can get no money out of *The Mohawk* so if you will put them in the County Court, it will cost you 2/- and I will attend and prove your case for you. Please do this when you are in the district, other clients will do the same, I now think the amount is £1.18.0. The agreement was a guinea per 1,000 so if you have the story, you might calculate the exact sum yourself."

This then, Crabbe commented, was the advantage of using a literary agent. You write deathless prose: he pelts you with exacerbating letters, and leaves you to do the dirty work. As Crabbe was not a dab at sums beyond Simple Division (except on his fingers, now occupied with more important work), he had no means of knowing what *The Mohawk* owed him. Besides, who was he that he should do so very fatuous a thing as putting a literary man in the County Court! The matter was likely to rest: but, on the fifteenth, Perkins fluttered him with this:—

"Don't trouble about *Mohawk* please I've got a cheque oddly enough and a very abusive letter from them this morning, directly I can cash it I'll remit."

On the sixteenth, he wrote again:—

"I got £2 from *Mohawk* and so now send you cheque value 30/-, as arranged with thanks."

On the twenty-seventh, he returned all the MSS. for which he had begged in April except one short story, with this statement:—

"I am now afraid I cannot sell any work of yours, I have tried in many quarters to get you orders but publishers will not give them, hence I advise you to push on with *Necessary Propositions* and finish that all ready for publication, the MSS. I have returned I fear I cannot sell at all at the present juncture. I have sent them about pretty widely and failed to get rid of them,

179

personally I believe oddly enough you will be able to sell *Necessary Propositions* almost on sight."

Finding Crabbe silent and unreproachful—as a matter of fact he was puzzling over the foregoing—another whimsy seized the creature; and two days later he wrote again:—

"Can you drop down and see me on Saturday say noon, I would run up and see you at studio only I have got neuralgia rather badly and am living a two hours' journey from L'pool St, on a farm. O. wrote you the other day and it was sent on to me I declined to receive it hoping to see you soon."

Crabbe went to see and to be seen. Perkins diffidently would know how hard up he was. He replied (without a blush) that the case was grave—it appeared likely that he would have to lay up his house-boat at once for the winter, and lose the ruddy golden splendour of autumn. Perkins thereupon gushed words.

"Well I must confess, Mr Crabbe, that I've been rather worrying myself lately about that advice I gave you *re* Oldcastle. Thought preaps I might have made an error. But day before yesterday oddly enough, I heard of two cases exactly like yours. In both, O. was trying to get authors to do work for him outside their contracts. He promised to pay them: but he wouldn't bind himself in writing. One of them caved-in and did the work—six weeks' work—because he'd literally been living on Hovis bread and Vi-cocoa and nothing else for four months on end; and, when he'd done, O. refused to pay him a penny—said he hadn't got an agreement:—but he had the cheek to offer him half-a-quid as a matter of courtesy he said, because he looked as if he wanted a dinner he said. Jever know such a swine? But the second man held out; and, in the end oddly enough, O. was obliged to do the proper thing by him. Couldn't do without him, don't you see? Now, what I want to know is, Mr Crabbe, how do you now feel about your own affair?"

"*Non deerunt tamen hac in urbe forsan unus, vel duo, tresve, quatuorve, pellem rodere qui velint caninam. Nos hac a scabie tenemus ungues*'," Crabbe spouted; and added a tralation. "I feel like the second man," he said. (*O superba responsio!*)

180

CHAPTER TWENTY-SIX

"But can you manage—I hope you won't mind my asking— but are you now able to hold out?"

"Look here, Mr Perkins, have you any idea of the quality and the quantity of the sweating and the insolence, to say nothing of the false pretences, which I have tolerated from that pustulous young man?"

"No: but I can believe anything that you might say that way, oddly enough. Oh I know O.! Why I've known him ever since he was a boy fresh from the University——."

"Which Varsity?"

"Why Oxford of course!"

"Oldcastle never was a member of the University of Oxford."

"Well all I can say is he came to town, so he said at the time, fresh from the University of Oxford; and set to work to teach us journalism in Fleet St. Goo-goo!"

"I don't care what he said. He never was a member of the Varsity: as you can see by the Kalendar. It's true that he did come from Oxford: but he was 'Town', not 'Gown'. He was spawned there. His connection with the Varsity is another example of his false pretences. However, I'm only here to talk about the frightful blighter in so far as he is concerned with me. If you have a general knowledge of the way in which he treats his authors, I needn't give you particulars of my own case. I'll only describe my present frame of mind. A year ago, you know, I was prepared to do almost anything to oblige him. But he has taken the meanest possible advantage of my circumstances, and my forebearance. *Et genus et virtus, nisi cum re, vilior alga est.* He is dyspathetic to me. He has on me the effect of a κρομμυοξυρεγμία. All my being, where the indestructible soul of ancestors slumbers, revolts at him, at the very smell of him, at the sound of his frightful name. I would like to make him eat his broken monocles. And I, on my part, am dyspathetic to him. 'Hoc habent pessimum animi magna fortuna insolentes, quos laeserunt, et oderunt,' as Seneca says. Oh, sooner than bend before his contemptible arrogance any more, I'll resist the insufferable little bounder—that's what they call him at the Taylor Galleries

181

of Oxford—as far as God has any ground, as Shakespeare or Bacon or Hall Caine or Francis Nunn (you can settle it yourself) says."

"Goo-goo-goo-goo!" Perkins laughed.

"But you know, if you'll consent to do this work for him, O. offers to consent to do other business through an agent afterwards——."

"That's simply vacuous, and rather impertinent into the bargain. If I deliberate to use a literary agent, Oldcastle will have to deal with him or not deal at all. The fact is the scurvy lout's so eaten up with overweening self-conccit that he really believes himself to be conferring favours by saying things of that kind. Why he said to me, last March in the Tivoli Bar, 'Look here, my dear sir, I'm sure I should always between ourselves you know be glad to privately see any work of yours, and to as far as in me lies and notwithstanding the doubtful opinion you've got of me courteously specify a generous offer.' Oumph! He fatigues me, *usque ad nauseam.* Would you yearn, for example, to spread your delicacies before an ostentatious tyrannical turpilucri-cupidous half-licked pragmatic provincial bumpkin who, first, stamps on your face as hardly as ever he can, and then, when he find you determined to rise (and what's more able to rise to the very top), actually has the brass to ask you for the gold of your brains to pay for his trips to Monte Carlo and for pushing him and his κυνάμυια of a wife into the fringe of the smart set? No: you wouldn't. Nor do I. Why, every time he buys her beads, ten authors die. Oldcastle has it in his power to kill me. Oh I know what I'm saying. He's been sucking my life-blood and promising to restore it twenty-fold. If he doesn't restore it, I shall die. And, if I die, I'll leave letters behind to cry aloud these words. Stranger, behold an author murdered by a publisher! If he had the decency personally to come to me, and to make me a subabject apology for the past, I don't say that I might not change my present opinion. I detest rows. Don't snigger! I detest and abominate rows with every fibre of my being: although I do take such meticulous and elaborate pains over them when once they're started. Oh my dear Mr Perkins, I can't tell you how frightfully violently and wholeheartedly I famish to be on good and equal and sensible terms with an honest publisher. I most meekly would take hints: I most gratefully would follow the lead of such an one; and I would give him stuff worth both our whiles. But never, never, under any possible circumstances, will I ever write even a single comma for an impenitent thief!"

"I quite agree with every word you've said. 'Impenitent thief' is excellent! And now I've found out what I wanted to know oddly enough. I'm firmly convinced, that, by holding out, you'll win and better your position incalculably. What I wanted to know was if you could and if you would. Well, now I know. My dear Mr Crabbe, I must say it gives me considerable pleasure to meet a man with such determined force of character as yours. Oh I mean it. Well then I'll say no more now on that topic. Well-well: keep up heart, and you'll win. O. can't possibly bring out the *Medici Book* without you. He must have your name on it, you know; and he can't oddly enough because of your prohibitions. Then again, he must have you to see the thing through the press. No one can possibly do that except the author; and, if the author won't, and O.'s still alive and in full possession of his faculties, then the book can't be issued; and that's all about that. Then there's another thing. You know the success of a book depends just as much on what we'll now call the passive exertions of the author as it does on what we'll also now call the active exertions of the publisher—after publication, I mean. Suppose O. issues the book without you. He can't possibly: but suppose he does. You've told him that it's an insult to the public intelligence in its present form. You say that he's garbling your MS. in the press. Suppose you denounce him for garbling. Suppose you expose him as the publisher who knowingly insults the public intelligence. Who'll buy his book then? No one. It'll be a frost. All his outlay will be thrown away, unless he can manage to swindle some American publisher; and he'll have gained the baddest of bad names. Do you see my contention? Take my word. I assure you that author and publisher must work together if a book's not to be a failure. Oh no, O. can't do without you, you take my word."

"Very well then. I'll take your word; and I'll do exactly what you tell me——."

"Well my advice now is 'Do nothing and do it as hard as you can.' Utterly ignore O. Return all his letters. Presently you'll find him sitting on your doorstep oddly enough."

"And then?"

"Then send him to me and I'll trounce him."

"It shall be done. Now just give me a bit of paper and ten minutes; and I'll make a note of this conversation while you write some of your charming letters. . . . Now then, please cast your glittering eye over that."

"Wonderful! What a memory you must have!"

"I hope that I get some sort of a grip on things."

"And how well it reads! It's as natural as life, and yet oddly enough it seems to have got such a literary flavour. Why you're quite a phrase-maker, Mr Crabbe!"

" 'It is me trade, kind sir.' '*Rem tene, verba sequentur,*' as Cato Major said."

Chapter Twenty-seven

O N the seventh of September, Perkins wrote:—

"The last phase of O. is now enclosed with this. (Enclosure) 'Dear Mr Perkins, I sent round to your office towards the end of August a letter addressed to Mr N. Crabbe by hand, a formal letter that I wished to legally be able to if necessary testify that I had sent to the only address that I had of his. The letter was not stamped and in forwarding it to me your clerk chose to discourteously do so without stamping it. If I thought that you were responsible for this I should think that it was a somewhat unfriendly act, but I can hardly believe that it is so, and think that you would like as a matter of common courtesy to as between one man of business and another having several not altogether unimportant interests in common have your attention drawn to this seeming slight. Believe me, dear Mr Perkins, yours very sincerely, Doron Oldcastle.' "

How that dear Crabbe did roar! How exquisitely all the antennae of his sensibilities worked, to disentangle the various ideas of this epistle, to select those which were capable of being put to useful purposes! How deliberately the great claws were cleaned and sharpened and exercised and, at length, how fiercely they snapped at and crunched and rent the prey!

In the fond belief (to which he still forced himself desperately to cling), that a literary agent is a person who acts on behalf of the interests of an author, generally *motu proprio* with his own power and discretion but particularly when he receives explicit directions, Crabbe deliberately and explicitly wrote to Perkins:—

"Please send these two enclosures to Oldcastle. How funny his letter is!"

(Enclosure I.) (A crossed cheque on the National Provincial Bank of England in favour of Messrs Doron Oldcastle Limited, worth Two Pence.)

(Enclosure II.) "Dear Mr Perkins, It is very difficult to gather the drift of Mr Oldcastle's pathetic and weirdly-worded letter: but I suppose that the young man wants to recover his tuppence, that being the fee which he has had to pay to the Post Office for the unstamped letter. I cannot conceive that he would have displayed so great anxiety in connection with so small a sum, unless he were harassed by a recrudescence of his pecuniary difficulties. Publishers and authors are mutually interdependent and indispensable. In financial straits especially, it is very meet, right, and a bounden duty, that the one should assist the other for the benefit of both. I therefore inclose a cheque for the amount in question; and request you to transmit it, with my compliments and condolences and this letter, to Mr Oldcastle. But, let it be understood clearly that this is an act of grace on my part, and not the creation of a precedent. For I admit no reason why Mr Oldcastle should address unstamped letters to me, "formal" or otherwise; and I also admit no reason why you should receive the same. There are no relations between me and Mr Oldcastle, except business-relations; and, as he well knows, communications on matters of business should be addressed (not to me but) to you. My attitude to Mr Oldcastle has undergone no mitigation since last April. It is indeed confirmed. I refuse to have anything to do with him, or to undertake any work for him outside the contract, until he shall have strengthened his verbal promises by a written agreement. And my attitude to the *Medici Book* was defined in the numerous letters which I sent to him in the autumn and winter of last and in the spring of the present year. In those, I formally prohibited him from using my name in connection with his garbled and gelded book. Faithfully yours, Nicholas Crabbe."

Perkins secretly disobeyed his principal's directions; and suppressed this letter and the cheque. This misdemeanour was of the greatest moment: for it left Oldcastle comfortable in the delusion that a poor author can be imposed upon with impunity by a preposterous publisher. All the straightforward elaborate efforts on Crabbe's part to make Oldcastle understand, completely were nullified by the congenital hybrist obtuseness of the publisher plus the unjustifiable disobedience of the literary agent. Oldcastle never had met a poor author who was prepared to sacrifice his time, his toil, his prospects, for his principles. He had not—and Perkins prevented him from having—the faintest notion that Crabbe was in deadly earnest, and meant at any cost, even ruinous to himself, to abide by every single word which he had said.

Toward the end of September, Crabbe found himself obliged to write with some formality to Perkins. He had seen, in *The Minervium*, that Oldcastle actually was announcing the *Medici Book* in his name. He reiterated all the facts and all his prohibitions, requesting Perkins to communicate the tenor of his remarks to the publisher, in order to avoid future unpleasant complications. Perkins replied:—

"*Re* O. I now strongly advise you to say nothing at this juncture."

Crabbe responded that he would follow this advice, much as he regretted it. He compared Perkins to the oil-lamp which gives light while the universe conflagrates. And now his calls for letters at Schelm's brought him inquiries from people at Oxford, Americans, editors of literary papers, concerning his forthcoming *Medici Book*. He began to go frantic. What was Oldcastle really going to do? What, in fact, was Perkins' little game? Though rigidly determined, Crabbe was by no means yearning to proceed to extremities. He asked Perkins to obtain from Oldcastle a definite statement of his intentions. And, on the ninth of October, Perkins answered:—

"I am now afraid that I cannot interfere farther in the O. matter."

Seventeen days later, Crabbe furiously wrote to him:—

"You will observe that that insufferable little bounder actually has filched my name, and attached it to his mangled caricature of my *Medici Book*, after all, and in spite of your assertions and manoeuvres. I would like to see my contract with him, if you will be so kind as to return it to me."

187

On the twenty-eighth of October, Perkins responded:—

"Herewith I now beg to hand you your contract with Messrs Doron Oldcastle Limited, I found I had it in a pigeon-hole oddly enough."

The next six weeks passed without communication between author and agent. Crabbe ensconced himself in his cave, cultivating his emotions, exercising his claws, watching for prey. That there would be grips, he was sure: but at what point could he clutch most fatally? He said nothing to Kemp. That one was tolerating torments of his own, feeling the burthen of his fetters. They both suffered silently and separately. There seemed to be no chance of relief.

Crabbe at length decided that the moment was come for the ceremonial invocation of the Divine Friend. He waited for a Monday: called on Saint Gabriel Archangel: armed himself with his chalcedonyx; and went and consulted the painter. Their relations had become rather aloof; the painter seemed to have bitten off more than he could chew: the writer was averse from taking anything for granted. Crabbe said that he wanted the Divine Friend's help in making up his mind as to whether Perkins had merited to be trusted with the now complete MS. of *Necessary Propositions*. He invited the Divine Friend to consider that, in seven months, the net result to him of that freakish gothamitish old fatwit's ineptitudes had been, (a) thirty shillings in coin of the realm, which was rather less than a third of the price usually paid for one of Crabbe's pseudonymous short stories of 1,500 words when Crabbe (under one of his pseudonyms) himself was the vendor: (β) venomous and rankling antagonism permanently consolidated between him and Oldcastle: (γ) a book had been published in his name, and hebdomadally was being damned by exasperate and purulent old-fogeydom (such as the reviewers of *The Anagraph* and *The Minervium*) as ignorant, pretentious, absurd,—and indeed it was all that, considering the monstrous form in which it had been produced after (what Carlyle calls) the nefarious garbling of the MS. by an obstinate illiterate publisher and an effrenate printer. Crabbe said that all the years and all the labour, which he had expended in trying to make a mark in literature, had been annihilated. He said that he must begin again at the very beginning now. The painter feared that he did not quite follow.

Crabbe confined himself for the present to *Necessary Propositions*. As for the *Medici Book*, he was in the dark: he did not yet know in which direction he would take satisfaction on account of that outrage. Just now he was concerned with his new book and his literary agent. Was Perkins to be deemed a fit and proper person to whom to intrust one's vital affairs? The painter implored Crabbe not to be so touchy, so suspicacious, so pessimistic: he assured him that Perkins was a thorough man of business, who knew all the tricks of the trade and all the rules of the game, who was toiling even now most earnestly and most incessantly on his behalf. Perkins had quite a handful of trumps up his sleeve, which he would play to Crabbe's very great advantage, if only he would be patient and give the chap a chance. More than this, the painter personally paid a visit to the literary agent, (in Crabbe's interest, he said); and he afterwards telegraphed:—

"Have just seen Perkins. He has done more for you than you credit and I am convinced it will be your loss if you break with him."

How Crabbe could have persisted in being such a perseveringly meek fool, I am unable to explain. But, partly through solicitude to do no injustice through impatience, partly through delicate scrupulosity of taste and habit, and partly through desire to catch some prey, on the sixteenth of December he wrote to Perkins:—

"I would be glad to know how my affairs stand. I know nothing whatever about the *Medici Book*, as to the actual effect on me of its publication; and it is very necessary that I should know this before entering upon fresh plans. I believe that you are able to say many things for my guidance; and I would be most happy to hear from you, or to see you at the studio."

189

Perkins replied:—

"I now take the opportunity of saying I am sorry I have not been able to sell that short story of yours called *The Inevitable Universal* that I had in hand and will return it if it comes back again to your address c/o Schelm's, I too oddly enough know nothing whatever about the *Medici Book* and should suggest you now call and see O. yourself on the matter when, no doubt, a great portion of the misunderstanding might be amiably removed. I now am so busy that I can't undertake any fresh representation for anyone."

Crabbe thought that that would do nicely, thank you, Mr Perkins; and set to work. He did not expose his soft shell to the insolence of the Archsplitter of Infinitives: but left that matter where it was. He began to clothe himself in new armour. He seriously cultivated confidence in his own opinion. He fully intended to love his neighbour as himself; and, to that end, he would follow the advice of Nietzsche by first becoming one of those who love themselves, and *"occupet extremum scabies,"* he said. It was due to Kemp that he should do so: for to Kemp alone he owed the joy of living to serve. " *'Habere non haberi','* says Gabriele d'Annunzio citing Lionardo da Vinci, "is the rule from which the man of intellect should not swerve." It was due to Kemp, that he should not let himself be swerved by any storm— that he should, not be had, but have.

He wished to know the exact nature of the connection between Perkins and the painter. Was it a case of collusion—to harass his critical faculty and his exquisite sensibility with their trite platitudes, their frightful diction, their exiguous vocabularies, their merely maculose punctuation? Was it collusion, to distract his attention from the things which really matter— collusion, to divert his energies—collusion, to preclude him from profiting by his talents and his toil? Was it collusion to carry out his old enemy's threat of preventing him from earning a living ever? Both he who claimed to be the Divine Friend, and the literary agent were his nominees, were in touch with the friends of Crabbe's old enemy; and we all know (since Max Nordau told us) that a normal can be changed into a hysterical individual simply by tiring him. Was it a conspiracy to this end? Or, was it solely the fortuitous concurrence of a gaggle of inconvenient and inconstant geese? Crabbe, at the moment, had not collected sufficient evidence on which to base a valid and accurate sentence.

One thing, however, was as clear as day. He ought to take his courage in both hands, to go the holosialos (in vulgar language): he ought to sever himself from both these men. Should he cut the painter? Or should he silently let it slip? While he was perpending, the gods of his stars provided an opportunity.

On the first day of the New Year, Perkins wrote:—

"I now regret to say *The Perfect Lady* have mislaid the MS. of your short story called *The Inevitable Universal* and cannot find it oddly enough even after special search at my request. I trust however that you have another copy of it and no loss will ensue therefrom with the Best Compts of Season."

Crabbe sharpened his strong new nippers, while he flung back:—

"I have no copy of *The Inevitable Universal*; and the MS. must be found and returned to me. I never would have consented to sell it to a paper of the calibre of *The Perfect Lady*. I do not write for milliners: but for men—as you ought to have known."

Perkins replied:—

"Thanks for your letter, the matter is now evidently one for your solicitor."

Then Crabbe's great claws crunched together; and he severed the painter:—

"I must say," Crabbe wrote, "that I fail in understanding your peculiar idea of the office of a literary agent. In the beginning, you proposed to relieve me (in return for a commission which I myself benevolently fixed at 25%) of all trouble except that of the production of MSS. In practice, your professions egregiously have been belied. Your voluntary and gratuitous promise, to procure orders and advances on the strength of a few pages of MS., lacks performance. Your direction of my affairs with Doron Oldcastle Limited has been both fatal and absurd. In cases where your action has involved me (or has seemed likely to involve me) in loss, you airily propose to shift on to my shoulders the task of repairing your defalcations. In short, your agency has been to me nothing but a source of worry and detriment. I am unwilling (except in case of necessity) to disoblige your friend, at whose suggestion I consented to employ you: but I feel compelled to invite his attention to your singular unsatisfactory and vacillating method of conducting my literary affairs. I especially am unwilling to treat you with unduly austere severity, seeing that you are a brother in the Household of Faith: but my past experience of the extreme untrustworthiness of the Faithful in secular matters, and the additional evidence of the same which you appear to be providing, cause me to declare that (unless you promptly satisfy me in the present matter of *The Inevitable Universal* and *The Perfect Lady*, and furnish me with an assurance that such an imbroglio will not disturb me again), I intend, from the date of this letter to terminate my connection with you and the man whom I shall regard as your colleague; and to trust my confidence in people who, not being of our religious persuasion, are not likely to afford me fresh occasions of scandal. I assure you that I write thus with profound regret; and that I would be only too happy to have reasons for dealing leniently with you—reasons which you yourself are competent to provide at your own discretion. This is all without prejudice; and I reserve all rights in this letter."

Perkins' inept insulsity led him to reply:—

"I now beg to say your letter has comforted me greatly. *Pax. A.M.D.G.*"

That was what Crabbe wanted. The case was not the case of a feeble and silly old man, ousted by age limit from Fleet Street, desperately afraid of and contemned by publishers, trying to make an as-near-as-might-be legally honest living. Crabbe took the discursion into Latin as the defiant bark of disappointment on the part of a detected Jesuit's Jackal; and on the sixth of January, the Festival of the Manifestation of Christ to the

Gentiles, he finally fulminated:—

"Sir, The impertinent letter, in which you attempt to brazen out the Epiphany of your dishonourable culpability and incompetence, is now before me. After breakfast, it will be in its proper place—behind me."

Also he thrust the Demon False Friend down to his own place.

Chapter Twenty-eight

Ir was the beginning of the year, and of a new phase of things. Crabbe reviewed his situation, and erected new schemes.

All the good which had been promised to him, on which he had counted, which might have been achieved by the genuine publication of three fairly important books in one year, now was null and void. The *Kalliphonos* ought to have appeared in June 1900, *Daynian Folk-lore* in September, the *Medici Book* in October. Instead, Schelm had retarded *Daynian Folk-lore* till March 1901; and the *Kalliphonos* was hung up even now. The *Medici Book* came out in October 1901; and was a frost and a disgrace. And here was 1902. Two books practically were thrown away: for Schelm was not even advertising *Daynian Folk-lore*, and Oldcastle must be prevented from succeeding with the *Medici Book*. There remained only the *Kalliphonos*: but Schelm was such a scoundrel that it would be wrong to place any hope on that. No. Better to clean the slate and begin again, Crabbe said to himself.

He took heroic measures without any hesitation and with radical ferocity. He attached a new name to *Necessary Propositions*; and started its perambulations among the publishers, putting it out as the work of a new author.[1] He knew that he would have to suffer for that, although he did not know how frightfully: but he plainly perceived Schelm's dodge and Oldcastle's dodge. They were not going to boom his books until he had made his own name. Very well: he would make a name in literature, but not the name which was on Schelm's and Oldcastle's books. Oh no. He would consider himself. And he would begin again at the bottom of the ladder.

So he wrote in the first chapter of another book. It was a very modern novel, a deliberately low and sensational thing such as the publisher believes to be loved by the public; and he called it

[1] *Hadrian the Seventh* was the first book to be published under Rolfe's own name.

Amorroma. And then he broached the subject of collaboration to Kemp.

"O my dear man," that one cried. "I am so glad that you've spoken at last. My brain is simply seething."

"Why didn't you tell me?"

"Of course you know why. But there is something which I must tell you. Do you know that I can distinguish day from night? I know when the lamp is alight."

"Gracious Powers! When did this begin?"

"About Christmas."

"I say, Kemp, do go and see an oculist."

"No, I won't. I want to watch it a little longer."

"I do wish you would."

"Dear man, I can't. Look here, I'm quite content as I am. If I thought that there was any hope——. But just think—suppose that I did get back my sight. What good would it be? Think what I should have to see. No, no—I'm quite done for. Life holds nothing for me but this; and—the gods are kind—they have prevented me from seeing ugly and unpleasant things. Talk of something else, please. Talk about writing a book together. That would be really good of you."

Crabbe shot out both eyes; and looked the patient little creature over most pathetically. He well knew the pains of sight —mean streets crowded with clots of frightful anxious female, streaked with stunted male, all stridently shrieking—the vulgar attenuate fusky skimpiness of everything, toweringly roaring. For these and a great many other reasons, it was quite as well that Kemp should not see. Yet—compulsory terrible darkness—! But that was preferable to deadly bitterness or horrible howling or unmitigable cold, or piercing stink. Oh yes, of the Five Corporeal Torments, terrible darkness was most tolerable.

"What kind of book could we do together?" he said, at length. They were returning from a tramp over Highgate Hill and Hampstead. The night was a plum-bloom-coloured mist, thinning into clearness in the centre of vision. To Crabbe, it resembled a shimmering veil, sewn with little mother-o'-pearl discs of the arc-lights here and there in shoals, spangled with the yellow stars of incandescent and electric lamps, studded with the rubies of occasional doctors' and apothecaries' signs, barred with the black trunks and branches of young trees on the kerbs, loomed with splashes of reflected light. He wondered why no Whistler and no Trevor Haddon ever had treated a London street on these lines. The effect was that of the mysterious jewelled drapery of Orientals—Persians—Assyrians, for choice. It gave him a clue.

"Did you ever read a book called *De XXX Improbis Imperatoribus*?" he continued.

"Gad! What a title!" Kemp laughingly exclaimed. "*Concerning Thirty Naughty Emperors!* No: I never read that. But whoever could have written it?"

"A blighter called Rufus Teres Natator."

"How delicious!" Kemp again exclaimed, clutching Crabbe's arm with excitement. "Who was he? What's the book about? Where did you find it?"

"I haven't the faintest notion who the Red-haired Smooth (-skinned, understood) Swimmer was: but I found the book when I was rummaging at B.M. It's bound up with a pack of pamphlets; and uncatalogued. Everything else in the volume is catalogued except that; and I suppose that it has escaped notice. I rather think it a find, you know. Anyhow, I spotted it; and stored it up for my own purposes."

"Have you read it yourself?"

"Bits here and there. I managed to tralate the chapter on Elagabalus pretty well—'A Goat in Priest's Clothing' the author calls him."

"Oh I say Crabbe, you know, we really ought to do it."

"I'm willing. It's quite the funniest kind of serious history in the world, written in four shades of yellow by a man who knows how to paint. Nasty? Oh yes, it's frightfully nasty: but printably nasty, you know. I don't think that we shall have to expurge anything. Rufus Teres Natator wasn't a bestial old sot like 'Umar Khaiyam, anyhow."

196

CHAPTER TWENTY-EIGHT

"Let's begin directly."

"Very well. I'll go to B.M. every morning for a couple of hours and transcribe the text. Then, I'll read it to you—if you'll promise not to throw the chairs at my false quantities—and you shall dictate a literal tralation, which I'll take down and put into literary form. I shouldn't be surprised if the publishers jumped at it."

"There's something which I've had in my head for a long time."

"Out with it."

"Do you think we could do a little something for a magazine— something in the nature of a note on posthumous literature?"

"For example?"

"Well: for example, Caesar's 'Life of Napoleon'."

"Excellent. No. 'Men in their Multitudes muse on Beliefs and on Faiths: others, 'twixt Doubt and Knowledge, in a Torpor lie. Sudden then shouteth the vigilant Mage, O Fools, the Road ye seek is neither here nor there!' No we couldn't do a little something for a magazine. But a series called *Notes on Post-humous Literature* we will do—Cicero's *Oration for Joan of Arc*, St Jerome's *Tractate on Widows*, Tacitus *On the Manners and People of America*, Hesiod's *Nights and Plays*, Cardinal New-man's *Grammar of Dissent*—do I catch the idea?"

"Oh finely. I say, can't we find a bus somewhere, and get home and begin them to-night?"

"No. We have to settle terms; and I'm going to place a condition."

"Terms be hanged!"

"I'll have a clear understanding with you before I do a stroke."

"Oh well then."

"You will do all which I ask you to do, i.e., you will place your brains and scholarship at my disposal. I'll do all the hand-work, and as much head-work as I can; and I'll market the product. Then, I'll take a third of the proceeds; and the rest will be yours."

"Nonsense! You'll do most of the work; and you'll take two-thirds of the pay."

"Either I'll take one-third, or I won't do the work."

"Very well. Have your own way. When the stuff is sold, I'll take my two-thirds and respectfully return half of it to you."

"Which I shall refuse."

"Well, we'll see. And now for your condition."

"I want you to think favourably of the idea of seeing an oculist. Leave it all to me; and I'll arrange it. Will you?"

"O man, you are good. Well: if I say that I'll think about it, should that satisfy you?"

"It will have to. There's a splendid man at Oxford, you know. I'm sure that I can make some arrangement with him."

"I won't go to Oxford."

"You needn't. He comes to town once a week; and he shall see you here."

"Well; if you insist, I'll think about it."

"Oh, if you'll let me, I will insist."

"You'll regret it."

"No, I will not. But I want to be sure that you're able to keep on living somehow, safely, all right, doing something, in the case of my death."

Chapter Twenty-nine

A LETTER, in Thorah's handwriting, awaited Crabbe at Schelm's. He brought it home unopened, muttering curses, guessing at its content, waving his feelers, snapping his claws, and rigidly protruding both eyes. Finally, he flung it to Kemp, sweeping, with "Waste paper—for lighting the fire."

And he went on writing his novel.

He had hit on the dodge of making his hero always talk in hendecasyllabics. It was not the poetic prose of Dickens trying to be pathetic: for the hendecasyllabic measure is an almost unknown one; and, as far as he could see, it simply gave a characteristic keen sweetness to his hero's diction. He was rather pleased with the effect. It was quaintly delicate and sober, suited well to the figure which he was delineating: but it was difficult.

"Hard, hard, hard is it only not to stumble:
So fantastical is the dainty metre."

He knit his brow to keep his thoughts from wandering. They wandered, all the same, to Thorah's letter.

He wrote a short sharp note, (intended to pinch), saying that, having recognized the handwriting on the envelope, he had had the letter thrown into the fire: but he could not conceive why Thorah should address him, after the libellous statement to Arkush Annaly and the cruel heart-breaking neglect of the last two years. Did he wish to curse him for the *Medici Book*? Surely nothing was easier than to instigate the editor of the *Daily Anagraph* to damn it. Crabbe was quite ready for anonymous stabs; and would return them on the rawest and most secret sore. (He derived much satisfaction from posting a pinch of the distinct and gratuitous ferocity of this one.)

Thorah's reply came by telegraph. That, of course, Crabbe opened: because the cinnamon-coloured envelope gave no clue to the sender of its content.

199

"Impossible you should be serious in what you say but if you are come dine seven-thirty ock and talk matter over."

It perturbed Crabbe very gravely. He wondered whether he had snubbed a penitent. Still (though he was no Oratorian) he was not in a mood to try persuasion. He resented cruelty. As for permitting anyone to saturate curiosity by the spectacle of genius contortuplicating in mortal agony—that was not to be thought of. He had not the slightest intention of coming under Thorah's yoke any more.[1] He was a burnt child; and he dreaded fire. So he said.

Thorah wrote at length, being very much distressed; and offered to send some reasonably presentable clothes. Far from urging the *Daily Anagraph* to damn the *Medici Book*, he had recommended an important notice. One would appear to-morrow, or at least very soon: but the editor's reviewer "had not found the book quite so remarkable as I did—in which case the reviewer lacks perceptions," and Thorah would write a signed letter to the *Daily Anagraph* replying to the review. But oh!—if Crabbe only would come to see him, he was sure that all misconceptions could be cleared up.

"Kemp," Crabbe cried, on this, "do you remember an un-opened envelope which I gave you for the fire the other day?"

"Yes."

"I suppose it's burned?"

"No: I don't think. The fact is that I economize all your waste paper in order to have the wherewithal for the fires——."

"Could we find it?"

"No doubt."

The two went and rummaged in a neat little heap of paper stored in the kitchen cupboard. Crabbe pounced upon the rejected letter.

"Dear Crabbe, Your *Medici Book* is GREAT. To say nothing of the labour and the learning of it—the historic imagination, the big vision, the humour, the irony, the wit, the perverseness,

[1] This is a pun on the title of one of Harland's early novels, *The Yoke of the Thorahs*, written under the pseudonym of Sidney Luska.

the daring, the tremendously felicitous and effective *manner* of it!! It is like a magnifical series of tapestry pictures of the XV Century. Of course I think you are *advocatus diaboli*: but *what* an advocate! In any land save England such a book would make its author at once FAMOUS and RICH. It is GREAT. Yrs, Sidney Thorah."[1]

That was what he had given to be flung into the fire—that delicious and apparently generous praise. After treating him abominably and deserting him for two long years, the dicaculous Thorah actually had been forced to break silence with this spontaneous and explosive shriek of admiration.

Crabbe acknowledged that he had done one injustice. But Thorah must blame no one but himself for the effect of his conduct to a hypersensitive. It was nasty but natural. Crabbe supposed that he ought to be grateful for admiration. Well, he was not.

" '*Timeo Danaos et dona ferentes*'," he wrote. "And I knew it all before. I knew it (what I was doing) when I studied the subject and wrote the *Medici Book* in seven months at a pound a week, unaided by any of you. The whole work has been mutilated by Oldcastle. If the thing (as it is) is a success, I am not going to demur: but if I am damned, I am going to damn. Yes: I am sick of empty admiration. A little love, a little human sympathy, is what I am not yet able to buy. But I really would like to believe you kind; and I am prepared to do so, seeing that you (who never write a letter) have written two. I don't seek you: but I would be very nice to you genuinely seeking me. So say the word; and, if you'll promise not to gibe at me, or to dispute with me, I'll come and see you any night you like."

Thorah liked Monday; and Crabbe went after dinner. He was so flurried that he forgot to take his chalcedonyx with some aloes in his pocket. On meeting, the two men yelled at each other, "Why you've shaved!" and Thorah pattered on, "It takes ten years off your head! Doesn't it, Eileen?"

[1] This is simply a copy of Harland's letter to Rolfe on reading *Chronicles of the House of Borgia*.

"Oh I do think it such a pity," the lady said. "Do you know, Mr Crabbe, that Mrs Toovey used to go into raptures over your little beard and upturned moustachio? She used to say that you were the living image of Van Dyck's King Charles the First."

Crabbe's claws snapped about for a similar personal point to pinch. Meanwhile, he murmured, "That's what I did it for."

"What do you mean?"

"Well: I found that you all posed, and expected me to pose: so I did my face like that because I could do it easily. Nature made me that way. But now I'm not posing any more. I'm shaven and shorn and bald and naked and somewhat ugly—like Truth—; and I'll be taken as I am, or not taken at all. That's a new ring of yours, Thorah. Where did you get it? And what have you done with your jacinth?"

Thorah drew off the ring; and handed it to Crabbe, asking what he thought of it, saying that the jacinth was lost. Crabbe produced the tiny Codrington lens which he used for sigil-reading; and studied the very massive gold entypoma.

"One, two-three, four-five-six, seven-eight-nine-ten, eleven-twelve-thirteen-fourteen-fifteen tassels—well—a cardinal's hat and 'Deo Gratias' in late Seventeenth Century characters—1680 to 1700, I should say. Very funny! Whence did it come? And what does it mean?"

Thorah blinked queerly. "Of course you see what I mean it to mean?"

"M-yes. Perhaps I do."

"It came to me in quite a strange way." Thorah hesitated during a moment; eyed his wife: and continued, "Do you know what's happened to me since I saw you last?"

"Only that *Red Rappee* has gone into its fiftieth thousand, according to the papers."

"Ninetieth, now."

"Ninetieth? Gracious Powers! Why you're a made man!"

"Yes, I suppose I am. But the point is that I was made just at the very moment when I was quite undone." Thorah bounced up and down on his heel; and gabbled on as garrulously as a

clattering of choughs. "It was like this. You know that, up to
the time when we went abroad, my father had been allowing me
a thousand a year. That was all we had to live on: for my books
and journalism didn't pay my wine-bill. It was a pittance merely.
Consequently, we simply had to go. No sooner had we gone
than my father saw fit to die. Then, my mother came out to join
us; and 'Sidney,' says she, 'I'm grieved to tell you that I shan't
be able to do what your father's been doing for you. We all
thought him a rich man. Didn't we?' says she. 'Well: we none
of us knew how rich he was; and we none of us knew the
enormous sums he gave away. They're dreadful. And so of
course he's left little or nothing behind him. And, Sidney,' says
she, 'I shan't be able to continue your allowance, for I've only
just got enough to live on myself. All I can do for you is this—
I can give you a thousand a year for two years: or I can give you
two thousand now, and be done with you,' says she. And there
we were adrift, Eileen and me, in a foreign clime, with a paltry
two thousand pounds between us and the gutter. It was horrid.
I couldn't sleep. I thought I should go mad. I couldn't make up
my mind which of my mother's two offers to accept. One day,
in the hotel at Bergamo, I happened to pick up an English newspaper; and I saw that *Red Rappee* had gone into a fifth edition.
'Ha-ha!' say I: 'There'll be a penny or two coming out of that.'
A little later, we had moved on to Ventimiglia; and the same
sort of thing happened. Eileen and I were worrying ourselves to
death about money—whether to take two thousand down or the
two year's allowance—and trying to be civil to my mother;
and then, one day, by chance I picked up another English newspaper. *Red Rappee* had gone into its twelfth edition! 'Eileen!' I
screamed, what you said just now. 'Eileen, my ship's come
home!' For you know, Crabbe, that when once your book gets into
a twelfth edition your reputation's made for life. After that you
never have any more difficulties about your books. Every
publisher's only too anxious to get you. As a matter of fact,
within the next month, I got letters from every English and
every American publisher and literary agent offering terms for

my next book which I hadn't begun to think about. The minimum was £1,200 down on account of a 25% royalty; and I was only getting 15% on *Red Rappee*. But now this is where the ring comes in. Here was I dancing; and there was Eileen howling——."

"You can translate Sidney, Mr Crabbe?" the little lady demurely inquired.

"Well, Eileen: you won't deny that you were weeping, I suppose? So was I for that matter; and I take no shame for a little momentary weakness. But listen, Crabbe. In comes my mother from her drive, looking rather remorseful. I expect her internal or maternal conscience had been pricking her. And 'Sidney,' says she, 'I've bought a ring at a curiosity shop; and if it fits you I'll make you a present of it.' Of course it fitted me—me, as well as my finger—coming pat like that. The cardinal's hat stood for Red. That's my book. And '*Deo Gratias*' stood for me at that moment. I can tell you I was nothing but one great big bursting Thank you then. And that's all."

"Well, I'm sure that I'm very glad. I suppose you've made your fortune?"

"I've made four-thousand seven-hundred odd pound so far; and I shall make as much again."

"Well, I congratulate you with all my heart."

"Thanks, Crabbe. That sounds rather generous of you."

"Oh you needn't sneer. I really mean it. I think this business of writing is the most damnably dilacerating torture under the sun. Consequently when I hear of anybody getting the better of it, I don't care who he is, I feel a glow of triumph."

"It's what you ought to have done yourself, considering the quality of your stuff."

"Of course it is. But I haven't. I'm just where you left me, plodding through the slimiest mire that's made."

They went into particulars. Thorah produced shocks, when he heard of the villainies of Welbeck and Oldcastle and Neddy: although he naturally could not go all the way with Crabbe in ascribing villainy to Schelm. But he said some things which were

204

rather illuminating. He made a very strenuous effort to make his guest believe that he had spoken hurriedly in saying that he was Schelm's partner. What he had intended to convey was merely that he had an interest, as an author, in the good estate of his publisher.

The explanation seemed lame: but Crabbe made no verbal difficulty about accepting it. He turned to inquiries about people. The mouse-mannered sub-editor, he learned, had disappeared with Thorah's *Encyclopædia Britannica*. Annaly had come a financial cropper; and the Thorahs did not know him now. The lovely Florentine—well: the Thorahs thought that they were better out of her society also. Ha-humn! The witty Irishwoman—she actually had had the brass to present her husband with a triplet, all alive and kicking, if you please. And Welbeck—Crabbe had heard all about him of course? On the contrary, he had heard nothing at all.

Thorah began to walk delicately, and to pick his words. Welbeck had made a slight mistake between his own bank balance and Schelm's. Schelm had turned up suddenly in New York: found things all over the place; and sent Welbeck to the right-about on the spot. It was a great pity that Crabbe ever had had anything to do with that Hebrew Jew.

But Crabbe was very much amused. He knew what his connection with Welbeck actually had been; and he began to perceive why the little man had shewed such anxiety to make friends with the mammon of uprighteousness. No doubt the MSS. which he had accumulated eventually would attain the honours of print, over a name which was not Crabbe's.

Thorah gave the impression of thinking that Crabbe was Welbeck's ally. Knowing the skeptical habit of the man before him, Crabbe bluntly stated the facts of the case; and left them there to be accepted or rejected. As usual, he made no effort at persuasion. Also, although he was conscious of (and revelled in) the charm of Thorah's personality and of the social amenities which surrounded him, Crabbe deliberately played the game. He was genial, agreeable, brilliant: but he gave no vital confidences. He felt his way. He said nothing of Kemp; nothing of the literary agent or the painter; and not much which was really definite about his work. Thorah was pumping him all the time—whether on behalf of Schelm, or in the interests of the people in Farm Street[1] who like to know everything, or whether out of proper inquisitiveness, he did not know. But he knew that he was being pumped; and he exuded enough information to prevent leading questions which he might dislike to answer.

They talked of the *Medici Book* just then damned by *The Minervium*. Crabbe shewed Thorah how unfair a personal attack was made upon him; and indicated several bad blunders on the part of the reviewer. Thorah dwelled on the inadvisability of noting reviews; but deemed the present an exception. Misrepresentation was so gross. He drew up a remonstrance for Crabbe to send to the editor—a respectful and convincing remonstrance, beginning, "I write in defence, not of the book, but of myself." But, as for the book, despite all Crabbe said about its emasculation, it really was a masterpiece, in Thorah's opinion. No matter where you opened it, there was always good reading in it. He had given away nine-and-thirty copies as Christmas presents. It actually was far and away the best thing on the market at present. How was it selling?

Crabbe knew not. He had not inquired; and Oldcastle had not told him. But all the newspapers were damning it—bar the *Largest Circulation*.

Thorah snorted.

"For my part," said Crabbe, "I think it an honour to be told by you that the *Medici Book* is majuscularly GREAT, and a distinction to be told by the *Largest Circulation* that my work is full of novel and unexpected attractions and like an icy shower-bath after the tepid ablutions of modern historical research. You see the *Largest Circulation* agrees with you so I don't know why you should snort. However, if Oldcastle wants to sell the book, why

---

[1] Here Rolfe is referring to his fellow-Catholics at the Jesuit Church of the Immaculate Conception, in Farm Street, Berkeley Square.

can't he quote the *Largest Circulation* in advertisements. But he doesn't want. He has sold 750 copies· to an American publisher under false pretences—I mean that he has not mentioned the fact that I had withdrawn my name from the frightful thing. That way he has cleared cost of production; and now he will let things slide. He doesn't want to let me have any benefit from my work: which is to say that he doesn't want to sell.''

"No. You're all wrong. You take such a perverse view of things. The fault's your own. The fact is, Crabbe, you're what the Jews call a *'schlemiel'*. Nothing ever prospers with you; and everything goes wrong. Of course a publisher wants to sell his books.''

"Yes: under ordinary circumstances. But, in this case, you must ponder the personal equation. That's the stumbling-block. Don't you see that I'm personally antipathetic to Oldcastle— and to Schelm too, for that matter. *Oderis quem laeseris.* Of course they would like to sell their books: but they are irritated and sore; and they have recouped their outlay; and, because they are disappointed at not finding me sufficiently servile, they will break all their solemn promises and do no more. The next thing will be the sale of the remaining copies at remainder prices. There, will be the end; and all my labour will have been thrown away. However, I'll see whether *The Minervium* is going to do the fair thing by me. I'll make that effort to reinstate my literary reputation; and, if it fails, I'll denounce the book and Oldcastle even if I kill myself. Thorah, I'm in a mood to pull down the pillars of the Philistines——.''

"Gently, gently! Why don't you do something else, and let bygones be bygones?''

"For the simple reason that I'm distracted by poverty and starvation and the impossibility of paying my way and living in peace. How can I do brain work while my body's being broken on the wheel?''

Thorah looked with meaning at his wife; and there was a passage of communicated thought from eyes. He turned again to Crabbe.

"I've got a proposition to make to you, if you'll promise not to be offended."

Crabbe shot out both his own eyes. "Go on," he said, glaring.

"What you want is quiet and ease and a comfortable home while you use your perfectly astounding genius to write some more books."

"Yes."

"Well: when we came back from Italy, we stayed a few weeks in a gorgeous country house belonging to a friend of Eileen's. And do you know the first thing I saw in the library was a pile of new books with the *Medici Book* on top. Didn't I pounce on it and ask questions, Eileen? Our hostess said that Bumpus had *carte blanche* to send her all important new books. That's how it came there. So you see what the booksellers think of it! She'd read it; and she'd been wondering whoever you were to have written a thing so devilishly distinguished. Of course you know, Crabbe, I didn't tell her anything to which you could possibly object; but I told her a great deal. And now she's burning and yearning to know you—burning and yearning in fact for you to go and stay there and do what you like as long as you like."

"Gracious Powers!"

"So there you are. There's a great big house, in lovely country, big boxes of cigarettes on every window-sill, plenty of horses and shooting and fishing, five automobiles, charming people—she and her husband too—as much privacy as you like, meals when and where you like to order them, and the run of the place."

"What does the woman want?"

"Want?"

"I mean, what am I to do for all this?"

"Nothing. She admires your work and wants to know you. Her house and all the rest is yours for the honour and pleasure of your acquaintance."

Crabbe turned over his affairs in his mind—his clothes, the appearance which he could make among people's servants, his responsibility to Kemp, his work. He decided to face the unpleasantness of a poor and scanty wardrobe. The chance of ease for work was most desirable. If, in the course of a few days, no opening should appear for Kemp as well, he could return to Lincoln's Inn Fields. Anyhow, the thing must not be rejected without trial. Lord! What a godsend it might be! His heart opened; and he went back to Thorah with, "Well, it sounds excellently. You'll understand what I mean by preliminary difficulties; and I would like to hear what you propose. Mind you: I'm frightfully obliged to you, and I'm as willing as possible."

"What I propose is this. Eileen and I are going there next week to stay a bit; and we'll arrange everything exactly as you'd wish to have it. When our friend comes up for the season you shall meet her here. She shall ask you to use her house when and how you like; and there you are. They've got oceans of money. She's a perfect lady. And she adores your Greekness. In fact, you'll find her all that we've been looking for for you. And that reminds me that I want your advice. I'm sick of modern literature. There's nothing improving to the mind about it. So I'm thinking of rubbing up my Greek, and I want you to put me in the way. Tell me something fairly easy—something which you think I ought to read and which I should like to read——."

"Read Longinus *On the Sublime*—and read the Gospel according to Saint John. You could do them with a lexicon and a primer, easily. Order them at Bumpus's. Have you got a lexicon and a primer?"

"No."

"Well: I'll lend you mine, if you'll return them in a couple of months."

"Can you spare them?"

"I would be delighted—for two months."

"It's awfully good of you."

"It's frightfully good of you."

The next day, Crabbe sent the lexicon and the primer (two of the tools of his trade) to Thorah; and waited very hopefully for a happy issue out of all his afflictions. But Schelm and his (shall

I say) partner, or (shall I say) spy, possessed full knowledge of Crabbe's condition now.

Thorah retained the books: closed his door upon Crabbe; and kept silence. As for the woman who wanted to offer a home to a writer, needy and worried—she (I suppose) was the bait for insnaring one so credulous, one so easily spoiled by the spoiler. That was the end of it all. Letters and visits were useless.

Chapter Thirty

THE *Daily Anagraph* damned the *Medici Book*, by means of a tissue of misquotations (from passages which by chance the publisher had not castrated) with a corruscating display of the reviewer's historic ignorance. Thorah belied his promise of a signed demurrer.

The Minervium agreed to admit the letter of remonstrance; and volunteered to send a proof. No proof came: but the letter appeared, surreptitiously and completely distorted in the publisher's (and advertiser's) interests. For, whereas Crabbe had written, "I write in defence, not of the book but of myself," the editor made him say, "I write in defence of the book"; and nothing would persuade Mr Burnand Burstall[1] to amend so gross a perversion. If *The Minervium* had been bought by Oldcastle, it would not have acted otherwise.

The great claws crashed and quivered with the fury of outraged impotence. There was no truth and no honour and no righteousness anywhere in literary London. Crabbe did not know a single writer or a single publisher or a single journalist who was not a liar or a thief or both. He printed, in America, a ferocious denunciation of his book and of its London publisher; and gained the consolation of having an editorial article devoted to his case, emphasizing all his points and gibbeting Oldcastle as the stealer of an author's trade-mark. It gave the deathstroke to the *Medici Book* which instantly became obtainable in second-hand bookshops at a third of its published price. Oldcastle's comments could not be set down here.

Before Crabbe finally was convinced of Thorah's perfidy, the question of the *Kalliphonos* came to the front again. I think that Schelm was terrified by Oldcastle's fate: for he also had in hand a book of Crabbe's. Schelm perfectly knew that he had been playing the fool with that for a year and a half; and, when he saw

[1] Vernon Rendall, editor of *The Athenaeum.*

how wholeheartedly, how ruthlessly, how carelessly, this author tore to tatters an offensive publisher, he conceived a yearning for protection against a similar disaster. He must clear cost of production, anyhow—by means of a little blandishment perhaps. He invited Crabbe to tea at his private house in barbaric Bayswater.

Crabbe got up himself with elegant negligence; had his head and hands groomed and his face made by Clarkson;[1] and deliberately presented such a very good appearance that no beholder possibly could have guessed his actual condition. And also he used an air of quick and independent geniality.

Schelm was not at home when he arrived; and, after waiting ten minutes in a dingy unused study, he rang the bell for the maid and said that he would wash his hands, by way of expressing his opinion of his publisher. Before lavation was complete, Schelm of course turned up and said, "Hullo!" There was something novel and enlarged in Crabbe which he did not quite understand: but still—he was delighted to renew acquaintance; and offered tea in the dingy back room.

"What I mean to say is have you heard from your friend Welbeck lately, Mr Crabbe?" he promptly began.

"You may as well understand that Welbeck is not and never was my friend. He was a publisher's manager perspicacious enough to recognize the value of my work. It would have suited him to be intimate with me: but I had little or no intimacy to give him. What my business relations were with him, you know. Perhaps you don't know that, privately, he has not treated me any better than he has treated you."

Schelm bounded a bit. "What! 's he been robbing you too?"

"Oh I didn't know that he actually robbed you. Thorah didn't say quite as much as that. I understood that there only was a slight confusion between the firm's account and his own."

"Slight confusion, indeed!" Schelm spat. "The man was a rank swindler. I suspected something was up, from the rude letters he wrote me; and I ran over without warning just to see. What d'ye think I found, Mr Crabbe? A bum in possession

[1] An allusion to the firm of theatrical costumiers and wig makers.

of—my—office! That Welbeck had paid himself his own salary first out of the funds at his disposal; and, because there didn't happen to be just then somehow what I mean to say is enough to go round, he had permitted—my—bookbinder—to put in a bum-bailiff into—my—office. Cost me one hundred and twenty-five dollars to get rid of him: what I mean to say is—one —hundred and twenty-five—hard dollars, Mr Crabbe. The rascal! If it hadn't been for his wife, I'd have put him in prison, I would! However, he had to quit—sharp! What did the scoundrel rob you of?"

Crabbe could not perceive any salient iniquity or criminality in all this. No doubt Schelm had been trying to starve his manager, and his manager had contrived to get his knife into Schelm; and the latter had winced so very violently that the former had lost his footing. Crabbe was smiling to himself as he responded,

"Well: he got a lot of MSS. out of me; and didn't pay."

"And I'll be bound he kept the stuff?"

"Yes."

"I thought so! I—thought—so—Mr Crabbe. Thecheatthe-ruffianthethief! Swindled all of us all round! If I could only put him in jail——."

"Well, why don't you?"

"What are you going to do about these MSS. of yours he's stolen?"

"Oh, just let them go," Crabbe disdainfully decided.

Schelm looked for a minute; and saw no sign of a co-prosecutor in the grim noncurant face—not even a token of a tool for wreaking revenge. He addressed himself to another subject. "What I mean to say is you know, Mr Crabbe, we really must begin to see about getting that book of yours out."

"Well, I'm sure that I'm not placing obstacles. You've had the book for eighteen months; and I've corrected all the proofs. What do you want?"

"I know, I know: but what I mean to say is this Welbeck affair's put the whole thing quite out of my head, till I saw that you'd been writing in the *New York Thunderer*. Have you seen the letter? D'ye know they've printed it?" Schelm whipped the print out of a prepared table drawer by his elbow.

"Oh yes: I see all those things," Crabbe said, grimly smiling.

"You know that is a very terrible letter, Mr Crabbe. It'll kill your book."

"Oh I hope so."

That struck Schelm dumb and staring. Crabbe continued, "You see the book's not mine. It's Oldcastle's: as *Kalliphonos* is yours. And I and Oldcastle are not friends. He tried to stand in my way; and I am striking him out of it. I don't at all mind getting hurt if I can do that. You know how you yourself feel in regard to Welbeck. By the by, what about the preface to the *Kalliphonos* which that blighter was going to write?"

Schelm licked his lips. "I've got a better man than ever Welbeck will be to write it. Do you know Mr David Askew Lype?"[1]

"Never heard of him."

"Well he's the first authority in the world on the subject; and he's got some unique information about *Kalliphonos* which he's going to embody; and I've paid him five-and-twenty dollars to write me a preface. I'm sure, Mr Crabbe, you'll admire that as much as he admires your translation. Now what I mean to say is I think it would be greatly to your advantage if you were to pen me a nice little letter saying that you——."

"Have you a piece of paper? I'll write you a nice letter with pleasure if I know precisely what you want me to say. Thanks. Go on."

"Well—say that you appreciate the honour of being associated with Mr David Askew Lype——."

"(Appreciate associated with D.A.L.)"

"And some little compliment about his being a gentleman and a scholar——."

"(Gent. and scholar.)"

[1] Rolfe's elaborate version of Omar contains an Introduction by Nathan Haskell Dole.

"And you're sorry you don't know him personally: but perhaps he'd let you see a proof of his preface——."

"(Sorry no personal acquaint. like see proof of preface.) Of course I expect to see it."

"And you'll leave the revising of the Greek revised proofs in his hands——."

"(D.A.L. read Greek revise.)"

"Well and then there are one or two matters of scholarship which you differ on. If you could see your way to concede a point or two——."

"What sort of point?"

"He says something about accents. Ah yes: here it is. I'll read you what he says. 'I must say I'm sorry to see that Mr Crabbe decorates the text with the eye-confusing accents that are not generally used nowadays. These were only invented by Arístofains——' is that the chap's name—Arístofains?——"

"Aristophanes."

"Well then Arrystoffanees—'and mean nothing, and personally I prefer'——."

"My dear Mr Schelm, I don't care a scrap for the accents. They're usual; and the text will look queer to modern eyes without them. But they really don't matter."

"Then you wouldn't mind omitting them?"

"Look here. You promised to make me a commercial success. If you really are going to do that, you are at liberty to do whatever you please with the book."

"I'm most glad to find you so agreeable, Mr Crabbe. And most surprised——."

"Now why 'surprised'? "

"Well you see—the way you've treated Oldcastle——."

"Ah but you see, you haven't treated me yet quite so badly as Oldcastle has."

"No, Mr Crabbe! I should think not indeed! Ah, you'd far better have stuck to me."

"But I have stuck and I am sticking and I will stick. I say that, in view of your promise of eighteen months ago, which you renew today, I'll consent to all these alterations in the *Kalliph-onos* and, in order to hasten matters, I'll do the revised proofs directly you let me have them."

"Yes now about those revises. What I mean to say is you see they've got to be printed in America, and then sent here, and then sent back: and that takes time; and I want to get the book out in a month. Now I'll promise you that, if you'll waive your right to a revise and leave it all to me, everything shall be done exactly as you wish and you shall net four figures by this book. I give you my word."

Crabbe shivered for a moment; and then bounded forward plunging headlong, as his manner was. "Very well. In order not to prevent you from realizing your desire to publish within a month, I consent to waive my right to revised proofs; and, on your assurances that you will make me a commercial success, and that you will not make me responsible for a book which (after publication) I should be compelled to denounce, I consent to leave the *Kalliphonos* in your hands. And to-morrow you shall have all this in the letter for which you've asked me."

Schelm was gratified; and said so. And he wanted to know what Crabbe was doing now.

"Oh, writing. No: not to order. I'm able to write to please myself now, you know."

"I'm sure I should be very happy to see anything you might like to shew me, Mr Crabbe. Why when I look at you now and think how you've got on since you first came to me three years ago————."

Crabbe snipped the thread of the brute's thought.

"Thanks to no one but myself. Perhaps I'll think about sending you something, some day."

"If you had anything ready————."

"Oh I have two or three things ready; and I haven't quite made up my mind as to where I shall place them, yet. I'll see what you do with the *Kalliphonos*. You know, in view of your notorious talent for making very great successes of very slight things, I expect—expect you to make a very great success of that. I don't believe in fantastic rhythmic prose myself: but you do, or you would not have asked for it. Well: you've got all you asked for; and now let me see what you can do with it."

"Then there's another thing, Mr Crabbe. You see a great many MSS. come into my office every day. I've often thought I should like to have your valuable opinion on some of them. But I'm afraid I can't go into that now—the fact is I must ask you to excuse me, Mr Crabbe—a most pressing appointment."

"Well you only have to let me have your MSS. with the usual guinea apiece. That's the price of my valuable opinion," Crabbe concluded, from the door-step.

So now the *Kalliphonos* really was coming out at last; and Schelm had repeated his promises. Perhaps after all this was the way of success. Crabbe went home; and talked it all over with Kemp, who did not seem particularly sanguine.

"Yes," he said. "I suppose you should do nothing else with this fellow: but, if you'll take my tip, you'll be very wily in writing, making it clear that you write by request, in compliance with orders—no—suggestions on Schelm's part. Then, if he means to be honest, well and good—what you put in your letter won't matter a tittle: but, if he plays any hanky-panky dodges, you've got him. You make concessions upon conditions, by Schelm's own suggestion. As he suggests the letter, he never can plead it against you."

Chapter Thirty-one

THE two hermits went on impetuously working together at their *Notes on Posthumous Literature* and the stories of the *Thirty Naughty Emperors*.

Their task was a tremendous one: because of the brilliant versatility, the multifarious knowledge, the intellectual perversity and the salient individuality of each of the minds engaged upon it. The stuff which they turned out was as rich and as pregnant and as aromatic as a Christmas-pudding. It was all plums and almonds and spice and candied peel. It had no negligible residuum whatever. Not an allusion, nor a word, nor a letter, nor even a comma, but had due value. In consequence, it was frightfully indigestible by feeders and readers used to bolting. Prolonged mastication was essential, in order to arrive at its essential savour, and in order to prevent mental dyspepsia.

In course of the work, the workers themselves came closer together, closer in amazement at and admiration of each other's extraordinary genius. Crabbe was astonished by the nimbleness, the profundity, the dazzling wit, the chaste taste of Kemp. Kemp shouted applause at Crabbe's mordant irony, his delicate certainty of touch, his patience and dexterity in producing beauty of form.

"I wish," he remarked one day, "I wish I could say big things simply. You say I fulminate. Yes, I know. I lose my way in my own words. But you have the power of speech. 'My song is in the mist that hides your morning.' I cannot travel on your wingless and unnavigable way."

MS. after MS. was written and emended and revised and rewritten again and again and again, until the two keen minds were wholly satisfied. Arguments and quarrels took place, without a vestige of ill-nature; and no difference was passed over until it had been threshed out thoroughly and solved. Each was willing to give in. Each was open to conviction. Neither was too

218

proud or too stupid to learn. This was ideal collaboration. No pains were shirked.

Crabbe reserved to himself the frightful gnawing suspense and pain of the knowledge that they were, and long had been, living solely on credit. True, there were a few pounds in the bank. True, there was a good stock of stationery and a fair amount of food in the house. But insolvency was actual; and the debts were huge. The gods of his stars in mercy made him oblivious to this horror during most of the hours of the day, in order not to impede him in his work. But his pauses and his sleepless nights were filled with apprehensions. Once, being oppressed in a most poignant money-famine, he emitted a slight squeal: but Kemp's sightless eyes regarded him with such dignified and unapproachable gravity, that he became aware of the indecency of naming the mere mundane. He often wondered how much his companion perceived, realized, knew: but he kept his wonderment with his pains and both to himself.

Kemp's physical affliction also caused anxiety. It became evident that a change was being effected: for he plainly could distinguish the movements of masses. Crabbe continued to persuade him to take an oculist's opinion; and, at last, he consented. I suppose that the temptation, to recover a lost sense, is more than even a Stoic can resist.

Crabbe corresponded with the Oxford specialist: used up the remainder of the bank balance in paying a reduced fee; and arranged for an examination in London. That was brief, simple, and quite decisive. The cause of blindness had been a shattering of certain nerves. Time and circumstances had been enabling Nature to replace what had been destroyed. A couple of touches from the stopper of a vial, and a week with bandaged eyes in a dark room in the doctor's private hospital, sent Kemp out into Beaumont Street in full possession of sight.

The beautiful little creature leaned on Crabbe's arm, dazed by the noise, sparkling with joy, and chattering like a schoolboy fresh from the river. The day was one of those brank-new days of April which make you thankful for being clean and alive. Its vigour gradually crept into the stiff limbs of Kemp; and steadied his dizzy brain. As they walked along, Crabbe was wondering how things would strike him; and noted (with enormous content) that his own aspect brought no twinge of surprise or disgust upon his companion's sensitive face. He had been frightfully afraid of that—that Kemp would consider him haggard or shabby. But the latter was strangely indiscriminate of particulars as yet. Only things in general excited his attention so far—the surge of the traffic, the bright movement of the world, the self-preoccupied people streaming by. There were some detachments of Horse Guards crossing the road into the Park; and the two men waited on the kerb.

"My God, Bobbie! Is that you?" The question dropped from aloft, from an officer, who leaped off his charger, flinging the reins to an orderly; and impetuously dashed at Kemp.

"Oh Theo, Theo!" came from Kemp. At the first sound of the voice, he had shivered: looked this way and that; and tightened his hold on Crabbe's arm. But now he was shaking the stranger's hand with rather more effusion than is usual in England.

Crabbe perceived that this was a meeting of long-lost friends; and he effaced himself with a lateral step or two and a gaze directed elsewhere. Impulse prompted him instantly to sidle away to his cave, and to reconnoitre from that akropolis: but second thoughts taught him the civility of immobility.

The two were chattering as vividly as possible, giving and receiving news; and, in a few minutes, Kemp returned with, "Crabbe, do let me present to you my very dear friend Theophanes Clayfoot."

"Pleased-to-know-you-Mr Crabbe," the captain jabbered. He [was] a sallow wiry-haired athlete, all sinew, and solemn of mien.

"Bobbie-tells-me-that-you've-been-very-good-to-him; and-I'll-come-and-thank-you-this-afternoon-if-you'll-let-me-catch-up-my-troop-now."

"Ninety-six Lincoln's Inn Fields, top floor," Kemp cried, as the other mounted and galloped away. "You remember I told you once that I had given my only two real friends the slip?" he continued to Crabbe, with vivacious animation. "Well: Theo was one—the first—the most important. And do you know, he's actually been hunting for me ever since. He really did want me after all. Oh he is a good man, I can tell you!"

"Who and what is he?" Crabbe impassively inquired.

"Well I suppose we may say that he's really a howling swell—got a lovely place of his own in Cornwall, J.P. and all that sort of thing in the county, and a commission in the Guards. He and I were at the House together. Birmingham of the Puseyum made us known to each other. And can't you see what he is to look at. But of course you don't know the splendid soul of him yet. Neither you nor I are worthy to lick his boots——."

"Boot-licking is not a habit of mine," Crabbe interpolated.

"No doubt that is a joke: but the taste displayed in such a joke is like a blow in the face to me."

"Sorry."

"Dear man, I want to bring you and Theo together. But you are going to make it difficult. I suppose you don't understand that: because you don't know him."

"I'm sure that, if your friend gives me a chance, I shall do my best to know him—for your sake."

Crabbe now instantly and instinctively felt that he was going to be robbed again; and he naturally became a little glum. But Kemp dilated on the double wonder of the day—yes, by George, a Wednesday—which gave him with both hands his sight and his friend. The circumstances of the journey home, the home itself, the restrained apathy of his companion seemed to go quite unnoted. Kemp had leaped backward into his past; and, with one bound, had taken up the threads of his former life at the point of rupture. And the ends appeared to be in a fair way of becoming joined together.

Clayfoot anon arrived; and was charmed; and was charming. Crabbe did not perceive a reason for raving about him in dithyrambics: but he accorded full value to the man's exquisite grace and urbanity (in Cicero's sense of the term). He wrote him down as a fine specimen of the product of freedom plus ease. Kemp babbled of old times; and described his connection with Crabbe most properly. Clayfoot thoroughly appreciated everything. And he wished to take Kemp away from him.

"There's my flat in Margellion Street which you can have all to yourself, until I'm free to take you down to Sonorusciello. That'll be in a fortnight's time. And I'm sure Mr Crabbe will be glad to get rid of you."

Kemp looked at Crabbe. The claws were folded neatly, the eyes fixed and imperscrutable.

"If you're thinking about our work," the crustacean said, "you may be easy. I've got enough stuff in hand to occupy me for a fortnight or so. And the change will do you good. Write as much as you like, when you're able to use a pen again; and send it on to me to manipulate."

"I hardly like to leave you."

"Oh I do wish you would. What am I to do with you during your convalescence. Don't you see that this solves all our difficulties? I don't want to have you disgusted every day by living in this slum. And besides, if you're happy and comfortable, you'll be able to do ever so much better work; and we both must be at our best if we are to make our fortunes."

Not much urging was needed. And Kemp passed over to Clayfoot.

Chapter Thirty-two

OF course the work went on; and of course they met again. Crabbe went twice to tea in Margellion Street; and found Kemp luxuriating in a new unexpurgated French edition of the *MI Nights*. Clayfoot was doing him magnificently: the wan stare of terror was almost faded from his face—that brilliant grave little face, with the low wide forehead which looked as though it owed its being to the turning back of the short silken silver curly hair. Crabbe watched the two strangers—yes, strangers to him—he watched them together. He perceived the natural sympathy which knit them together heart and soul. The Virgin mates with The Twins: not with their successor. He sometimes wished that he possessed a like capacity of sympathy: but the lack of it gave him no more than momentary trouble. It was frightfully pretty to look at; and he truly admired it: but, as wearing apparel, he did not deem it convenient to a person of his complexion. Nor did he succeed in getting to know Clayfoot very well: though there was no reticence on either side. (I regret that I can give you only an outline drawing of this captain: but he is not a person of any conspicuous character, and merely bounds into my story and out again.) Once they all dined together at the Carlton. Crabbe pawned the last of his treasured sigils in order to redeem his dinner dress; and spent a heavenly evening in the palm court, with Chartreuse (combined in the Carthusian formula) and cigarettes, listening to the music, watching the antics of Miss Mary Ann Beardstone in pink satin and loose hair studded with jasmine, and talking to his two intelligent and eager listeners about his works and about himself. Clayfoot vowed that he instantly would buy *Daynian Folk-lore* and the *Medici Book*, and read them at once. It was an exquisite night, while it lasted; and it led nowhere.

Another time, Crabbe lunched with Clayfoot alone at the Berkeley: but the meeting was unnotable. Its sequel was not.

About the middle of the afternoon, they meandered up Dover Street. When they emerged in Bond Street, Clayfoot suddenly said, "Now I'm going to show you something truly elegant. Observe the military gent. across the road. You'd think he was one of Ours, at least: now wouldn't you. Well: in the gorgeous creature which I have the honour of introducing to your notice, you behold an Imperial Yeoman. It parades here daily from eleven to four, with an interval for refreshments; and we mock it till it swears. Observe the cock of its tile. Observe its corsets and its puce gloves. Observe its superior side."

"Gracious Powers!" Crabbe exclaimed, as the Flower of the British Army came nearer. "Why it's Neddy Carnage!"

"You know him?" Clayfoot rejoined. "Accept my congratulations. Don't introduce him to me though: because yesterday I asked him in passing whether he put on his beautiful bags with a shoe-horn!"

More than a year had elapsed since the fray. And Time is said to heal scars. So Crabbe unhesitatingly crossed the road alone; and accosted an animated fashion-plate: "Hallo Neddy!"

"Hullo Crabbe, begad!"

"What's all this?"

"All this what?"

"Why you and these sumptuous paludaments?"

"Cursed nuisance, don't yah know. What I mean to say is been to South Africa with Kitchenah. Got potted eleven times, begad: nine bullets in this foot, and one here, and another up here. What I mean to say is got my gory boot all shot to ribbons in a glass case in the dinin-room at the flat. Come into Truefitt's and I'll have their rottah of a cheiropodist take my boot off for you. Not—want—to see—my—wounds? Yah always were a beast, Crabbe. Well then, come up to the flat and see the skiagraphs of my leg. The drawin-room's full of them. There's a bally splintah back of my knee, now. See how cursedly I limp, begad. Admire this coat? Neat waist, my tailah says. Not—like —a grey Newmarket—with a—supah—velvet—collah? My —deah—chappie, its the only thing in the Service. What am I doin now? Why goin to be skiagraphed, of course. If yah like to come with me, yah'll have a chance of seein my bally leg bare——."

"No, no, no; I mean what are you doing for your livelihood?"

"Oh nothin. Chucked my partnership, yah see, when I got my commission. Live? Oh, live at the flat. Yes: on the guvnah, if yah like. Thenks, Crabbe: yah're just as cynical as evah. Marathonisi? What *are* Marathonisi? Petroleum? Oh I thought I told yah the cursed lease expiahed long ago. We got sick, yah see; and let the bally thing slide. Dropped a mattah of a cool eight thow ovah that, begad. No, I know it's not cricket. Well what I mean to say is I think I must be movin on now, Crabbe——."

As Crabbe scuttled in the opposite direction, he pondered whether the whole oil scheme had been merely chimerical, merely megalomaniacal illusion: or whether it really was one of those good gifts which the gods (with inextinguishable laughter) frequently send to fools fore-ordained to behave as pigs to pearls.

He turned away from the contemplation of the disgusting and unprofitable; and withdrew into his cave.

There, he buried himself in his writings, after Kemp and Clayfoot had left town.

In his mind, not a shadow of doubt existed—and he examined all the evidence most meticulously and quite impersonally—but that he and his collaborator had hit upon as novel and as taking an idea as could be. Both the *Notes on Posthumous Literature* and the *Thirty Naughty Emperors* had the one salient quality which had been absent from all his previous work—they seized the reader in the first few lines, gripped his attention in the first few pages, set him rubbing his eyes and wondering whether he stood on his head or his heels, caused him to explode in yells of laughter, and kept him in a simmer of giggles and guffaws till Finis. It was an amazing thing to Crabbe that so much dainty undeniable merriment should be the offspring of his soured soul and miserable condition. Which of the gods of which of his stars was responsible for this caprice, he often asked? For May, June, and July were months of unmitigated wretchedness.

Nothing was heard or seen of the *Kalliphonos*. *Necessary Propositions* and *Amorroma* continually were coming back again and going out again. The loneliness of his life was worse than crucifixion. He was nailed to his room; and there was no one at all with whom he could exchange a single word. And Kemp's absence immensely increased the difficulties of collaboration. The MSS., now, had to travel a dozen and twenty times between London and Cornwall, for correction and discussion in diverse coloured inks, before they were pronounced perfect and set aside to be fair-copied. Gradually all clothes and everything else which were pawnable were pawned; and all books (except a few indispensable lexicons) were sold, to pay for postage. Crabbe used to curse Thorah, in those days, for depriving him of a couple of books on which he might have raised a couple of shillings.

Once he briskly walked for a whole afternoon about the open spaces in Hyde Park, trying to clear the cobwebs from his brain: but the sight of the phallos of Westminster Cathedral, rigidly piercing the horizon, dragged him back to consciousness of the predominant ugly. Rigid inanity is so loathsomely meek. Of course it made him chant to himself,

> "*I wish that God would reconstruct the world:*
> *I wish that He would do it now;*
> *So that I could see Him at the work:*
> *I wish that He would blot out,*
> *From the Book of Life, my Name:*
> *Or that He would increase,*
> *From His mysterious Store,*
> *My Means of Livelihood.*"

And he sidled away to the left, raging against men.

His work was so exigent that he had no time to knit new towels to sell in Finchley Road, or to exude pseudonymous rot for sixpenny magazines—at least, he could not make a practice

226

of these trades, although he did not shrink from them now and again. But the sitting on the pavement was utterly odious in summer. The suburban woman's boots do stink so foetidly. And, on a day when he ventured to stand by the railings hawking his wares, not a single purchaser came near him. People will give you anything, and will do anything for you, if you are in (and, shall I say, to keep you in) the gutter: but nothing— nothing to prevent you from sliding to that facile descent.

True, Clayfoot anon invited him to Cornwall. But, though he had no clothes save those on his back, all tatters, very unseemly, and though his boots' soles and heels were worn away, yet, he would have brazened out these degradations if he could have afforded a railway ticket, and if he had certainty that (at the conclusion of his visit) he would be able to regain his own cranny in town. He returned thanks for the invitation, regretting that acceptance was impossible. It did not occur to him to walk to Cornwall.

Not only was he troubled by all these things, and weakened by starvation—two closed fistfuls of raw oatmeal a day formed his ration with unlimited water—but all the time his creditors came and banged upon his door. He had not the solace of tobacco. That was paralysing. He sold all his pots and pans, at a marine store in the alley between Red Lion Street and Square, and all his furniture except a table and one Windsor chair: even his bed went; and he slept in a rug on the bare floor. For his stores were exhausted: his credit gone. On the day when he made five pence by the sale of a pile of old paper, he was almost delirious with joy. He gormandized on a two-penny Hovis loaf and two pennyworth of apples; and posted a fresh packet of MSS. to Kemp.

I am perfectly ignorant of what was in Kemp's mind all this time. I do not know how much of a clue to his condition Crabbe gave him. I am under the impression that (when he was not writing about the work) he merely said bluntly that he was having a damnable spell with his loneliness and his debts and his lack of necessaries. But of course, when people tell you that sort of thing, you take it as only a proper fashion of speech, and pass by on the other side. However, Kemp was a singularly perspicacious creature, as a rule; and, although those three months passed as described, I am sure that his sensibilities were not inert. For one day, the last day of June, when Crabbe came home from fruitless humiliation in Finchley Road, he found inside his front door an unposted and personally-delivered letter from Clayfoot. Out of it issued a cheque worth a hundred guineas and a ten-pound note.

The man wrote, with the huge stiff fist of one used to writing on arenas with cudgels,

> My dear Crabbe,
> I feel diffident and unhappy. I cannot express these subtle difficulties on paper. Know, at least, it is done in a humble and diffident spirit. A man who appreciates and loves beauty and genius hates to see the very fount of it, where he has drunk and benefited, clogged with vulgar dust and world scrapings, altogether undesirable and undeserved.
> Do not let pieces of paper break the harmony of our trio. At least let this note be as though it were not—nor ever had been.
> *Tibi, fonti lucidissimo, clarissimo, dulcissimo humillimus ego.*
> Theophanes Clayfoot.

How deliciously the sensitive antennae stroked that quaint ascription—To thee, O well-spring full of light, very clear-shining, very dear, I, most humbly——. And yet Crabbe was frightfully angry at the proffer of alms. And yet it was impossible to offer alms more gently. And he did want money so. And the gesture of the script was so strong that the scribe must have meant his words. There need be no acknowledgement. There could be no humiliation. The claws closed upon the filthy lucre.

Not a word was said: save this, a month later, to Kemp, "You and Clayfoot have done well."

"Dear man," Kemp answered, "I was sorry for all your troubles, and glad that I happen to have been a link in the chain which hauled you somewhat out of them. Theo said that you

228

should not write to him because he told you not to write. I said you should write nevertheless."

But Crabbe did not write. He was quite sure that such exercise would have been most indecorous; and, as for his relations with Clayfoot, he left them in Clayfoot's care. He had declined the invitation to Cornwall for good and comprehensible reasons. That no longer was open to him. It was his duty to wait until Clayfoot would address him on another subject. And he waited.

His first act, on the morning after that last evening of July, had been the reopening of his account at the bank. Next, he divided ninety-five pounds among his most persequent creditors to keep them quiet. And, with twenty pounds in hand, he went on working. Out of this sum, he had his boots repaired, and bought a sovereign's-worth of postage stamps and a mattress to render the floor less cruel during sleep. By means of his revived credit, he accumulated a new store of oatmeal, Sunlight soap, and lamp-oil. As for his ragged clothes, he deliberated to make no alteration. He never left his cave, except in the dead of night: but he kept his body in health by a system of gymnastics indoors; and sometimes, on a Sunday, he washed and darned and mended his garments. So, he remained clean and wholesome and just whole: but, of course, utterly unpresentable anywhere. That means that he could do nothing else than the thing which he did. His correspondence with Kemp caused him to perpend. He never saw Clayfoot; and never heard from him. Every now and then, Kemp wrote of his old friend as being with him. Evidently, the Captain divided his time between Whitehall and Sonorusciello where Kemp seemed permanently to be established. Anon, Crabbe was given to understand that Clayfoot was in trouble: but the information was couched in such hieroglyphic language that he could gather no more than the bare fact. He naturally felt very kind-like toward Clayfoot; and so he said. Further, he inquired whether it would be within his power to render any service.

The response to that was so carefully cryptic, or so rankly and deliberately romantic, that it nearly drove him cranky.

"I cannot tell you the reason of Theo's unhappiness. But you shall sympathize with the feeling of the wounded beast which wants to hide in a corner and die alone. I don't mean that he is going to die: only that he prefers to remain in his corner. His troubles are different from yours and mine, because they are free from pecuniary associations. But his delicate thin *animula* feels them more poignantly than we do. Pray for him. Oh yes, I know; I don't suppose your prayers are efficacious. But prayer postulates sympathy: at least, in you it would postulate it.

"You say that I am human and nearer to you than Theo. I am glad you said that. It is true. Be sure of that. Through all 'he is the God of my idolatry!'"

Crabbe had no light on these men or their affairs; and he blundered on, sideways, as usual. He thought that there must be some sort of amusement to be obtained from making oneself miserable under such circumstances. But of course he did his best in accordance with Kemp's petition, drawing the mystic circle and performing due ceremonies, burning a penny-worth of saffron (the day being Thursday), and praying, at the east:

"O Great and Most High God, Honoured, world without end:" at the west:

"O wise Pure and Just God and Divine Clemency, I beseech Thee, Most Loving Father, that I this day perfectly may understand and accomplish my petition, work, and labour, O Thou Who livest and reignest world without end, *Amen*:" at the north:

"O God, Strong and Mighty, and without Beginning:" at the south:

"O Mighty and Merciful God:" and, in the centre of the circle, the conjuration:

"I conjure and confirm upon you, ye holy angels, and, by the name Cados, Cados, Escherie, Escherie, Escherie Hatimya, Strong Founder of the Worlds, Cantine, Jaym, Janic, Anic, Calbot, Sabbac, Berisay, Alnaym; and, by the Name Adonay, Who created fishes and creeping things in the waters and birds upon the face of the earth and flying toward heaven in the fifth day; and, by the names of the angels serving in the sixth quire before Pastor, a holy angel and a great and powerful prince; and, by the name of his star which is Phaeton; and, by the name of his sigil; and, by the Name Adonay the Supreme God Creator of all things; and by the names of all stars and by their powers and virtues; and, by all the names aforesaid, I conjure thee, O great angel Sachiel, who art the chief ruler of this day of Phaeton, that for Theophanes Clayfoot thou labour and fulfil all his petitions according to his will and desire in his cause and business. *In Nomine Patris et Filii et Spiritus Sancti. Amen.*"

I really do not know that any man or mage could have done more for his very dearest friend. And, when you consider that Clayfoot, by aloofness and by silence, actually and indeed was doing all which he could do to do that which he had begged Crabbe not to do, viz., to let those damnable and infernal pieces of paper break the harmony of the trio, I think you must admit that Crabbe, though clumsy, was behaving very well for a crustacean. But he went further. In the simple hope of getting into focus with those men, so as to range his powers with theirs for their benefit, he recalled (to Kemp) Clayfoot's invitation, saying that (if agreeable) he now was able and willing to accept it.

But all he got was, "As to Theo, you know nothing. You don't know him and you don't know how wonderful he is. His counsels are beyond all. I can't explain him to you. Perhaps the chance will come some day and you will find him. You ought to have come when you were asked. Theo does not want you now. That is not a message from him. It is my own statement. He does not want anything new. Also we are going to climb tors on Dartmoor on Monday. And in the following week Theo is due at Whitehall. You shall meet him some day. Meanwhile, write to him if the spirit moves you. The *Notes on Posthumous Literature* and the *Thirty Naughty Emperors*—well, as a question of importance they are not paramount. They are only two of the second things in the world. Theo is the first thing."

That swirled over Crabbe's head; and drove him out of his

depth, entangling him in the weeds of the wildly ideal. He emerged, at length, and swam back to his cave. He knew that he didn't know. So he placed a lot of questions; and demurred to barks which bite.

Kemp responded: "I suppose my last was very disagreeable. You must forgive. Remember that to you I write straight out what I think and feel. If you were less important to me I could make my letters more pleasant. What I said about Theo must have been singularly silly. Oh he does not need me to keep him on his feet. It is just the other way. But though he does not need me, it gives him pleasure to have me here with him. For that reason only I would deny all other delights to stay with him. But I don't think there are any joys open to me greater than to be with him. For duty—you seem to make duty the proper test— it is my duty to serve Theo always. You don't realize what I would have been without him. I never can pay my debt to him: but if I can approach near to the paying of a little portion of it, my duty lies there. I have been talking to him again about you. It should give him pleasure if you were to write. We are all three agreed that that paper ought not to come between you two. Therefore you must write. But mention neither the money nor his troubles. There is a task for you."

Crabbe's habit, as I hope I have explained, was receptive: not diffusive. He seized flotsam and jetsam floating by: but he did not go rampaging on the prowl for prey.

> *"Ask me no more of this World of Change,*
> *Ask me no more of future Hope:*
> *Vex not thyself for the Past:*
> *Seek not to know the Future:*
> *And treat the Present as a Spoil*
> *Which thou hast won."*

That expresses his habit of mind. He held on to his own, until you tore it from him. And the losing of a claw (or claws) with the torn-away matter was, as you must have seen by now, a common occurrence. He plainly perceived that he had lost

Kemp. He was not unconscious of what he had done and was doing for that one: but, when a sane keen critical dainty-minded and purely selfish creature (as Kemp was) wrote as he had written of Clayfoot, it was quite clear that Clayfoot had been able to do what Crabbe had not been able to do. The morsel was torn away, and (with it) the usual claw. Crabbe accepted the fact without disguise or demurrer. Decency and uncommon sense demanded acquiescence in the inevitable, and the prompt culture of a new forceps. So he placed no futile regrets: but engaged in his obvious duty. At the same time, there remained the question of his own relations with Clayfoot. From Kemp's rhapsodies, he extracted the fact that Clayfoot was too shy on the one hand, or too unconscious of his mental attitude on the other, to dare to approach him. So, if bits of paper were not to rupture such harmony as there was, it became necessary for Crabbe to take Kemp's tip to write to Clayfoot.

He wrote a short note, on things in general. He knew that it was artificial (in the second intention of the term); and it seemed to him sterile. But it was all which he could do, at the moment, in his condition. It was an opening whereby an approach might be made to communion. He was most willing, desirous. Clayfoot remained unresponsive.

Chapter Thirty-three

As soon as he and Kemp finally had agreed up and finished the text of *Notes on Posthumous Literature* and *Thirty Naughty Emperors*, Crabbe devoted his remaining energies to practical commerce.

He had heard printers objurgating the illegibility of ordinary typescript. He also had seen the brutally casual way in which editors of magazines and publishers' advisers were wont to judge the blood and brains of authors. The owner of a name notorious in both hemispheres once had bragged blatantly to him of a custom of trusting entirely to the first impression obtained from the sense of Touch.

"When MSS. come to me, I open the packet, shut my eyes, and finger the first page or so. If I like the feel of the paper, I glance at the first few pages and the last few and perhaps the middle few; and, if they please me—well. If I don't like the feel of the paper, I scribble N.G. on the back and chuck it."

"For what does N.G. stand?" Crabbe inquired.

"No Go!"

Crabbe abruptly laughed. "Then I'm wondering why you should have accepted my first MS. before you even had heard of me."

"Darling old boy! When I first opened your first MS., I shrieked in a moment 'This is going to be damn good!' A man who would dare to send a tiny tiny packet containing a story typewritten in blue italics on Japanese silk copying paper, should be worth reading. So I read. And you were. But *per l'amore di Dio* (if that's right) don't do it again."

Crabbe's scheme was to produce the new work in such a form as would compel attention. To this end, he devised simple artifices. First of all, he used fine paper: secondly he wrote beautifully and far more plainly and blackly than any modern print: thirdly, he spaced boldly and exactly: lastly and in chief, he cast his stuff in narrow columns, so that an intelligent be-holder inevitably must grasp and seize the gist of nearly a whole page at a glance. The result was magnificent. He knew the fatal stupidity of those long lines which involve head-swinging, eye-rolling, and infinite losing of places; and he avoided everything which did not allure and entice to fair con-sideration. He made three copies of *Thirty Naughty Emperors*; and had them strongly bound (as books) in violet buckram with white labels. He took great care that they should open and lie flat at any page. As for the twenty-seven essays called *Notes on Posthumous Literature*, he made three copies of the first two as specimens of the rest; and packed them flat, in full-sized foolscap envelopes, with a list of the titles of the series. Late at night he delivered the three bound books at the offices of three separate publishers, and the three packets of essays at the offices of three separate editors. The idea of triplicity was that the earliest bird should catch the worm.

Without pause, he spent the days in writing innumerable copies of all the *Notes*; and, every night, he deposited his day's work in literary letter-boxes. He acted as postman in order to economize postage: for the cost of producing his wares, and the postal rates on the packages with which he bespattered America, exhausted all his ready cash. As the *Notes* came back, thumbed or torn or crumpled or pencilled by rhypokondylose violent stultified editors, he recopied them; and dispatched them on new travels. He worked like a machine.

One perspicacious Friar sent for him; and said that the *Notes* were most brilliant: but, would he kindly write three new ones, to make a series of thirty. Crabbe went back to his crevice; and, saying nothing to his collaborator, squeezed out of himself Notes on the Venerable Bede's *History of the Jesuits*, on the *Autobiography of Theodora Senatrix et Meretrix*, and on Shakespeare's *Lamb's Tales*. He sent in the series of thirty; and never saw or heard of them again.

Another Savage admired the idea: but wanted somefin upter-dight. Crabbe (in a fever to justify his connection with Kemp) emitted, all alone, a whole new series of Notes on Maurice Hewlett's *Adventures of Sherlock Holmes*, Conan Doyle's *Forest Lovers*, Alice Meynell's *Heavenly Twins*, Sarah Grand's *Dolly Dialogues*, Alfred Austin's *Barrack-Room Ballads*, Henry John Newbolt's *Quatrains of 'Umar Khaiyám*, Hall Caine's *Cardinal's Snuff-Box*, Henry Harland's *Eternal City*, Max Beerbohm's *Light that Failed*, Rudyard Kipling's *Happy Hypocrite*, J. M. Barrie's *Harry Richmond*, George Meredith's *Little Minister*, Dickens's *Esmond*, and Thackeray's *David Copperfield*. He did them in eleven days—the experience of a lifetime expressed in 21,000 words; and the editor was afride he couldn't foind rewme f'th'm neow.

Several times the books came back: innumerable times the essays came back. Instantly, at midnight, they were taken elsewhere. Crabbe discovered that most publishers and several editors did not maintain letter-boxes large enough to reçeive a foolscap packet. In these cases, he used to deliver his goods to the housekeepers, very early in the morning, before the clerks in starchy vests and rolled-gold sleeve-links arrived to sneer at his shabby carapax.

The pace of this period was terrific. It told upon his weakened frame, making his sleep a paroxysm of successive nightmares, or a torpor from which he arose with a palate tasting of hot and rusty sin. Daytime became even more hideous than night: for it brought the postman with insults and spoiled work to be done again. Crabbe trembled at the sound of his footsteps coming up the stair: and conceived a most fervent dyspathy against these essays which, now, he knew by rote. As for his own two books, they made their periodic reappearances, and instantly were dismissed again. As for the *Kalliphonos*—he placed it with *Daynian Folk-lore* and the *Medici Book*, in the category of Things Lost. He was indeed at the bottom of the ladder of literature.

Kemp behaved beautifully; and that was an enormous consolation. Crabbe of course kept him posted with news that the things were on their rounds; but he never manifested even the

slightest symptom of impatience. Yes: he was an ideal collaborator—and, no doubt, an ideal comrade.

But, as the months and months went by, Crabbe began to be
troubled very violently by Clayfoot's continued silence, and by
Kemp's seeming lack of interest in the interesting thing. It
was frightful to suspect: but—was it possible that Kemp's
apparent patience should hide indifference? There was no need
(except an intellectual need) for him to care, now: for the paltry
pounds, which the collaboration might earn, were quite unimportant to him—now. All the same, Crabbe did think that
the exquisite little creature had been truly in earnest in desiring
a literary opening, such as the publication of these works could
not fail to bring. He was frightfully troubled on both these
points, Clayfoot's and Kemp's; and, leaving the secondary
matter alone, he wrote his mind to Kemp. His excuse for writing
was that, after keeping the *Notes* for three months, the editor of
the *Albemarle Review*[1] had at last promised to give them favour-
able attention.

"I long for Albemarlian news," Kemp wrote in reply. "Oh
my dear man that should be grand. And you should have done
well. But you drivel of my suspicions here. Oh why? Have I said
a word? Man, can't you believe me? I tell you I trust you entirely: for is not the huge bulk and all the pain of the work yours
alone. I tried to shew you this by never asking one question
about the *Notes* or the *Emperors*. Did you think I have not
searched each letter as it came for news of them?"

That settled that. Next, Crabbe would know whether Clayfoot knew of his letters. He wanted to see the soul of this god of
Kemp's. He asked the question a dozen times; and at last pro-
voked a snarl.

"Why can't you leave unanswered questions alone? When I
have avoided with candid and naked obviousness the answering
of certain questions I presume you have some compellant reason
for asking them again. Very well then: Theo knows of your
letters anything which I think shall interest him. I don't shew

[1] *The Monthly Review.*

him your letters. I tell him if you have any news. There is a certain amount of things in your letters which I don't tell him. I tell him that there is a certain amount which I don't tell him. Your letter to him seemed to him and to me to be silly. If I had thought you were going to write like that I should never have urged you to write. This house is full of visitors. Dinner-parties succeed successive luncheons. I grow stout and air interminable platitudes. I am most useful. Man, it is wearisome. But the food is good."

That was enough. Crabbe understood nothing. He was prevented, by those two, by eight–nine months of wearisome labour, by the necessity of continuing heart-sick and lonely, and by the fact of long starvation—he was prevented both from knowing and understanding what was expected. Nothing happened: nothing mattered. This was the end of his tether.

Chapter Thirty-four

DURING one more month, he contrived to keep on his feet: but he was senseless and done for. Then, occurred the final clash of events which finished him.

Let it be quite clear that I make no excuse for Nicholas Crabbe. I find it interesting to describe the methods by which he was slowly tortured to death by inches during a matter of nearly four years. I simply am telling you patently of the things which he did which he ought not to have done, and of the things which he left undone which he ought to have done: and, that there should be no health in him, is not singular.

These last days mainly were occupied in giving audiences to his creditors, and in tolerating their tiresome abuse. The order of the ceremony was for these tradesmen (wearing their hats) to sit down in the only chair, while Crabbe meekly supported himself by the table and elaborately explained. He had five books finished and in the hands of publishers. From these, he hoped to earn the wherewithal for fulfilling his obligations. At the present moment he was slightly unwell and unable to attend to things. He only asked for time. Then the creditor, or the creditors, would recite litanies or antiphons, scornfully acclaiming him as a pretty feller, demanding whether he called himself a man, jeering at his etiolated appearance. It did not even make him angry, now: nor did judgment-summonses, distraints, unexecuted warrants for arrest, have any alarms for him. They were so common. He was rather run down at the present moment, and obliged to let things slide. He only asked for time.

The house agent at the corner sent a polite note, reminding him that his lease was about to expire, inquiring his pleasure in the matter of a renewal. He had strength and wit to reply that he would perpend and communicate his intentions without unnecessary delay.

But the night of this day brought him a rictus of terror. If he had no luck within the week, he would become an outcast again—a homeless outcast, with no secret place where he might agonize decently alone. People would crowd round and stare at him. Horrid little girls would yelp comments on his twitches. Dear kind souls would poke at his soft shell; and the claws, now, were far too weak to pinch gratuitous pokers. The wildest phantasies whirled and tore through his brain at the thought of such outrage. The gods of his stars seemed to have deserted him. All the conjurations (which he uttered) failed to bring an answer to his prayer, or an angel to mitigate his pain. The gods of his stars were deaf, or reluctant; for 'who could see with his eyes a god who was unwilling, going either here or there?' Even the divine ones were averse from him.

And, if he were to end thus, then all his past toil would become wasted and annulled. Oh no: that must not be allowed to happen. He could swear to God that he never had been idle or drunken or abnormally base—that he had worked hard, denied himself every amenity, generally done his best all round. Surely he was not to be deprived of the fruits of his labour? Surely he was not to be made a public spectacle? The very notion of such a fate drove him crazy: and nerved him to one thing more—the only thing which occurred to him in his extremity.

He wrote to Kemp: and told him how he was. Also, he made over to him all rights in the *Kalliphonos, Necessary Propositions, Amorroma, Notes on Posthumous Literature,* and *Thirty Naughty Emperors,* begging him to put his own name to them, and to use their success (if it should come) as the basis of a literary career. He made the offering as a token of sincere regard, and in thanksgiving for companionship; and also to give himself the satisfaction of knowing that he had not laboured in vain.

God forgive him: but I believe Kemp thought that he was being got at. He said that what Crabbe suggested was out of the question.

Crabbe went from craziness to phrenzy. He tried hard to refrain himself: but it was no good. Then he remembered, and made his own, what Cardinal Newman once said to Sir William Cope about the controversy with Kingsley: "When I speak in an ordinary tone, no one listens". So Crabbe shouted. He implored Clayfoot to come and save him from ruin.

He knew all Victor Hugo's invaluable aphorisms:—

"Never let anyone do you a service. They will abuse the advantage which it gives them."

"Never permit yourself to be caught in the article of inanition. They would relieve you."

"To be obliged, is to be sold."

"The happy, the powerful, make use of the moment when you stretch out your hand to place a penny in it; and, at the crisis of your weakness, they make you a slave of the worst kind—the slave of an act of charity—a slave forced to love the inslaver. What infamy! What indelicacy! What an assault upon self-respect!"

"The slime of a good action performed on your behalf, bedaubs you and bespatters you with mud for ever."

"An alms is irremediable. Gratitude is paralysis. A benefit is a sticky and repugnant adherence which deprives you of free movement."

But he knew also that the Preacher says:—

"Have thou patience with a man in poor estate: and delay not to shew him mercy."

"Lose thy money for thy brother and thy friend: and let it not rust under a stone to be lost."

"Make not an hungry soul sorrowful: neither provoke a man in his distress."

"Add not more trouble to an heart that is vexed: and defer not to give to him that is in need."

Clayfoot had wished those bits of paper not to break harmony. So he said. Clayfoot hated to see the very fount of beauty and genius, where he had drunk and benefited, clogged with vulgar dust and world-scrapings altogether undesirable and undeserved. So he said.

And Kemp proclaimed him as wonderful—counsellor—god.

It would be unfair to refuse him a chance. Crabbe implored Clayfoot to come and save him from ruin.

And Clayfoot begged to be excused.

But Kemp came, some days later.

Just before he arrived, Crabbe heard the postman drop a letter (not a packet) in the letter-box. He staggered round the room by the walls, to fetch it; and returned to his station by the far window. Presently he listlessly opened the envelope; and glanced at its content. The luck had turned. The editor of the *Albemarle Review*, with the most handsome of words, accepted the *Notes on Posthumous Literature*, would pay well for the English serial rights, would arrange for their serialization in America, and subsequently would get them issued in book-form.

Crabbe grasped the facts with his brain: but they had no interest for his heart. He laid down the letter on the table; and reeled across the room again: for someone smartly rapped at the outer door.

It was Kemp. He came in, looking as mystically pure as a moonstone and as cold and severe as snow. Perhaps Crabbe's eyebrows flickered up a sixteenth of an inch in noncurant inquiry. But nothing mattered. No: nothing.

In the front room, Crabbe proffered the chair. Kemp left it unnoted; and stood by the table end. Crabbe leaned against the wall in the shadowed corner beyond the window. He knew that he had committed the unpardonable sin of asking for help; and, try as he would, he could not feel a trace of shame, or of regret. On the contrary, he was rather proud of it. He would submit to arraignment, and to sentence. The idea of asking for mercy never entered his mind.

"Crabbe," Kemp began, "you and I must agree that we have made a mistake. We thought we were friends. We did not know each other. I did not know that you were the man to write that letter to Theo. You did not know that I was a man to disapprove of it. Disapproval is a mild term to express my feeling."

Crabbe felt thrills of pleasure at the very sound of the clear virginal voice, at the mercurial lightness and decision of touch, at the pretty breathless severity of the sentences.

Kemp continued, "This strikes at fundamentals. I have waited before telling you. I did not want to say that of which I would repent. I am quite certain that we cannot go on."

He paused. Crabbe said nothing: because just then he happened to be pondering the doctrine of Appulejus: "Men are then most bewitched when, with often beholding, they direct the edge of their sight to the edge of their sight that bewitch them; and, when their eyes reciprocally are intent one upon other, and when raies are joyned to raies and lights to lights, then the spirit of the one is joyned to the spirit of the other and fixeth its sparks. So, strong ligations are made."

But Kemp's eyes were fixed upon the table; and he went on reciting his lesson.

"There remains the wretched little question of our mutual MSS. I would be glad if you keep them all; and erase my name from them. But I suppose you shall refuse. Or, shall you keep the *Notes* as entirely yours; and let the *Emperors* be entirely mine? Or, if you like, I am content that the original agreement would hold as a simple commercial arrangement. Please let me know which of these three suggestions displeases you least. I myself would prefer the first, or the second."

Crabbe emerged, with his wits, from a maze: took the editorial acceptance from the table; and handed it to Kemp, speaking gravely and impassively.

"You once said that, if I got the *Notes* accepted by the *Albemarle Review*, it would be grand—and that I would have done well. The grand thing is done, and done very well indeed. When these *Notes* shall have appeared, there never will be any more difficulty about selling work."

"I do not want anything more to do with them. I refuse to touch them. They must be yours entirely. Our way is now open to a literary severance as well as a social one."

It was rather hard. Lips from which cups are dashed, utter strange things. Crabbe became lightheaded; and raved awhile of treachery, embellishing his denunciations with copious quotations, nipping, pinching, tearing, and rending frightfully.

"The fact that you hold the MSS., makes it possible for you to dictate your terms to me to some extent," Kemp said. "It seems useless to appeal to your generosity: but you should do me a great kindness if you could bring yourself to accept one of my three proposals."

"You place me in a disgusting position in regard to the editor of the *Albemarle Review*. And you reject a literary opening for which many a man would give his ears."

"There is nothing further from my wishes than to prejudice you with Mr Orchardleigh.[1] It does not follow that, because we have ceased to be friends, we have become enemies——."

"(It does not follow—on this side.)"

"I do not desire this opening with the *Albemarle Review*: nor, if it is mine, shall I allow it to be of subsequent use to me. I therefore once more beg you to make it your own."

Crabbe pulled himself together; and delivered his ultimatum. "You withdraw your friendship from me. You rob me of the pleasure of making myself and you independent. And you reject the chance which I have gained for you. To get you what you wanted was the reward for which I worked. Nothing more——."

He stiffened a little; and added in a lower voice, "I swear that —by the Nine Orders." Then he continued, "Well: the *Notes* will have to appear. You may break my agreements. I will not——."

"I don't break them. I offer to keep them. My third proposal is that the original agreement would hold as a simple commercial arrangement——."

"And, to that, you adjoin an expression of opinion which makes it impossible for me to accept it. You prefer your first or second proposals——."

"So I do——."

[1] Sir Henry Newbolt. The sobriquet derives from the fact that Sir Henry's father-in-law, the Rev. W. A. Duckworth, lived at Orchardleigh Park, Frome.

CHAPTER THIRTY-FOUR

"So do not I. I unconditionally reject them both; because I will not sail under false colours—a false friend's colours. The *Notes* must appear: but, as you disdain me, and, as I disdain your invitation to pose as the sole begetter of stuff which you helped to write, and, as you deliberately and insistently prefer—prefer —to break your agreement, they must appear anonymously. You don't seem to know even now that your will—even your preference—is my law. You prefer to break your agreement. It is broken. You wish for literary and social severance. You have them both. Good-bye."

He came out of the shadow; and sat down at the table, beginning to draw paper and pen toward him, with a negligent and preoccupied air. He moved slowly in order to conceal the trembling of his hands.

Kemp stood quite still during several minutes. After some thought, Crabbe began to write in an absent-minded way. He was quite unconscious of what he was doing. His was not the brain which directed his pen.

Kemp turned; and went out.

Crabbe heard the slamming of the door. It roused him a little; and he studied what he had written:

"Robert, famous in counsel: Fulgentius, the Radiant One: Kemp, the Champion:"
and these verses of Tusser:

"As hatred is the serpent's noysome rod,
  So friendship is the loving gift of God.

The drunken friend is friendship very evill,
The frantick friend is friendship for the divell.

The quiet friend, all one in word and deed,
Great comfort is, like ready gold at need.

With brawling fools that rail for every wrong,
Firm friendship never can continue long.

NICHOLAS CRABBE

In time that man shall seldom friendship miss,
That weighs what thing, touch kept in friendship is.

Oft times a friend is got with easie cost,
Which, used ill, is oft as quickly lost.

Hast thou a friend, as heart may wish at will?
Then use him so to have his friendship still.

Wouldst have a friend? Wouldst know what friend is best?
Have God thy Friend, Who passeth all the rest."

That was all. He dropped to the table, hiding his features. He was alone and naked—all alone with The Alone.

ExPLICITUR

DATE DUE